LEGACY

ANDREW BILLINGS

LEGACY

2024 Copyright © – Andrew Billings

Unless otherwise identified, all Scripture quotations are taken from the New King James Version, copyright © 1982 by Thomas Nelson, Inc. Used by permission. All rights reserved.

Scripture quotations marked KJV are taken from the King James Version of the Holy Bible.

Scripture quotations marked NIV are taken from the Holy Bible, New International Version®, NIV®, copyright ©1973, 1978, 1984, 2011 by Biblica, Inc.® Used by permission. All rights reserved worldwide.

Scripture quotations marked NLT are taken from the Holy Bible, New Living Translation, copyright © 1996, 2004, 2007 by Tyndale House Foundation. Used by permission of Tyndale House Publishers, Inc., Carol Stream, Illinois 60188, USA. All rights reserved.

Scripture quotations marked AMP are taken from the Amplified® Bible (AMPC), Copyright © 1954, 1958, 1962, 1964, 1965, 1987 by The Lockman Foundation. Used by permission. Lockman.org.

LEGACY

GOD'S DREAM MAN'S INHERITANCE

BY

ANDREW BILLINGS

WITH A
FOREWORD BY

JEREMY RIDDLE

CONTENTS

Foreword		1
Dedication		3
Introduction		7

SECTION I: WHAT IS LEGACY? — 12

1	God's Dream, Humanity's Inheritance	15
2	The Original Design For Adam	23
3	The God of Abraham, Isaac, and Jacob	29
4	Jesus: The Firstborn of Many Brothers	39
5	The Legacy of Jesus: The Great Commission	47

SECTION II: WHY IS THE MODERN CHURCH FAILING? — 56

6	The Plan and Purpose of the Church	59
7	Legacy And The *Ekklesia*	71
8	How Paul Stewarded the Early Church	81
9	Why Is the Modern Church Failing?	95
10	Faltering Church Models	107
11	Compromised Fathering Roles	119
12	The Good and the Bad: Fathers and Mothers	133
13	The Counterculture of Legacy, Part 1	147
14	The Counterculture of Legacy, Part 2	159

SECTION III: WHY IS LEGACY FAILING? — 168

15	The Good and the Bad: Sons and Daughters	171
16	Disconnected Generations	179
17	Dealing with Parent and Leadership Wounds	189

SECTION IV: HOW WE RETURN TO LEGACY — 200

18	The Hope of the World	203
19	Healing the Generations	215
20	My Personal Journey	227
21	Discipleship: The Vehicle of Legacy	235

Long Live Legacy	249
About The Author	252

FOREWORD

As is likely the timing of the Lord, I happened to read this book in the middle of a season where my own heart was in a broken and hurting place over the state of the church. In that season I had encountered more pain, dysfunction, brokenness, and betrayal than I ever could have dreamed I would in my ministry life. It left me fighting to keep my head above water and to hold on to faith, hope, and love. In the middle of this fight, I had been crying out to the Lord asking "Where are the mothers and fathers of the faith?" "Where are the voices of clarity and reason in the midst of insanity and confusion?" "Where are the ones who carry His Spirit, His wisdom, and His authority to not only address the great brokenness and dysfunction in the Church today, but to lovingly bind up her wounds, remind her of her true identity and purpose, and set her back on the firm foundation that is Christ and the path He pioneered and calls all who believe in Him to walk on?"

I believe the book you hold in your hands is an answer to that prayer.

I met my friend Andrew Billings under very unique circumstances. And perhaps that's fitting because he really is a most unique man. I remember feeling prompted to ask him questions about his testimony and ministry during the course of our first meeting. As he began to share about his encounters with the Lord and the ways the Spirit was leading him and his family, I began to feel the presence of the Lord so strongly. In that moment, I remember distinctly thinking "Here is a man who has been uniquely marked by God for a special purpose." When he asked me to write the foreword to his book "Legacy", I knew that I would not just be recommending a work to people, but I would be recommending a trusted spiritual father and a faithful son in God's house.

This work "Legacy" he has labored to bring forth is a critical work for our day. The issues addressed in it must be communally and prayerfully engaged by all those called to lead the present and future church. I believe the church is the most important institution in the world and the weight of her mission sobers me on a daily basis. We cannot continue to turn a blind eye or adopt a passive stance towards any area of sin, compromise, or disobedience in our personal lives or communities. Nor can we allow the church to be led by any directive, vision or model that is earthly, sensual, unspiritual, unbiblical and not firmly rooted in the person and ministry of Jesus Christ. A harvest of souls hangs in the balance!

Any builder worth his salt knows the most important part of any building is its foundation. A faulty foundation can live undetected for a time, but only for a time. At some point, it will always disclose where it was poorly or wrongly laid. I believe the church is in such a moment—a moment where the flaws, the shortcuts, and the lack of diligent obedience on behalf of the builders to the clear foundational blueprints given to us in scripture, *is being seen.*

This "seeing" is painful. But this "seeing" is critical in order for the structure to rightly undergo a corrective, restorative, and reforming work. As every home owner knows, you can afford to overlook a poorly painted wall, or a scuffed up floor, but you cannot afford to ignore signs of structural damage that point to a weak or faulty foundation.

My friends this is not a moment for small, subtle course corrections. This is a time for a deep work of reformation to take place. A time for radical obedience and wholehearted returning to the Lord! I believe times of great refreshing from the presence of the Lord are awaiting a repentant church! Let us delay them no further.

Let us have ears to hear what the Spirit is saying and HEED it with all our hearts.

– Jeremy Riddle

DEDICATION

TO MY HISTORY AND MY PRESENT:

This book is written with deep and humble gratitude to those who have fathered and mentored me, examples both good and bad, the Davids and the Sauls. I have learned from both. You have taught me so much—how to live and how not to live, who I want to be and who I don't want to imitate.

TO THE FUTURE OF MY PERSONAL LEGACY:

I dedicate this book to my three sons—Benjamin, Jonathan, and Joel. I am so proud of you. God's hand is on your lives, and each one of you has a key role to play in future history. I am confident that you will go further and achieve much more than I have, building on the rich foundation I have been able to cultivate, steward, and pass on to you. I have counted myself beyond honored and privileged to not just be your dad but, most importantly, your father. I have found so much joy and blessing giving you what I never had as a son and sparing you the many pains and hardships I endured. The curse of past generations breaks in this legacy—it transforms, and it will result in you changing the world.

TO EVERY SON AND DAUGHTER WHO IS BEING RAISED:

I want to encourage you so that you do not just live, but that you live with purpose, success, and passed-on legacy, no matter who raised you. Stop reflecting the culture of your generation; instead, strive to pursue heaven's culture—to be shaped by it and reflect it to the world. Don't filter heaven through your culture. Never let what has happened to you negatively define who you are. Forgive those who irresponsibly used their positions and hurt you. Learn from their failures and make it your goal to bless those who come after you with a much healthier leadership than you experienced.

Learn who God is—discover your identity in Him. Pursue God to heal your heart of all father and leadership wounds. Realize you cannot grow without a father or mother who will mentor you with wisdom. Find someone who is walking in purity of heart, a person you would like to be like someday. Find someone who will correct you, not just compliment you. Pursue them with value, submit well, learn honor and how to serve them in their mission so that one day you will be entrusted with your own. Learn how to grow from correction and not become bitter. Seek truth over comfort. Learn how to humble yourself and subdue your pride and ego. Prize integrity and character at the highest level. Value the pursuit of truth in every situation, belief system, and mentality you have, above personal comfort zones.

Run well. Be fruitful and multiply. If you learn to be an excellent son or daughter, then you will have the ability in time to disciple the next generation as you have been discipled, but only better. Remember that you will never be able to be an authentic father or mother until you have learned what it is to be a son or a daughter. If you are in the kingdom of God, then you must become a son or daughter.

And lastly, to the would-be and existing fathers and mothers:

You will never be validated or deemed successful in your role until you have raised sons and daughters. Your purpose for being a father is not so that you can be lifted on to the backs of your sons, but to serve them and lift them up into greatness, so that they will go further than you ever could in your pursuit of establishing the kingdom of God. Remember that we never own anyone; we merely steward the King's children. We labor over them until Jesus is formed in them.

Your discipleship as a son or a daughter should have removed insecurity out of your mentality, and your walk should now be stable and intentional. You cannot assume influence and not have somewhere to take a son or a daughter. You are in the room to be a coach to the next generation, not to be approved by them. Stop trying to be their best friend and be a loving yet focused coach.

Like Paul, we labor over people until the maturity, dedication, and focused mindset of Christ is formed in those we steward. Fathering and mothering are crucial foundations in the kingdom mandate—so know who you are called to disciple. Equally, know who you are not called to disciple. Stay grounded in your focus, be down to earth, and have fun along the journey. Remember, it's a family culture we are creating.

To us all:

We are the hope of glory, the hope of the cloud of witnesses, and the hope of the fathers and mothers who have gone before us. We are the hope of the reward worthy of His suffering that is due to Jesus. We are His legacy.

—Andrew Billings

INTRODUCTION

JESUS CAME TO EARTH AS THE ONLY PLAN OF THE FATHER—there was no plan B. He came with no personal agenda, never once enforcing His rights. The Scripture tells us that "when the fullness of the time had come" (Galatians 4:4), "God so loved the world that He gave His only begotten Son" (John 3:16).

In Jesus's brief thirty-three years on earth, He spent thirty of those years in preparation for His mission. This is a far cry from what the modern church calls preparation. Jesus did not use anointing as His validation; He walked in perfect character and integrity; He learned by the things He suffered. And yet Jesus waited until His appointed time to enter public ministry.

Throughout His earthly life, Jesus prized one thing as His utmost value—His relationship with His Father. Jesus honored the Father and gave all credit to Him. In John 5:19–20, Jesus expressed that He could not do anything unless He saw His Father do it or say anything unless He heard His Father say it. In an equal measure, we see the Father holds Jesus in the highest honor too. Jesus, on the day He was baptized by John, God the Father audibly spoke in a booming voice from heaven, declaring, "This is My beloved Son, in whom I am well pleased" (Matthew 3:17).

The unity, honor, love, and submission between the Father and the Son is beyond remarkable.

WHAT IS LEGACY ABOUT?

Legacy is about more than receiving something from those who have gone before us. It's about seeing past just us and our influence. It is about being relationally interwoven into God's great story of generational creation.

Jesus was, and is, so perfectly submitted and discipled by the Father that He could boldly declare, "He who has seen Me has seen the Father" (John 14:9). Jesus could not understand why the people were still asking for Him to reveal the Father to them. In other words, Jesus had been so perfectly discipled by the Father that we are practically looking at the exact same attributes and value systems in Jesus as we would see in the Father. This is why the writer of Hebrews tells us that Jesus is "the brightness of His glory and the express image of His person" (Hebrews 1:3).

Imagine if we raised disciples who were so confident in their representation of us that they could boldly say that others have seen us when they have seen them! And on the flip side, how differently would our lives be if we were so confident in a spiritual leader pouring into us that we could declare that we correctly represent him or her in all that we say and do. But this is only half of the story of how legacy operates.

You see, Jesus was not just coming to minister and share His good news for three and a half years, and then die and resurrect in Jerusalem to fulfill divine redemptive justice. No, it is far deeper than this. Jesus came and gathered twelve men and invited them into proximity with Himself, a lifestyle of friendship and mentorship with Him. Jesus invited these men to experience His way of life, saying what the Father said and doing what the Father did, so that they would begin to see, experience, and then model what legacy is supposed to do, which is to extend the kingdom of God. God is a God of generational relationship, which is a culture where fathers teach sons and mothers teach daughters.

Jesus came to build and initiate a new dispensation. He didn't leave cryptic prophetic messages; rather, He lived the literal model both as a Son to the Father and as one who disciples the disciples, so that all could see and understand what He was about. And yet, we have become blurred in what true discipleship means.

As a twelve-year-old boy, Jesus recognized who His Father was and that He must be about His Father's business (see Luke 2:49). As soon as Jesus was anointed for public ministry, He allowed God to handpick His twelve disciples in order to teach them about God's kingdom and to model how they were to live once He was gone (see Matthew 12:1–4; Luke 6:12–16). Jesus reiterated this right before He ascended back to heaven: "Go therefore and make disciples of all the nations" (Matthew 28:19).

BELIEVERS OR DISCIPLES?

Jesus's ministry focus was not the crowds or the prestige from His miracles; *it was investing into the twelve* men for three and a half years, twenty-four hours a day. And after He ascended into heaven, the eleven remaining disciples took the pure message of Jesus to the entire world, bringing transformation and the reality of God's kingdom to earth.

> *If Jesus's eleven remaining disciples had each created twelve disciples in their lifetimes, and each of those 132 disciples had discipled twelve.*

If Jesus's eleven remaining disciples had each created twelve disciples in their lifetimes, and each of those 132 disciples had discipled twelve more, then that would be 1,584 disciples in the matter of a few years of Jesus's ascension. So, shouldn't the bride of Christ, the church Jesus spoke to Peter about, have converted and dominated the entire world by now, some two thousand years later? It is apparent that the church is currently far from this model. We desperately need to return to the model Jesus gave us before another year or decade passes, before another generation is raised fatherless and motherless.

One of our failures in the church that we must recognize, acknowledge, and correct is that we have raised believers and not disciples. What's the difference?

> *Believers admire Jesus, while disciples obey Him.*

Believers show up for the food and the miracles; disciples stick around for the cleanup and the learning that reveals the real miracles and transformations that have taken place. Disciples are changed by the power of God, not entertained by it.

> *Jesus focused on disciples more than believers.*

Jesus focused on disciples more than believers because a son or a daughter will do so much more—and do it willingly—than a servant will ever do. This is because he does this for the interests of his father's estate, not his own glory.

As you read this book, I want to show you the legacy of how we take back our cities, our states, our nations, and even our continents for the glory of God. Jesus intended to spread His kingdom across the face of the earth through His sons and daughters. And how we fulfill this mandate is by reintroducing true legacy, allowing God to teach us again about the legacy of fathering, mothering, and discipleship, and about what being a son or a daughter means.

This message of legacy is God's only plan to save the world.

I pray that you are blessed as you read these chapters. I ask that the Spirit of understanding and revelation will be with you as you digest these words.

—Andrew Billings

Please share and recommend this book with as many people as you can.
We need to see the body of Christ dismiss distraction and become incredibly focused
and dedicated to God's plan of discipleship.

#LegacyBook

WHAT IS LEGACY?

SECTION I

I HAVE A DEEP LOVE FOR THE CHURCH THAT JESUS BUILT. In fact, I have served her in various ways for most of my adult life. In times gone by, in notable moments of history the church has risen to the occasion that God was calling her to, and God has received the glory. We must do the same in our generation with the legacy that God is passing on to us.

> In this section, we will look at God's ideal plan and dream for the church Jesus commissioned, the current state of the church, and how we can realign our lives, churches, and ministries to His blueprint for winning the world back to His heart. I have the privilege of revisiting the story of God's romance with humankind and His legacy that He has passed on to us. Understanding this will allow us to fall in love with the poetic and majestic perfection of God's generous love and mercy that has been lavished on us as sons and daughters of God through the tapestry of this legacy.

This legacy has been built into and carried by generations of humanity who have partnered with Him. It is my hope that we will rediscover His flawless plan to save the world and His extreme passion for us in the midst of that. This section will set the tone for how we will perceive and grasp the overall message of this book.

CHAPTER 01

GOD'S DREAM, HUMANITY'S INHERITANCE

WHEN WE HEAR THE WORD *LEGACY*, it is easy to conjure up the idea of a mythical baton we are handing down to successors to live their lives just as those who have gone before them. For example, I want my kids to go further and do more than I was ever able to do. I want them to stand on my shoulders and go where I only dreamed of going. This is what we think about when speaking of passing on a legacy. However, if there was widespread understanding of what legacy truly is, then we wouldn't see most of the issues we face in the church today. Let's look at the industry of construction as an example of the concept of legacy.

There have been countless large cathedrals and architectural achievements throughout history that have been built over three to four generations. The first generation began building, knowing that they would never see its completion. This lack of vantage did not deter their workmanship. If anything, it made them work with more diligence, knowing that they were laying the foundation upon which their descendants would install the final pieces. Imagine being the last generation placing the finishing touches on the structure, being able to look up and see the work of your father, your grandfather, and your great-grandfather. The pride instilled in you to be a part of that living chain of events would be indescribable.

These large cathedrals have a magnificence and precision that is still marveled at hundreds of years later. At seven years old, I remember marveling as I stood on the steps of St. Paul's Cathedral in London. Even then, I began to grasp the concept that fathers would work on this and die while not seeing it completed, all the while knowing that their sons or grandsons would finish the work.

Why would people start something they would never see finished? What made them connect with something so massive? I concluded that people have an inherent desire for purpose and significance, and so they build dreams so much bigger than themselves and larger than their lifetimes. In comparison, it appears as though the church has mostly lost this value of generational building toward true compounding kingdom advance and growth.

APPRENTICESHIP: GENERATIONAL BUILDING

Imagine a huge mural that is highly detailed. It's so big that it takes thousands of years to paint. Think of the logistics of a project like that! In essence, each painter would have to do his part and paint his delegated section of the wall for it to be completed. Each father would need to train his son for years, so that when he could no longer paint, his son would pick up the brush and follow the original dream for the mural, with the same creative understanding. No matter how well a painter could paint, when he passed away, if there was no successor to continue the painting, then that section of the mural would suffer and not be fully completed.

A successful ministry without a successor is a tragic failure.

Likewise, a successful ministry without a successor is a tragic failure. All too often leadership figures realize too late that they lack successors. And so there is a scramble during the last part of their leadership to install the next generation. But the serious flaw with this approach is that the successors were not enabled to work alongside the leaders long enough to truly obtain the full benefits and training. Not just in an assistant posture, but in the scenario of being entrusted with lesser levels of leadership and responsibility and being coached through their failures and successes.

If this is not realized in the context of the generational mural, then things will begin to degrade and wander from the purposed dream. For instance, the painting may wander from a landscape portrait and get remolded into an abstract expression painting. This would completely dishonor the master painter's dream and betray the intended message.

Through this illustration, we can clearly see that it is not about the skill and technique of just one painter, but rather the generationally honored and stewarded dreams, skills, accumulated tricks of the trade, and the transitional art of passing on each of these assets to the next generation. This is a process we call an apprenticeship.

An apprenticeship is the practical school or internship where artisans who are masters take on young protégés who know nothing and invite them into their world and workplace to teach, coach, and instruct them over several years. This is not a skill level learned by watching a YouTube video or doing a Google search. It is hands-on.

While an apprenticeship may not be able to teach everything that one may encounter in life, it does equip the student with the framework and mindset to be able to perform well and thrive when they are entrusted with greater responsibility. And even then, the more mature young artisans will still need the input and presence of mature artisans as they are raised up.

WHAT IS LEGACY?

Legacy is often recognized as the sum of a person's assets and accumulated value that is passed on to the next generation. For some people, that could be money, a business, or even properties or assets; sometimes they pass on valuable or sentimental heirlooms that have been handed down for generations. For some, legacy looks like teaching their children the pursuit that brought them joy or success, like a father teaching his children how to fish so his children can carry on the tradition of what brought him joy. Or it could be a mother teaching her children and grandchildren family traditions, passed-down recipes, or even cultural and spiritual values.

These examples are better described as inheritance. But legacy is something that is passed from fathers and mothers on to the next generation. It is passed on to sons and daughters, who in turn steward the inheritance into growth and increase, not merely just to be consumed in their lifetimes. In the kingdom of God, legacy is seen in building upon a previous wealth of establishment that has been passed on from the previous generation. It's an accumulated wealth of experience, wisdom, and anointing. To put it more simply, inheritance is what you give someone, while legacy is what you invest into someone.

*Inheritance is what you give someone,
while legacy is what you invest into someone.*

A father who builds wealth for his children to inherit doesn't work hard with an expectation that his children will become lazy and squander the money and do nothing with their lives. No, the father has a dream that his children will honor what has been passed on to them by building and growing wealth upon his life's labor and sacrifice expressed in the inheritance, so that the coming generations would be advantaged and established. A father dreams that his gift of legacy would empower his children to have a better life than he had, if they steward it wisely. However, not all sons are willing to steward the fruit of their father's toil and struggle that was passed to them. This separates the entitled from the honorable.

In our generation, privilege has been made a shameful word.

But privilege is the honor given by a parent to a son or daughter in various forms, one form being monetary or property-based inheritance. The abuse of that inheritance is called entitlement and squander, which is what the prodigal son did with his father's financial savings with complete disregard for his father (see Luke 15). The abuse and lazy embrace of inheritance, in whatever form it comes in, is an unacceptable response.

Likewise, privilege is a good thing. It truly is a humbling and honoring responsibility to be entrusted with the life efforts and fruits of a life well lived and a legacy well built. Never be ashamed of the privilege you have; rather, be humbled and accountable for the entrusted enrichment from others who expect you to be a wise and noble steward.

GOD'S DREAM TO POPULATE THE WORLD

Our God—the Creator, the great Architect of the universe, and the Father of humanity—has a dream. He has a plan to unfold that involves each of us playing our parts and roles. We are reminded in Jeremiah 29:11, "For I know the thoughts that I think toward you, says the LORD, thoughts of peace and not of evil, to give you a future and a hope." God has an amazing plan and dream for each of our lives personally.

While God sees each of us uniquely and personally, there is also a much bigger picture in that each of our lives is made to work together in a larger dream. It looks like a fabric being woven together—the lateral strands are the peers of our generation while the vertical strands are the batons passed between generations that tie us together in relationship, partnered with God's dream.

Legacy is God's dream given to us to steward generationally. The goal is to see the lost get found, convert orphans into sons and daughters, and raise sons and daughters into fathers and mothers. And then to repeat this over and over again, down throughout history.

God's dream is to populate the earth with children. Paul reminds us, "And we know that in all things God works for the good of those who love him, who have been called according to his purpose. For those God foreknew he also predestined to be conformed to the image of his Son, that he might be the firstborn among many brothers (and sisters)" (Romans 8:28–29 NIV).

His dream is for sons and daughters to be populated throughout the earth. And discipleship is the perfect vehicle He designed to produce this.

We are foolish to think we can rebrand, modify, or reinvent God's perfect design. Church programs, popular worship teams, appealing preaching, and impressive buildings are not acceptable substitutes for this. God's mission that is given to us is discipleship through relationship, which produces legacy that is passed from generation to generation. There is no other way to achieve this goal.

But discipleship is risky. It is hard and requires commitment. And we know that people naturally veer toward the paths of least resistance and greater ease and comfort. This greater ease and comfort can be observed in modern alternative church cultures and values, and it focuses as these new models and examples have been rolled out with the appearance of great numerical success. These models have established influence and been followed and replicated by generations of church culture over time. As time has progressed, these new models have been accepted as the benchmark standard of God's design.

Over time, this has slowly shifted the church away from its intended purpose. But God will periodically call us back to His original design. I believe this is one of these moments in which God is calling us back into true purpose, focus, and agreement with His legacy, which is our inheritance.

Jesus told us that if we wanted to follow Him, then we must deny ourselves, take up our cross—death to self and being in control—and follow Jesus. He did not live for Himself or His own ideals, but He received from His Father every instruction that He lived out. Even Jesus was stewarding the architecture of the Father's plan, and so we must too.

THE COMPOUNDING WEALTH OF LEGACY

Jesus didn't live validated and qualified because He had an important last name or great potential. Jesus's gifts were evident as a young boy, but His preparation to truly walk in the significance of His calling and responsibility took time. He was not released into public ministry until He was thirty years old. And He only ministered for three and a half years. It's important to note that Jesus spent nearly ninety percent of His earthly life preparing and being discipled by the Father to spend only ten percent of His earthly life to change natural and spiritual history by teaching, fathering disciples, and ultimately laying His life down for us at Calvary.

If Jesus spent all that time preparing before He led others, then we need to realize two things: First, Jesus, the very Son of God, needed to be discipled and led by the Father well before He discipled others. And even after He began fathering others, He was still being led by His Father in His mission. Second, it's important that we ensure we are being discipled by the right people. Not people who just have gifts and charisma, but rather people who have a personal culture of being discipled.

> *No one can authentically lead someone else where they have not been.*

As Jesus said, this is like the blind leading the blind.

There is an amazing invitation to every single believer to follow Jesus's model of being discipled and making disciples.

> *Following this model of legacy*
> *is the kingdom family heirloom.*

Kingdom legacy is about partnering with God's dream within His model and strategy, not our good or progressive ideas. Discipleship transfers the gained wisdom, experience, and guidance from the learnings, successes, and failures of a father's life invested into his sons. Once stewarded well and implemented in the son's life, he will in time replicate this, becoming a father who is investing into a newfound son, the new father needing more depth of input and advice than ever before. Once this begins to perpetuate, we discover the compounding wealth of inheritance that discipleship can build as it passes through multiple generations without a relational interruption. This compounding effect establishes legacy from a dream into a reality.

The saints who have gone before us in heaven can no longer build the legacy of the cross but can only watch and observe, praying that we honor it by holding to God's perfect design to fill the earth with sons and daughters of heaven. This is the great cloud of witnesses observing how we steward our part of the story that they worked on prior to us. The writer of Hebrews tells us regarding them:

> THEREFORE WE ALSO, since we are surrounded by so great a cloud of witnesses, let us lay aside every weight, and the sin which so easily ensnares us, and let us run with endurance the race that is set before us, looking unto Jesus, the author and finisher of our faith, who for the joy that was set before Him endured the cross, despising the shame, and has sat down at the right hand of the throne of God. (Hebrews 12:1–2)

Legacy requires a partnering of generations, where fathers and sons partner up and mothers and daughters run together. This is a crucial message God has for us in these last days. This is why Malachi prophesied, "Behold, I will send you Elijah the prophet before the coming of the great and dreadful day of the Lord. And he will turn the hearts of the fathers to the children, and the hearts of the children to their fathers, lest I come and strike the earth with a curse" (Malachi 4:5–6).

And he will turn the hearts of the fathers to the children, and the hearts of the children to their fathers.

It's obvious this isn't a suggestion that Malachi is giving to us—this is a mandatory command for God's sons and daughters in these days. Kingdom legacy is to establish God's kingdom in His way, not through our own egos or notoriety. Legacy is God's dream. But it is also our inheritance.

CHAPTER 02

THE ORIGINAL DESIGN FOR ADAM

To fully understand what heaven's legacy is about, we must first understand the *why* of legacy as it has been established by God, as well as the *purpose* of God's intentions surrounding legacy. From Scripture, we see that before the earth was created and humans inhabited it, Lucifer rebelled against God and seeded an uprising in heaven's city, an event that failed miserably. Lucifer was polluted. And in this process, he was sentenced for two things: his pride and his trading.

LUCIFER'S DOWNFALL

Lucifer must have been a sight to see. Ezekiel 28:11–19 details what would have been Lucifer's former splendor and describes his prideful downfall:

> Moreover the word of the Lord came to me, saying, "Son of man, take up a lamentation for the king of Tyre, and say to him, 'Thus says the Lord God: "You were the seal of perfection, full of wisdom and perfect in beauty. You were in Eden, the garden of God; every precious stone was your covering: the sardius, topaz, and diamond, beryl, onyx, and jasper, sapphire, turquoise, and emerald with gold. The workmanship of your timbrels and pipes was prepared for you on the day you were created. You were the anointed cherub who covers; I established you; you were on the holy mountain of God; you walked back and forth in the midst of fiery stones. You were perfect in your ways from the day you were created, till iniquity was found in you. By the abundance of your trading you became filled with violence within, and you

sinned; therefore I cast you as a profane thing out of the mountain of God; and I destroyed you, O covering cherub, from the midst of the fiery stones. Your heart was lifted up because of your beauty; you corrupted your wisdom for the sake of your splendor; I cast you to the ground, I laid you before kings, that they might gaze at you. You defiled your sanctuaries by the multitude of your iniquities, by the iniquity of your trading; therefore I brought fire from your midst; it devoured you, and I turned you to ashes upon the earth in the sight of all who saw you. All who knew you among the peoples are astonished at you; you have become a horror, and shall be no more forever."""

These verses tell us that Lucifer was inlaid with beautiful stones and musical instruments. He was possibly the most beautiful of the angels that directly served God. Specifically, Lucifer was the anointed cherub that made offerings before the Lord's courts of heaven and orchestrated the adoration to God of all created beings.

Ezekiel 28:17 says, "Your heart was proud and lifted up because of your beauty; you corrupted your wisdom for the sake of your splendor" (AMP). Lucifer's position of privilege corrupted his heart, and so he began to take credit from the glory he had been entrusted to direct to God from all the citizens of eternity.

When the theft of God's glory entered his heart, Lucifer began to take credit for something that was not his. Because of this, sin and darkness were initiated. Lawlessness, violence, and sin entered the scene. It was never enough for him to just pollute himself with this corruption of purity into pride and insurrection—he had to share his revelation of greed, pride, and rebellion with others. Revelation 12:9 tells us that he was able to deceive one third of the angels to follow him, and thus they were all cast out of heaven.

The second conviction against him that caused him to commit the high crime of treason against God was his trading. The Scripture does not go into depth as to what this trading was specifically, but I would suggest that Lucifer had begun to interfere with areas of God's creation—angels and commodities—in his role of service to God. There are aspects of this that we may not even understand until we reach heaven.

Lucifer began to trade things to leverage himself into power in various facets of his responsibility. This is simply defined as theft and corruption. We can sadly see similar attributes in our fallen world today. Just look at corrupt governmental, political, and global figures who use their positions for personal gain. They use bribes, manipulation, and leverage societies toward certain outcomes for hidden agendas. They take advantage or "trade" by using those who are ignorant, weak, or defenseless to accept or endorse intended outcomes.

Satan attempted to overthrow our invincible, undefeatable, and almighty Father. But he was quickly defeated. When the Bible tells us that war broke out in heaven and a third of the angels rose up and fought alongside Lucifer, I imagine they were all silenced and stripped of their fight when the Father simply raised His finger from the throne and pointed at Lucifer. I imagine the scene like an immensely powerful lightning bolt of power coming from the throne of God and impacting Lucifer and all the angels, and, in a flash, catapulting them out of heaven and down to earth. Even though this is speculation, it is close to the truth because Jesus told us that He "saw Satan fall like lightning from heaven" (Luke 10:18).

Satan fell to earth and was its inhabitant, even though at that time he was not yet the god of this world as we know him. But he was still a powerful being.

ENTER HUMANITY

What did God do about Satan's rebellion? Because of Satan's treachery, God refused to let him rule any part of His universe. God didn't just leave it there, however. Lucifer was fallen, banished, and reserved to an outer prison to wait out his judgment. And God saw fit to put a new master over him.

God had a discussion with the Holy Spirit and Jesus. He said, "Let Us make man in Our image" (Genesis 1:26). Why did God make man (and woman) in His image? The answer is amazing to me.

God knew that Lucifer was on earth, and therefore God put a delegate to rule the planet. Just anyone wasn't enough to be this delegate, however. God would create a being who looked like Himself, a man He named Adam. God then pronounced Adam with five major blessings: "Then God blessed them, and God said to them, 'Be fruitful and multiply; fill the earth and subdue it; have dominion over the fish of the sea, over the birds of the air, and over every living thing that moves on the earth'" (Genesis 1:28).

Contained in this verse are five kingly keys a father gives to a son. As Adam opened his eyes for the first time, there was the face of God that had just breathed life into his lungs, looking at him eye to eye. And God said to him, "Be blessed, be fruitful, multiply, have dominion, and subdue the earth."

The Father's desire was for Adam to have dominion and subdue the earth with the blessing and endorsement of his relationship with God. Adam was given the command to be blessed, but he also and equally was to have dominion and to subdue the earth. The words *dominion* and *subdue* relate to a governance and dominance, but we are not ever given a command to subdue something that is perfect. This word indicates that Adam's task was to contain and subjugate a negative or contrary element in the environment.

Now, every time Lucifer looked at Adam, and eventually Adam's descendants after him, he would see Jehovah's image and be reminded not only of the God who conquered him but also the delegated authority from God on the life of Adam.

This was in essence an early picture of legacy—God the Father passing on blessing, mission, and purpose to a son, Adam. And, in time, this also extended to Eve.

THE CONCEPT OF LEGACY

Every day God would talk with Adam and Eve in the cool of the day, fellowshipping in relationship (see Genesis 3:8–10). Even though the Bible doesn't say what they talked about, I believe that God coached Adam on his inheritance.

Adam was given a legacy by God to rule. The interesting aspect of the declaration of this legacy is the final key God gave Adam: "subdue the earth." Isn't that interesting? Most of us are taught to believe that everything was perfect on earth before the Fall, but one can't subdue perfection. Adam was entrusted with subduing the enemy. To Lucifer, Adam was a huge insult—a jailer who looked like God, who conquered and imprisoned him.

As we all know, unfortunately, instead of Adam subduing and having dominion over the earth, Lucifer subdued Adam and Eve through disobedience. He tactically and strategically targeted them with the same trading culture that caused him to deceive a third of the angels when he was cast out of heaven.

When Adam and Eve disobeyed God, there was a moment of transfer where Satan became the ruler of this world (see Ephesians 2:2). The convict stole the authority from Adam and enslaved him into the corruption and the consequence of sin. Through disobedience, Adam and Eve forfeited their potential for a healthy legacy. Instead, being subdued under the law of sin and death, there was an immediate change in awareness and integral character, expressing shame, deception, pride, and blame shifting. This is the moment where Satan deceived his way out of being an inmate to becoming the god of this world, which is only a temporary role for him.

Jesus reinstated the authority God gave Adam at the beginning in Eden to believers who would truly stand in the victory of the cross. Authority was reinstated because Jesus's death created an open invitation for everyone to be born again and grafted back into the legacy of God. This is why Jesus could say after His resurrection, "All authority has been given to Me in heaven and on earth. Go therefore and make disciples of all the nations" (Matthew 28: 18–19).

God's legacy is all about reinstating relationships, reinstating sons and daughters who rule through that relationship. God wants to see the earth subdued now through kingdom sons and daughters who will enter regions and push back darkness and establish kingdom Edens in our cities and countries.

When we take our places of ruling in the earth as God's people, God's original intent of having a subduer over Satan builds strength. Now, when the enemy sees us, we remind him of God who defeated him in a microsecond. But he doesn't just see one; rather, the enemy sees billions of human faces every day. We, redeemed sons and daughters of God, cause Satan to see a multiplied face of God ruling on the earth. There is not just one representative, but there are hundreds of millions of us.

JESUS RESTORED LEGACY

Jesus conquered sin and death in His death and resurrection, thus restoring the lost blessings and empowerment from Adam, by crushing Lucifer. But we need to be aware that while Jesus paid the full price for our redemption, restoring what Adam lost, Satan and his fallen angels are still at large, awaiting their final judgment. Paul reminds us that Jesus "disarmed principalities and powers," and "He made a public spectacle of them, [by] triumphing over them in it" (Colossians 2:15).

Jesus's great sacrifice and victory restored our legacy with God. So, we must carry our God-given authority by pushing back darkness by ushering in heaven as a way of walking in the blessing, the dominion, and the subduing that God mandated us. The church has a purpose to defeat and bind up the works of the enemy.

We are not just saved sinners; we are God's children who are here to enforce His dominion and authority on the earth.

We are here to subdue the spiritual atmospheres that are opposing our Father's kingdom, driving them out and establishing His kingdom. We are here, inviting His atmosphere and presence through worship and kingdom culture. That is why personal kingdom identity is so important in our hearts and minds.

Jesus returned to heaven and has now sat down at the right hand of the Father until God the Father makes Jesus's enemies His footstool (see Hebrews 1:13). Here's the question: Who is God going to use to establish the kingdom and defeat the enemy? The answer? God is going to use authentic sons and daughters of the Father. We are the redemption story of the legacy that Adam lost and Jesus restored. This is because God intended humankind to rule, subdue, and have dominion in every area of life. In fact, it was God's original design for Adam to rule.

CHAPTER 03

THE GOD OF ABRAHAM, ISAAC, AND JACOB

When God first met with Moses in the burning-bush encounter, He identified Himself as "I AM," and also "the God of Abraham, Isaac, and Jacob" (see Exodus 3). I have always marveled at these statements. God didn't say, "Hey Moses, I am the King of the universe, or the Creator of everything you see and know." He said, "I am the God of generational legacy. I am a covenant keeper who honors lineage. I am the God who builds promises by partnering with family legacy."

This statement—"I am the God of your father—the God of Abraham, the God of Isaac, and the God of Jacob" (Exodus 3:6)—was not just simply God showing that He had history with Israelite lineage. God identified Himself as the God who had a covenant of lineage starting with Abraham and flowing on to Isaac and Jacob, and then to all who would come after them. He was referring to a specific multigenerational covenant and legacy that He had initiated and upheld.

GENERATIONS LINKED TOGETHER

God's plans are too big to be played out in one person's lifetime. It takes generations linked together, working together, to realize and build upon the foundation of God's dream through obedience and faith. God starts this lineage with Abram by leading him and his family out of Ur of the Chaldeans. Then, when the story picks up, God is suddenly asking him to leave his father and go to the land that God would show him (see Genesis 12:1–3).

Please read this next passage closely and put yourself in Abram's shoes. Can you imagine the magnitude of this encounter?

> WHEN ABRAM WAS NINETY-NINE YEARS OLD, the LORD appeared to Abram and said to him, "I am Almighty God; walk before Me and be blameless. And I will make My covenant between Me and you, and will multiply you exceedingly." Then Abram fell on his face, and God talked with him, saying: "As for Me, behold, My covenant is with you, and you shall be a father of many nations. No longer shall your name be called Abram, but your name shall be Abraham; for I have made you a father of many nations. I will make you exceedingly fruitful; and I will make nations of you, and kings shall come from you. And I will establish My covenant between Me and you and your descendants after you in their generations, for an everlasting covenant, to be God to you and your descendants after you." (Genesis 17:1–7)

I can just picture Abram's mind being completely blown when he heard this. But equally I think about God's perspective, as He is making this covenant to Abram that God, who is not confined to time, is staring through the future bloodline and legacy of every single person who would result from and be connected to that sacred covenant of blessing and redemption.

When speaking this well-known statement, God was looking deep into the pupils of Abram's eyes and He saw Isaac, then Jacob, then Joseph, then Joseph's sons, Moses, Joshua, and David, all the way down to Mary, the mother of Jesus. And He is still looking through the generations, even as far as your eyes. Yes, He saw even you in that moment.

The legacy that God is passing down is architected. Once we begin to understand that while every person has free choice to reject God or be a part of His family, it helps us clearly grasp that God foreknew us, predestined us, and justified us (see Romans 8:29). It is here that we see a significant relational interjection into the timeline of humanity's redemption since Adam and Eve left the Garden of Eden. And it is here that we see the redemption described to Eve about her seed crushing the serpent's head really being set in a greater level of motion. It is here that we see for the first time since Eden, God cutting a covenant to create a nation out of a man who would eventually produce a redeemer.

God, the great artist, began to accelerate this beautiful mural that would take the color of lives and hearts painted with His brush over thousands of years to create a depiction of love, sacrifice, and redemption. God didn't just bless Abram for his own life, but he blessed him as a patriarch, that he would be a father of many and that many would be blessed through him.

God calls Abram to leave his father's house, the only land and country that he knew, and go somewhere that he would be shown later. In the course of time, God changes Abram's name to Abraham. After being obedient to God's call, Abraham begins to prosper; he is living under the covenant of God's blessing, and he starts to increase and become rich.

But there's something missing if you are going to have a covenant with God and wealth—that is a successor. You can have all the wealth, wisdom, and blessing you want, but if you have no one to carry on your legacy, then your life will fade away into a forgotten and pointless existence, and all your progress and work will crumble and wash away into time.

God fulfills His promise to Abraham that he will become a father when he is ninety-nine years old, a physical impossibility at that age. But God is faithful to His word and Abraham and his wife have a child, whom they name Isaac. Abraham exemplifies the covenant with God, the blessing of God, and the legacy of passing those on to the next generation: "And Abraham gave all that he had to Isaac" (Genesis 25:5).

This is a statement that sounds like a regular inheritance, but it's interesting that the Bible notes that Abraham gave *all* he had. This—"all he had"—indicates assets, possessions, and money. But by far, the most valuable asset passed on to Isaac was the covenant blessing Abraham blessed Isaac with. Abraham became rich under this covenant of blessing, but here we see something of significance—Isaac receives Abraham's blessing and, as time progresses, Isaac becomes very rich with monetary blessings and generational blessings (see Genesis 26:13).

Isaac goes on to have twin sons, Esau and Jacob (see Genesis 25). Esau was the firstborn of the twins, but he was flippant with the sacredness of his birthright.

Jacob coveted the birthright, and even though he was shrewd and walked in horrible deception, God honored the value he placed on the birthright.

While Isaac was on his deathbed, Scripture tells us that he requested a special meal of Esau prior to pronouncing his blessing. Esau went out to hunt wild game, and while he was away, Jacob impersonated Esau and made a meal with a goat from the herd (see Genesis 27). Isaac blessed Jacob on his deathbed, and Jacob continued a rather colorful journey. But I want to point out that the covenant blessing greatly influences his life. It is noted that Jacob becomes exceedingly rich (see Genesis 30:43).

THE BLESSING FOR MANY?

The covenant blessing doesn't finish with Jacob, however. God identified Himself as the God of Abraham, Isaac, and Jacob, but this covenant does not dilute with time; it compounds through each generation that stewards it correctly and passes it on to its successors. Hebrews tells us, "By faith Jacob, when he was dying, blessed each of the sons of Joseph, and worshiped, leaning on the top of his staff" (Hebrews 11:21).

This compounding effect is incredibly different than it was with Abraham blessing Isaac in a singular sense. It doesn't mean that certain people are not blessed. Ishmael still received a lesser blessing even though he wasn't the child of promise; Esau still received a blessing even though he devalued and sold his birthright; some of Jacob's sons didn't receive what anyone would call a blessing because they made terrible decisions.

But when Jacob blessed the sons of Joseph, which were his grandsons, he was multiplying that blessing out to more than just one son, such as the oldest. The blessing that Joseph carried saved a nation and the surrounding nations. The grain stored in Egypt, because of Pharaoh's dream and Joseph's interpretation, that was distributed in the famine, was more about preserving the covenantal bloodline than about saving the surrounding nations. The surrounding nations were blessed and preserved as an *overflow* of the covenant extended to Abraham's lineage.

What I want you to grasp is that this covenant blessing that God birthed into Abraham's life had a period where it was singular—a father passing it on to his oldest son. From what we can see, it remained singular, with a recipient receiving blessing until Joseph, where we see a multiplication of the endowed blessing. Abraham is the father and patriarch of this covenantal blessing, and it passes from father to son until we see it multiplied. Then we see the children of Israel enter a hard period of four hundred years of slavery in Egypt.

To see this in an amazing poetic parallel, we look forward in time from this Abrahamic era to the birth of Jesus. At approximately the age of thirty, Jesus was baptized at the Jordan by John the Baptist, His cousin. And with a booming voice, we hear the approval and blessing of Jehovah, Father God, being declared over Jesus. Again, just like Isaac, who was the son of promise, there was a singular transference of blessing and empowerment from the Father to the Son.

Near the end of Jesus's earthly ministry, however, we observe that Jesus breathes on all His close disciples: "And when He had said this, He breathed on them, and said to them, 'Receive the Holy Spirit'" (John 20:22). This perfectly mirrors the same sense that was modeled from Abraham to Jacob, who then transitioned to bless multiple sons. Now we see Jesus, the only Son of the Father, blessing multiple sons and empowering them to imitate Him. And that blessing goes down the line to us, who are called to spread and multiply this gospel and His kingdom.

The covenant that God cut with Abraham is potent. While there is a lineage that God has established with intention to redeem lost sons and daughters, anyone who holds it and understands it can discover the blessing compounded in their lives and lineage that tracks all the way back to Abraham.

In the book of Genesis, we see that this legacy dynamic God is operating with is a compounding blessing. Abraham becomes rich, Isaac becomes very rich, then we see that Jacob becomes exceedingly rich. It is kingdom compounded growth, potency, and discipleship, not just in numbers but in quality. Numerically and developmentally. And this is one of the greatest keys that the modern church is missing: legacy. Jesus architected the growth of His kingdom on earth through discipleship.

Second Corinthians 3:18 tells us that we as believers reflect God's glory in ever-increasing measures—going from glory to glory. What that means in simple language is that God advances every time He moves. He never moves backward,

He never retreats, and He never is lost in the valley. Every time the clock ticks, God has increased and expanded His glory. And if that is His language and culture, then the challenge is how we can adopt that more into our own lives today. Because sons look like their fathers and daughters look like their mothers.

The church should be growing and increasing numerically every year. This is because God is the God of Abraham, Isaac, and Jacob. Covenant is meant to live, while legacy is the framework for it to continue. Abraham's sons honored the legacy of covenant that was passed down from their father. That same legacy of covenant flows through the generations to Jesus on the cross and, both naturally and spiritually, to each one of us today. That's why we can clearly see that there is a stark difference between believers and disciples.

GENERATIONAL DISCIPLES

Believers admire Jesus, while disciples obey Jesus. Mere believers tend to think of themselves as individuals, whereas sons and daughters think in value systems around family interests and family heritage. Believers look for Christian celebrities to lead them. Many are even deceived into trying to make themselves a personal influencer to become a type of celebrity themselves.

Relationship with God requires vulnerability.

Many believers are happy for someone else to have intimacy with God while they just admire the glow of that person who is in love or on fire.

They do not pursue and do not desire the process that is required to become a son or daughter.

These people flock to large churches where they can hide in the pews and avoid intimacy of relationship with others, with leadership, and with God. And they do this while appeasing their consciences that they attended church, are immersed in "community," or are true servants of God who are serving people. These are not true sons and daughters of God.

Mere believers create followers with low-level commitments, like the five thousand who ate loaves and fishes when Jesus multiplied them. Believers leave no spiritual legacy footprint after they die. They are consumers who are intrigued by Jesus but not committed enough to die to their old nature and submit to a relationship that can train and equip them for more.

They will usually never endure or authentically receive any loving correction, because at the root they have an orphan mentality. This mentality is the result of a heart not connected to fathers or mothers, one that does not embrace kingdom family culture, one that sees correction as an evil enemy instead of a wise friend taking risks for their personal benefit.

The orphan heart is one of rejection, independence, hate, and fear of authority; it is one of survivalism, isolation, and loneliness.

Their accumulated learning and experience die with them and is not passed on to the next generation.

We must wake up and recognize this mentality as the enemy of the church of Jesus Christ. This trojan horse is an insult to the sacrifice of the cross. Sons look out for their father's interests, how the kingdom can be expanded, and how they can serve more. Daughters are fashioned into maturity by the careful guidance, example, and correction of a mother. And in the process, sons and daughters become fathers and mothers who replicate themselves in the lives of others.

Ten of the eleven remaining disciples who walked with Jesus all laid their lives down for Jesus in martyrdom because they had seen Jesus die in that way. They each became spearheads into new nations and territories, taking the gospel to the Jewish and non-Jewish world, taking the message of the Master to the lost and broken. They did not return to their own interests after Jesus ascended to heaven, but rather they pursued the interests of heaven. They followed the model of Jesus, who had become their father figure over three and a half years of discipleship.

THE ULTIMATE GOAL

When we hear someone say, "I ended up just like my father or mother," it usually carries a negative connotation along with it. But the disciples became like Jesus their father to the same extent that they also were executed like He was for their faith and in pursuit of building God's kingdom.

I don't know about you, but I want to end up just like my heavenly big brother and Father. That's the goal of passing on a legacy to the next generation. Sons and daughters will take ownership of a father's interests, values, and goals. It will be a personal conviction. That's why Jesus talked about the difference between a shepherd and a hireling (see John 10). Read hireling as an employee or contractor and shepherd as sons or daughters.

A son who is a shepherd has personal ownership of the sheep; he carries the responsibility for the flock. An employee is in the same situation but for their personal gain and benefits. The outside job or situation looks the same, but the heart is much different. The actions are the same, but the investment is not.

Jesus is not looking for orphans who want a paycheck; He is looking for sons and daughters who will take personal ownership of their Father's kingdom.

This is one of the reasons Jesus called Judas the son of hell, because Judas was just in it to find ways to personally benefit from the situation. This does nothing more than reflect the culture of Lucifer. Most of the remaining disciples eventually paid the ultimate price for the expansion of the kingdom of God.

You see, good sons will create good sons. Unless a son has spent a significant portion of his life under the training, instruction, and covering of a father, he simply does not qualify to be a father. While it is not impossible, there is a low probability that someone can lead someone else where they have not been led. How can anyone take others where they have not been themselves?

If someone doesn't have a spiritual father, it's likely they are operating in an orphan mentality and will become a spiritual tyrant should they get into a position of power or influence. All the unhealed pain, insecurity, and immaturity will manifest in control, ego, abuse, and narcissism, especially in someone who has not learned how to follow a healthy leader. It will then replicate the same type of culture in those following him or her. In essence, it is just like Jesus said—the blind leading the blind, which is a perverted counterfeit of legacy.

Sons and daughters are the building-block expansions of legacy; they are the surety for longevity. Fathers and mothers ensure that those blocks are correctly placed into the foundation and walls of the house of God. In order for legacy to thrive, there must be fathers who teach sons and mothers who teach daughters, passing on the lifetime of experiences they have accumulated.

Once we learn how to honor the culture of this concept—of passing on wisdom, training, direction, and influence from generation to generation—then we can finally get on this road of the kingdom that can result in true legacy that becomes our generational heritage. That is the power of our generational legacy, the God of Abraham, Isaac, and Jacob.

CHAPTER 04

JESUS: THE FIRSTBORN OF MANY BROTHERS

God's whole kingdom model is family-based and family-focused. God formed Adam from the dirt in His own hands and breathed life into his lungs with His own breath. But He was separated from relationship with Adam through Adam's decision to sin. Adam was born into the privilege of legacy, but he gave it up for a cheap deception. Legacy was lost but not gone forever. God foretold Eve in the Garden of His plan of a child who would come from her seed and bruise the head of the serpent (see Genesis 3:15). Legacy had hope.

We can sometimes become so familiar reading John 3:16, that "God sent His only begotten Son" into the world, that we lose sight that God is not limited to only having one singular Son. It has always been God's intention that He would have a family, many sons and daughters who would expand His kingdom. In the last chapter, we looked at how God the Father has built our whole perception of Him around just that—God as a Father. He has demonstrated and communicated that family is the platform upon which He intends to build His kingdom.

LEGACY REBORN

But how does a perfect, holy God connect a broken, sinful race to His world? He adopts them into His family by building a bridge between our worlds through the cross that Jesus redeemed us on. In John 3:16 we read that "God so loved the world that He gave His only begotten Son, that whoever believes in Him should not perish but have everlasting life." This is arguably the most well-known passage of Scripture where we read that God the Father sent His one and only Son to save the world. And yet we read that Jesus rose from the dead and ascended into heaven as "the firstborn of many brothers" (Romans 8:29 NIV).

> *Jesus came to earth as the only Son of the Father,*
> *but He returns to heaven as the oldest brother of many siblings.*

God said to Noah after the flood, as long as the earth remains, so shall remain seedtime and harvest (see Genesis 8:22). God implemented a spiritual law that would influence a natural law. Reading this passage and understanding the power of it, we see that God created an environment on the earth that would bear the harvest according to the seed that was sown.

Then we go on to the passage where Jesus was prophesying His death: "Most assuredly, I say to you, unless a grain of wheat falls into the ground and dies, it remains alone; but if it dies, it produces much grain" (John 12:24). Most of the listeners that day probably thought Jesus was speaking powerful philosophy. And He was, but He was directly referring to His death. In doing so, Jesus also prophesied about the powerful multiplication that results in many other seeds being born out of the "seedtime" of Jesus laying down His own life.

Thus, legacy is born because one Man became the seed for everyone who would come after Him. For that legacy to continue, we too must learn to die to ourselves. That's why Jesus said if we want to be discipled by Him, we must deny ourselves, take up our own cross, and follow Him daily. Or, to put it differently, we are invited to follow His example (see Matthew 16:24; Luke 9:23).

Have you ever had a garden or worked on a farm with crops? If so, then you understand that a seed is a powerful and fascinating thing. A tiny little grain can produce unquantified numbers of plants that produce replicated seeds of the same species of crop. And it can do this repeatedly.

Take the apple seed, as an example. If stewarded and cultivated well, we can take a single apple seed and multiply it to limitless numbers. We take an apple seed, properly plant and tend it, and in time we will have a single young apple tree. That tree will produce apples and seeds within those apples that can replicate and bear the exact resemblance of the first seed we started with. Over time, we can continue this process until we end up with an orchard—exponentially more apples and countless apple seeds. The orchard can then propagate over the local area, then a national area, then globally if tended properly. And all this fruitfulness comes from a single seed. If those seeds are left untouched or not interfered with—no hybrid or splicing with other apple or fruit species—then we will have the exact same apple a thousand years later.

The legacy Jesus gave us needs to be honored in its pure form without our help or modification. Just like the apple seed, but on a much greater level, the gospel and the blood of Jesus works all by itself; it doesn't need us to tamper with it or adjust it. The legacy Jesus gave us was designed in heaven to replicate a perfect DNA of His Spirit across the globe, to propagate sons and daughters of heaven who look just like Jesus.

Discipleship is the vehicle that Jesus gave us to replicate the seed of His life, message, death, and resurrection. This is one of the reasons Paul wrote, "My little children, for whom I labor in birth again until Christ is formed in you" (Galatians 4:19). This removes the concept that "it's just me and Jesus," and brings us back to the need for a father or mother to labor over us, modeling and demonstrating the kingdom of God to the end that the subsequent generations would replicate the kingdom's DNA and culture.

Just like the single apple seed turning into an orchard, Jesus was the first seed that was sown among His people. But He wasn't meant to be the only Son—God's desire was for a family. God's dream was that Jesus would produce many sons and daughters to populate the earth with kingdom family. Jesus was the firstborn among many brothers. God is looking for a harvest of ever-increasing family members. And He has an invested focus and mindset to this end.

Do you remember the parable Jesus told when He described Himself as the "true vine"? In the same parable, He describes His Father as the Vinedresser. Jesus said,

> I AM THE TRUE VINE, AND MY FATHER IS THE VINEDRESSER. Every branch in Me that does not bear fruit He takes away; and every branch that bears fruit He prunes, that it may bear more fruit. You are already clean because of the

word which I have spoken to you. Abide in Me, and I in you. As the branch cannot bear fruit of itself, unless it abides in the vine, neither can you, unless you abide in Me. I am the vine, you are the branches. He who abides in Me, and I in him, bears much fruit; for without Me you can do nothing. If anyone does not abide in Me, he is cast out as a branch and is withered; and they gather them and throw them into the fire, and they are burned. If you abide in Me, and My words abide in you, you will ask what you desire, and it shall be done for you. By this My Father is glorified, that you bear much fruit; so you will be My disciples. (John 15:1–8)

Considering all of this, let's now look at why it's extremely important that we see Jesus as our older brother who has gone before us.

THE EXAMPLE TO FOLLOW, NOT JUST ADMIRE

Jesus, during His time ministering on earth, did not come to display His own unique personality and ministry. Rather, He came to show us what the Father looks like. He said, "Most assuredly, I say to you, the Son can do nothing of Himself, but what He sees the Father do; for whatever He does, the Son also does in like manner" (John 5:19). And again, "For I have not spoken on My own authority; but the Father who sent Me gave Me a command, what I should say and what I should speak" (John 12:49).

Jesus came to demonstrate the Father's virtues and values by speaking of a kingdom that was at hand, a kingdom that was different from any earthly kingdom (see Matthew 4:17). Jesus did not point to Himself. Instead, He pointed to the Father, completely submitted and reflective of the kingdom model. This was to the extent that Jesus told us that if we had seen Him, then we had seen the Father (see John 14:9).

My point? While Jesus is unique, He set an example that we are to reflect another and not ourselves. We are called and shown that we are to reflect Jesus and Father God. But how do we do this? It only happens through discipleship and through learning kingdom family culture by mentoring relationships. For each of us, Jesus the firstborn means that we are born again, yes, but we are born *after* Him.

Kingdom leadership and mentorship should look like family! That family can look like a hospital, healing the brokenness of past damage for a new sibling's arrival. It can look like an academy to train and equip the healed siblings. Or it can even look like an army that has mobilized the equipped to go out into the world and bring God's kingdom in visible ways. I don't know how many billions of people have entered the kingdom since Jesus ascended to the Father, but what I can tell you is that you are one of them if you have given your life to the Father through Jesus's sacrifice.

Paul demonstrates this concept by saying, "Follow my example, as I follow the example of Christ" (1 Corinthians 11:1 NIV). Putting this differently, it means, "Imitate me, as I model Jesus." How did Jesus replicate the model the Father gave Him? He replicated it through doing life with His protégés, or disciples, not just His public teaching sessions. There was an immersive lifestyle proximity that His disciples were invited into where they learned from the way Jesus lived publicly *and* behind the scenes.

Jesus, the firstborn, strongly suggests that there are other siblings in the family. And siblings look alike because they share DNA, and they act alike because of time spent together. Jesus was clear when He referred to God as His Father. He referred to sons of God and sons of the devil. This entire narrative—the kingdom narrative—is about two families: the family of Jehovah and the family of Lucifer. There is no third family.

> *Jesus was clear when He referred to God as His Father. He referred to sons of God and sons of the devil. This entire narrative—the kingdom narrative—is about two families.*

When Adam and Eve rebelled against God's commands, they became slaves of the devil, and the family relationship was broken. In that moment, God in many ways lost custody of His kids. The Lamb slain before the foundation of the world was God's redemption plan to get His kids back. These are the ones, "the whosoevers" of John 3:16, who would believe in the Lord Jesus, the Lamb slain for our restorative family status.

Jesus inserted into the lineage of Adam, Abraham, and King David, perfectly answering the bloodline of the promise down through the generations from Eve. And we know that His birth was miraculous—He was conceived through the Holy Spirit by the virgin Mary. Knowing and committing no sin in His entire life, He was a perfect man. Standing before Pilate, a falsely accused Jesus is condemned by an angry mob and exchanged for an insurgent terrorist named Barabbas, whose name means son of a father. Jesus, the innocent, is sentenced to die, and Barabbas, the guilty "son of the father," goes free in exchange. Jesus dies on the cross, the innocent in place of the guilty.

But then Jesus rises from the dead, having defeated that serpent, that dragon of old, and He took back the keys that Adam forfeited in the Garden of Eden. Now, whosoever would believe in Jesus can have eternal life, which is through a rejoining of the family of God the Father. Now, He is also our Father just like He was Jesus's Father.

God wanted His kids back,
and He went to every length to make it happen.

BECOMING THE FIRSTBORN

This entire movement we call the church is not about celebrities of big-brand Christianity; it is about Jesus becoming the firstborn among many children, so that many people can now be called the sons and daughters of God. We—all nations, families, and peoples who believe in Christ—are the family of God.

I often imagine the first moment that Jesus walked back through the gates of heaven after returning from His resurrection, having accomplished all He was sent to do. And I see the thief who was next to Him on the cross, condemned for his crimes, but recognizing Jesus walking right next to him, he is no longer a criminal but a son. This is a picture of the kingdom of God.

We have all been reborn if we have believed in Jesus as Lord. We are no longer identified by who we used to be. We are now all siblings of our older brother, Jesus, the hero, savior, the firstborn of many brothers and sisters. This is why Paul could write:

> But God, who is rich in mercy, because of His great love with which He loved us, even when we were dead in trespasses, made us alive together with Christ (by grace you have been saved), and raised us up together, and made us sit together in the heavenly places in Christ Jesus, that in the ages to come He might show the exceeding riches of His grace in His kindness toward us in Christ Jesus. For by grace you have been saved through faith, and that not of yourselves; it is the gift of God, not of works, lest anyone should boast. For we are His workmanship, created in Christ Jesus for good works, which God prepared beforehand that we should walk in them. (Ephesians 2:4–10)

If the model of legacy that we have been given is full of leading a life of obedience, fulfilling our personal and collective ministries, and immersing sons and daughters into that environment, then we must ask ourselves: how are we doing? If what I leave behind in my life after I pass on into heaven doesn't look like personal prestige or recognition of my name, but rather how many followers of Jesus I have helped establish through my life, then the question we must ask ourselves is how many brothers and sisters are we personally responsible for bringing into the family?

It's going to be different for each of us; there is no corporate performance number that we are to measure our lives by. But God, who plans all things, has planned out each life we are supposed to touch, lead, and shape. This is not just a concept of being good receivers, but rather faithfulness to Jesus's mission: "Go and make disciples of as many people as you can, just in the same way as I have gathered and taught and modeled the kingdom for you" (see Matthew 28:18–20).

CHAPTER 05

THE LEGACY OF JESUS: THE GREAT COMMISSION

THE MOST IMPORTANT MISSION BRIEF

I have put significant thought into considering and meditating on the passage of Scripture found in Matthew 28:18–20, which is referred to as the Great Commission:

> AND JESUS CAME AND SPOKE TO THEM, saying, "All authority has been given to Me in heaven and on earth. Go therefore and make disciples of all the nations, baptizing them in the name of the Father and of the Son and of the Holy Spirit, teaching them to observe all things that I have commanded you; and lo, I am with you always, even to the end of the age." Amen.

Think about how Jesus, the King of Glory, stepped out of heaven and came to teach us about the Father and pay the ultimate price for our redemption. Right at the threshold of His ascension into heaven, Jesus had a conversation with His disciples in which He gave them some instructions.

These instructions were not mere suggestions; they were not a casual guessing at the best idea on how to keep the flame, which Jesus had lit, alive. Rather, at this last documented point in the earthly life of Jesus, with little time remaining before He ascended to the Father, every single word coming out of His mouth was intentional, pivotal, and important. He was leaving crucial instructions to

His trusted friends as to the only way to redeem as many people as possible. Jesus didn't die on the cross, sacrificing all He was and is, only to become casual about the potency of the redemption He had just purchased.

Jesus's last words give us a glimpse into His heart: "Hey team, this salvation cost Me literally everything. I am going home to sit at the right hand of our Father and to prepare a house for each of you. Please pay the utmost attention because what I am about to tell you is of eternal consequence to billions of people. We must save them, but it's going to be your responsibility now. This is the whole fulfillment of My heart and the heart of our Father who sent Me—to restore the relationship and the eternal life that Adam and Eve gave away. It's on you now. It's your turn to run with My baton to save the world. And here's how you do it."

God is the one who created the idea of multiplication; He created life to multiply—animals, birds, fish, plants, and even Adam and Eve. Even His command, "Let there be light," is still obeying God's word and multiplying and expanding in the galaxies in this exact moment. He came to Abraham and told him to look up at the stars, because his descendants would be more numerous than these. And now here is the resurrected Jesus, as a type of Abraham, birthing a new lineage of sons and daughters of God who are grafted into the family of God.

What we must understand is that Jesus's last commands are the starting point and the manual at which every believer is picking up His legacy. This is to redeem and save every possible lost soul. The way we embrace this proves if we really love Jesus or not. Like Jesus said to Peter after He rose from the grave, "If you love Me, then feed My sheep and tend My lambs" (see John 21:15–17). He also said, "If you love Me, then you'll obey My commands" (see John 14:15–17).

In some ways, our pursuit of souls and our pursuit of discipleship is really a way to express that we, in fact, really do love Jesus with our whole hearts.

THE GREAT COMMISSION AND LEGACY

Jesus said, "All Authority has been given to Me in heaven and earth" (Matthew 28:18). After having been raised from the dead, Jesus, having freshly conquered

Lucifer's hold and claim over Adam's lineage, having taken back the power of sin and death, and having been honored by the Father, was appointed as the name above every other name. He was given the ultimate authority in heaven and earth by the Father (see Philippians 2:9). Because of this, Jesus had incredible boldness and confidence to issue the following commands.

- "Go therefore and make disciples of all nations" (Matthew 28:19). I find it fascinating that Jesus boldly announces His risen power and authority as a prequalifying statement to this one. This looks like a political leader who wins an election and then goes straight to his desk and issues his first law. This first law is never casual or flippant, but it reveals the leader's most significant values, focus, and ideals. So here, Jesus says, "I've won; now go and gather every single person who will believe—we want them all back, as many as would believe."
- "Baptizing them in the name of the Father and of the Son and of the Holy Spirit" (Matthew 28:19). This is a statement of not just recruiting disciples but an urge to immerse these disciples into the culture and family of God, into relationship with each member of the Godhead—Father, Son, and Holy Spirit.
- "Teaching them to observe all things that I have commanded you" (Matthew 28:20). Once we are saved, gathered, and immersed, then we must teach His disciples to obey and observe everything He has taught us. This is not an optional gospel where we can select aspects we are comfortable or agree with; this is a kingdom with a King, and everything He says matters and holds up. Learning to be obedient to everything Jesus taught the disciples as if Jesus was standing right in front of us today is exactly what He meant.

We cannot water down or dilute the absolutes or principles in the culture and kingdom of heaven we are immersed in.

> *We cannot be in love with the benefits*
> *but despise the requirements.*

This is why authentic discipleship really matters, as we steward and replicate one generation to the next. We must ensure that we are walking in everything

Jesus demonstrated and taught. It's not enough for us to see blind eyes healed; we must also walk in integrity and moral purity in our relationship with God. We cannot dilute this legacy.

- "I am with you always" (Matthew 28:20). Finally, Jesus is empowering us to know that He is with us, to teach, comfort, empower, and supply and lead us. This is a mission with the accompaniment of resources.

Now that we understand the deeper aspects and perspective of this Great Commission, we can more easily grasp why legacy is inseparably paired with discipleship.

LEGACY IS ABOUT LONGEVITY

For decades, the Western church has taken a lot of false comfort in how many hands are raised or how many people respond to evangelistic altar calls in a church service or in stadium events. We have prized how many "sinner's prayers" we have prayed with people. But the reality is that there is no sinner's prayer in the Scripture—although the Bible teaches how we can acknowledge God before others and be saved and forgiven, thus responding to the kingdom to accept Jesus as our Lord and Savior.

The problem is that we focus on the sales aspect of the gospel and not in the fulfillment of the order.

It's like a service company putting ninety-nine percent of its focus selling its service or product installs, training its sales team to be the sharpest, most efficient at getting customers to sign the sales contract, with only one percent of the company's focus, priority, and expertise being resourced into the management of the customer, the organization of the project, or the execution and delivery of the service.

The church has become complacent in its boasting of a certain number of decisions for Christ, and we have made the grave mistake of using this statistic to gauge our success. The real focus must be, of the salvation prayers being prayed and the decisions being made, how many of those souls are still walking with Jesus one year later? How about five years later? How many of those people are being established, grounded, and planted in a local church? Encouraged and strengthened in their own personal relationship with the Father, Son, and Holy Spirit? How many of them are maturing instead of just attending church, battling the same bondages and wounds years later? Or even worse, how many of them have returned to their chains and chosen the world over Christ?

Let's look at this practically for a moment, using an example from the financial world. The financial world says that it is "not what you make, it's what you keep" when it comes to growing a business. In other words, just because you earn a lot of income doesn't mean as much as how much is left over after all your expenses and spending are taken into account. How much are you able to save after all your earnings are depleted?

We need to stop using crowds, personal evangelism, salvation prayers, and decisions to judge our success in the church. To be honest, too often it's self-validating boasting. It's not how many salvation prayers we can initiate; rather, it's how many souls are established and remain in the kingdom years later with Christ Jesus being formed on the inside of them.

Legacy is all about longevity. Decisions that aren't real converts at the end of the day aren't adding to the mandate that Jesus tasked us with.

SHEEP STEALING

I grew up in New Zealand, a nation with millions of sheep that are farmed for agriculture every year. We have a term for when a thief comes to steal the farmer's sheep—a rustler. These rustlers pay no price for the purchase of, raising, feeding, or caring for the sheep; they just want to benefit from the sheep. This is what has been happening in the church for many years, and it needs to stop.

Many churches have been following franchise models and have appeared to experience growth, influence, and success. We live in a time when people are more attracted to popular and exciting waves of fashion and trends than they are to the genuine presence and pleasure of God over them. This is destroying God's original intent for productivity and legacy. It seems as if few people care to steward what's in them to the next generation. Many only seemingly care about today's appearances, not the quality of tomorrow's established community in their church.

Ministers bypass the difficult narrow road of preparation and lifestyle by networking their way around successful, trendy, or popular circles of church ministry. They climb the invisible ladder to a platform of "secular influence," which is dressed up to look like they have God's approval. How sad to be trading the mountaintops with God for the idolatrous party of influence and fame at the bottom.

Upon closer inspection, these churches rarely function in the nature of the kingdom's intent. Few new souls are really getting saved and transformed. Instead, the leadership will find ways to be appealing to the crowd. They are not concerned about the one lost sheep or the less attractive individual. They instead want to attract someone else's ninety-nine sheep to relocate to their newly decorated pasture. So, they use the latest branding, associations, and marketing. They hire popular worship leaders or ministers with an intent to attract their desired demographic, which mostly means other church congregants. In essence, they rely on transfer growth, not organic growth. They want to look successful, but they do not want to pay a personal price for winning souls.

We cannot afford to herd sheep from one fold to another, deceiving them (and their leaders) that this is the kingdom model.

Legacy calls for children to be born and then raised—not stolen from other parts of the family.

UNPACKING THE GREAT COMMISSION

I love that God orchestrated four different individuals to write the Gospels depicting Jesus, so that we could get a glimpse through different eyes into His multifaceted nature and narrative. I love that we get to see Jesus for who He is, not just one person's view of Him. It creates a balanced grasp of Jesus's personality and establishes the details that matter in His early ministry.

THE LEGACY OF JESUS: THE GREAT COMMISSION

This is one of the most important moments in Jesus's story. Let's read through three of the perspectives of the moment the Great Commission was given to Jesus's disciples, in Matthew, Mark, and Luke:

> AND JESUS CAME AND SPOKE TO THEM, saying, "All authority has been given to Me in heaven and on earth. Go therefore and make disciples of all the nations, baptizing them in the name of the Father and of the Son and of the Holy Spirit, teaching them to observe all things that I have commanded you; and lo, I am with you always, even to the end of the age." Amen. (Matthew 28:18–20)

> LATER HE APPEARED TO THE ELEVEN AS THEY SAT AT THE TABLE; and He rebuked their unbelief and hardness of heart, because they did not believe those who had seen Him after He had risen. And He said to them, "Go into all the world and preach the gospel to every creature. He who believes and is baptized will be saved; but he who does not believe will be condemned. And these signs will follow those who believe: In My name they will cast out demons; they will speak with new tongues; they will take up serpents; and if they drink anything deadly, it will by no means hurt them; they will lay hands on the sick, and they will recover." (Mark 16:14–18)

> THEN HE SAID TO THEM, "These are the words which I spoke to you while I was still with you, that all things must be fulfilled which were written in the Law of Moses and the Prophets and the Psalms concerning Me." And He opened their understanding, that they might comprehend the Scriptures. Then He said to them, "Thus it is written, and thus it was necessary for the Christ to suffer and to rise from the dead the third day, and that repentance and remission of sins should be preached in His name to all nations, beginning at Jerusalem. And you are witnesses of these things. Behold, I send the Promise of My Father upon you; but tarry in the city of Jerusalem until you are endued with power from on high." (Luke 24:44–49)

These words were all recorded from the same event or conversation that we refer to as the Great Commission, but each one is a segment in that larger conversation.

If you think about it, there isn't enough room in the four Gospels to transcribe all the sermons or conversations throughout Jesus's three and a half years that He ministered. In order to have a holistic insight into the Great Commission, we need to put all the segments from that conversation together across the four Gospels.

The priorities of God's heart are easily evident and understood when we look at these three different accounts. God wants His kids back. Jesus didn't die on the cross at an incredibly high cost beyond our understanding and then arise to then not have a very clear intention as a result. He is clearly commanding we partner with that intention here.

It is interesting that Jesus never mentioned building big churches, great personal ministries, or finding ways to become the greatest church in the area, even though He grew in fame and reputation. Rather, He emphasized the importance and urgency of preaching and spreading this message of salvation to every possible person through every believer.

Jesus birthed the church. He had great rapport, and He demonstrated miracles so that we would have a lifestyle model to follow, not leverage to monetize or build our own empires. What He mentions, with vivid emphasis, is to make disciples of all people—Black, White, Asian, Hispanic, etc.—*everyone*. And this discipleship was not a mere sinner's prayer but a born-again transformation.

Jesus's focus is placed on His disciples replicating His model of discipleship, which was training through relationship and proximity. Jesus was not focusing on filling church seats with people who are semi-invested and still undecided. Jesus was interested in the legacy of His ministry on earth being passed on from generation to generation. He sought to ensure that the focus of heaven's throne would be met—the redemption and establishing of souls into the kingdom, not the church organization.

I need to add a caveat here, because one may think I am against the church. I want to be clear: I am not against the church. At least, I'm not against the church that Jesus ordained. I am, however, against the institution of the modern church that has forsaken Matthew 28:18–20 in order to become popular and to attain numbers and growth, all at the cost of authentic discipleship.

I think we all have an inner knowing that we have fallen short of what Jesus birthed. If it was not so, then we would have already converted and discipled most of the planet some two thousand years later using this model.

And because of this highlighted shortcoming, we need a reformation to truly honor what a revival would bring in our day and age.

While I love revival, revival culture has in most part become almost a nostalgic reliving of past moves. As you read through this book it's going to become clear that we need more than revival alone. We need reformation which is a place where we allow God to rebuild the foundations of our lives and churches, back towards His original design.

Jesus invited us to build His legacy through engaging in the Great Commission by the power of His Spirit. That means you and me empowered by His Spirit, being mothers and fathers to the next generation, teaching them all Jesus has commanded us, modeling for them kingdom values. This means we are calling to them, "Follow me as I follow Christ."

SECTION II

WHY IS THE MODERN CHURCH FAILING?

As we enter this second section, you will notice the focus changes from the poetic story of God to address some painful and problematic current realities and states of the modern church, which makes way for some difficult conversations. In order for hope and solutions to come, we first have to discuss and face dysfunctional realities. Walking through this section will invite each person to face conversations and realities that need to be addressed so that we can move into a future of generational legacy.

> The Lord is a jealous God, and He wants us to walk in the fullness of His culture. God only confronts those He loves, and He deeply loves His church. While a lot of popular culture ignores issues and sweeps them under the rug, Jesus does not do this. He will contend with any part of our culture that is in contradiction with Him.

As you read this section, please know that Jesus may need to turn over some tables in our generation for the world to see a glorious bride, without spot and wrinkle. The fear of the Lord is a much-needed attribute to be remembered in our culture. Please allow both the fear and grace of God to cover you as you read through this section.

> King Jesus never addresses issues in our lives and communities without offering hope and a path for restoration. This book has been written with a passion for the church, not from a place of criticism. Truth coupled with love is the only way to see heaven's reality. Love and grace alone cannot comprehend a healthy view of reality—only truth can unlock this. At times, truth can be extremely inconvenient and confrontational. So, this section has confrontational truth offered in love with the hope that if embraced by our generation, greatness would emerge in our destiny without the sabotage of compromise.

CHAPTER 06

THE PLAN AND PURPOSE OF THE CHURCH

Jesus left the church a clear mandate in Matthew 28:18–20: to disciple the nations and build His kingdom. The way that He accomplishes this mandate is through the church, through His sons and daughters who have been empowered by His Spirit. But before we can fully grasp God's desire for generational legacy to be passed on, we have to define the church and why He established it in the first place.

What is the church? Is it a community club where people huddle together and shelter themselves from the world? Is it a place where people can settle in and be isolated from reality? Or a place where people can live unchanged lives, always needing the same help because they are in the same situation in life without ever progressing? I would argue that the church is none of these things, although these are not uncommon realities in many churches today.

So, what is the purpose of the church? Why did Jesus establish it? Does church attendance or membership disciple and father people? Is this the legacy Jesus spoke of?

A major aspect of Jesus establishing the church was to facilitate discipleship. Contrary to popular belief, attendance, membership, or even sermons don't disciple people. Podcasts, teaching series, YouTube channels, and even books do not disciple people. Is there any benefit to them? Of course they are valuable tools. They inform people but do not disciple them. While church attendance may invite people to opportunities of preaching that convict, teach, and encourage, and membership creates community and gathers fellowshipping church members, mere church attendance does not disciple people.

Paul wrote to the Corinthians, "For though you might have ten thousand instructors in Christ, yet you do not have many fathers; for in Christ Jesus I have begotten you through the gospel" (1 Corinthians 4:15). Paul is making a line of clear distinction between teaching and fathering, between information and discipleship.

Fathers disciple sons and mothers disciple daughters. Proximity matters. Jesus's goal is not mere informational content transfer.

WHAT IS THE CHURCH?

So, what is the church, and why is it so important? Let's look at a short passage from Matthew:

> [JESUS] SAID TO THEM, "But who do you say that I am?" Simon Peter answered and said, "You are the Christ, the Son of the living God." Jesus answered and said to him, "Blessed are you, Simon Bar-Jonah, for flesh and blood has not revealed this to you, but My Father who is in heaven. *And I also say to you that you are Peter, and on this rock I will build My church, and the gates of Hades shall not prevail against it.* And I will give you the keys of the kingdom of heaven, and whatever you bind on earth will be bound in heaven, and whatever you loose on earth will be loosed in heaven." (Matthew 16:15–19)

Jesus clearly built the church as a hub and mobilized it on the foundation of the revelation of Jesus as the Messiah. This passage is where the Catholic Church believes that Jesus was saying that Peter was the foundation of the church, but that is incorrect. Jesus was referring to Peter's response being the foundation of the church, not Peter himself; specifically, that Jesus was the Christ, the Messiah, the Son of the living God.

Jesus said, "On this rock I will build My church," making the defining statement that there would be the establishment of the church, which also encompasses and implies growth.

But then He continued to expound further by saying that the "the gates of Hades shall not prevail against it."

Many believe that Jesus was implying that He was going to start a community church and darkness was going to attack the little church but not succeed. But gates don't attack things; they defend. I would propose that Jesus had recognized Satan as the lesser god of this world, that Satan's kingdom was like a fortress holding prisoners. And in the middle of the darkness, when hope was barren and rescue seemed impossible, Jesus, who is the light, entered the world (see John 1).

It was that light that put a stake in the ground and initiated a brand-new era, an era of hope coupled with power. He would bleed into the soil sinless, pure blood and pour out the only answer for our hopeless custody in the hands and stronghold fortress of Satan. In this plan, He would build a stronghold fortress of His own, a love centered, militant hub and call it His church. The church was never called to be powerless and helpless; it was called to be powerful and mission focused.

When Jesus said, "and on this rock I will build My church, and the gates of Hades shall not prevail against it," He was saying that from a place of revelation and enlightenment, He was going to establish His church.

Jesus is clearly starting a war here, and we the church are going to take the fight to the gates of hell, but the gates won't hold.

We are called to take hell's dominion from our cities by being spiritually proactive and aggressive. Behind those gates are all God's lost sons and daughters. He wants them back! We are like a military debt-collection force that is going to the gates and tear them open to get custody back. The blood of Jesus is our certificate and search warrant.

In most towns and cities today, the church looks like a passive country club trying to be relevant and fit in with the surrounding culture. This is not the church that Jesus commissioned. It is not the one capable of tearing down gates and besieging its fortress to get back lost sons and daughters.

The problem is that many people want to play church. Casual congregations are created by pastors and leaders who are too afraid to speak the truth because it may affect attendance and finances. This must shift.

God wants His children back, and the church is the mission hub and community He has chosen to be the kingdom vehicle for that purpose. Once people are saved into the kingdom (not church membership, I will add), then that is where discipleship can be recognized as the vehicle for kingdom maturing and development for individuals.

GOD'S PURPOSE FOR THE CHURCH

Let's take a closer look at what Jesus intended for the church, so we can best understand its purpose and function. Isaiah 61:1–4 is a blueprint for the church to get back to God's perfect model of discipleship. Jesus read this passage in Luke 4, confirming Himself as Israel's Messiah. I believe it's also a template of how the church is meant to function in our day:

> THE SPIRIT OF THE LORD GOD IS UPON ME, because the Lord has anointed Me to preach good tidings to the poor [evangelism]; He has sent Me to heal the brokenhearted, to proclaim liberty to the captives, and the opening of the prison [hell's gates] to those who are bound; to proclaim the acceptable year of the LORD, and the day of vengeance of our God; to comfort all who mourn, to console those who mourn in Zion, to give them beauty for ashes, the oil of joy for mourning, the garment of praise for the spirit of heaviness; that they may be called trees of righteousness, the planting of the LORD, that He may be glorified [healing]. And they shall rebuild the old ruins, they shall raise up the former desolations, and they shall repair the ruined cities, the desolations of many generations [government establishing]. (Isaiah 61:1–4, additions mine)

Simply put, the church is a hub that carries the heart of God where healing and restoration take place, where equipping, training, commissioning, and sending happen. This is somewhat of an ecosystem on its own. Our mandate in Matthew

28 is to go out and win the lost to Jesus. This should be present in every believer's life, whether one has been saved for one day or for sixty years.

There are three distinct departments to unpack and understand here: the church as the hospital, the academy, and the army. You must first be healed, then equipped, then you have a job to do. Just like the parable of the vineyard, each branch or person in the kingdom is called to be fruitful (see John 15). So, let's take a closer look at each of the departments that people will progress through and thus more clearly see God's purpose for the church.

THE CHURCH AS A HOSPITAL

When new believers first enter the church, their first season as a believer and church member is usually a season of healing and restoration. The church must be more than a geographical place that represents healing and restoration; it must be a family, team, culture, and process that facilitates healing with compassion and wisdom. The church builds up lives and sees people's hearts made whole.

The hospital establishes worth. If stewarded rightly, the hospital facet of the church begins to convey and establish worth to the soul of a new believer. Often it constructs an environment of care and safety in which someone who prior to being saved experienced the brutal treachery of the world where no one really cared for them, and they were on their own to fend for themselves. In that environment, a person is not vulnerable with anyone in their circle in case it makes them a victim of betrayal. This same person, now in authentic community, has people genuinely interested in their story, helping them with healing and deliverance from past pains and strongholds. Spiritual leaders begin the process of discipleship.

When the church has compassion on the wounded, abused, and weak, then we truly become strong. We must remember that Jesus came for the sick and all in need of healing.

*Authentic healing **always** precedes establishment.*

We cannot raise up those who have not been healed or at least those who have experienced significant deliverance and healing in their walk with God. We cannot commission those who have learned to navigate using church language but have not embraced healthy healing and deliverance, or it will only be a matter of time before the dormant strongholds wreak havoc at the worst possible moment.

Jesus called Satan Beelzebub, which means "lord of the flies" (see Matthew 12:27–29). In that region, it had significance in a way we need to pay attention to. Flies are drawn to cuts and wounds in animals, and they will lay larva into the dead flesh around the wound. Essentially, the wound is like a doorway for the fly through the protective skin and into the flesh of the animals. In some cases, this can lead to significant problems and occasionally even death.

Jesus compared us to sheep, and sheep were a valued flock in that region. The only way to treat these wounds so the flies could not get in and invade the sheep was for the shepherd to pour oil on their wounds from a flask that he would carry with him. The oil would be like a salve for healing and promote tissue repair, but equally it would create a membrane that the flies could not lay larva in.

Healing matters. If left unchecked, not only does a person continue in torment and misery, but that wound attracts demonic oppression, strongholds, and attacks in other areas of life through the access points. Healing is not an event or a class that a person takes; rather, it is often a long-term process. Discipleship is not an option if someone will not embrace this aspect of the kingdom. It's why Jesus, when Peter tried to resist his feet being washed, said to him, "If you will not let Me clean you up, then you cannot participate in what comes next. In fact, you'll have no part of My legacy" (see John 13:18).

The church as a hospital is to walk people through a deep healing and restoration when those people are saved or join the church.

This is a receiving posture for the new or young believer.
It's a humbling and vulnerable process and season.
It can feel messy and frustrating, even overwhelming at times,
as it can feel like he or she is constantly being healed
or delivered for a season.

As a result, this must be a place of great compassion and care for those who need help in their lives and hearts. But it was never meant to be a permanent season or posture. We are called to move from glory to glory, which looks like empowering people toward freedom and maturity, not enabling them to remain in the hospital.

People must understand that they are not in need of years of deliverance and healing. Rather, we must encourage them to pursue healing and deliverance, but to equally teach them how to maintain it, not slipping backward into old patterns.

> *We do not want a constant re enrolling into metaphorical rehabilitation clinics, going through a process only to need it all over again a few months later.*

Give and man a fish and you feed him for a day, but he is going to need you to give him another fish tomorrow. Instead, teach individuals to value the process of healing and how to maintain it, and thus we will set them free for a lifetime in Jesus's name so they can go and help others experience the same freedom!

THE CHURCH AS AN ACADEMY

The church is not just a hospital; it is also a place of equipping and training. The academy establishes identity and understanding. In the Great Commission, Jesus emphasized this aspect of the church:

> AND JESUS CAME AND SPOKE TO THEM, saying, "All authority has been given to Me in heaven and on earth. Go therefore and make disciples of all the nations, baptizing them in the name of the Father and of the Son and of the Holy Spirit, *teaching them to observe all things that I have commanded you*; and lo, I am with you always, even to the end of the age." Amen. (Matthew 28:18–20)

As we fulfill this mandate and teach people about faith, it will impart identity to them. If healing has begun and progress is made around restoration and care, the next phase is the natural progression.

Paul talked about laboring over people until they looked like Jesus: "But it is good to be zealous in a good thing always, and not only when I am present with you. My little children, for whom I labor in birth again until Christ is formed in you" (Galatians 4:18–19).

God is in the business of using the church to take orphans and raise them up into sons and daughters. This is kingdom transformation!

Authentic community and connection, good teaching, and mentoring, as well as personally engaging in all we are being fed and taught, will cause us to grow, develop, and mature. Again, this is done in a receiving posture. It's easy to fool a naive and gullible person, but someone who knows how the kingdom operates, their King, and their part and place, as well as their rights, is much harder to deceive.

There is a lot to grow into and learn. Do not allow this to be an intellectual transfer of data, but rather a spirit-to-spirit teaching, training, and equipping season of not just knowledge but also skills and experience. The church isn't only a classroom but also where discipleship excels in the caliber of sons and daughters who are raised and growing through this season of their lives.

THE CHURCH AS AN ARMY

The church is a hospital, an academy, and an army. It is a place of mobilization, maturity, and living out the gospel outside the four walls of the church building. The army establishes service that reflects our faith, making way for purpose to become realized. The truth is that each of us will continue to need moments of healing for the rest of our lives.

Equally, if we are wise, we have realized that the academy was not something we graduated from but rather a learning and equipping season that taught us to never stop learning, developing, and maturing in Jesus from a place of intimacy.

When the hospital and the academy have done their job and each of us have responded intentionally and diligently, the natural progression is that what has been healed and formed in us will begin to express itself in action. Those who have walked through this process of the hospital and academy will start to be commissioned into this next phase of mobilization. Put hands on equipment and get involved in the work.

James 2 says that faith without works is dead. We are to have an active posture. Remember that there are no spectators in the military; believers cannot hide stagnant in the hospital emergency room or in the classroom—there comes a point where all that investment needs to start proving fruitful in life.

What does an army do? In an army there are many roles and ranks, much like in the kingdom of God. In the church there is a significant variety of tasks, roles, and areas of utilized giftings, both natural and spiritual. God made us all a little different from each other because each of us has unique tasks and assignments He has equipped us for: "But to each one of us grace was given according to the measure of Christ's gift. Therefore, He says: 'When He ascended on high, He led captivity captive, and gave gifts to men'" (Ephesians 4:7).

Here are just a few roles an army has that I have compared to kingdom roles needed in and around the church so we can begin to see that there is a lot to do:

- **MEDICS** *(inner healing and miracle healings),*
- **ENGINEERS** *(those who build where others couldn't),*
- **RECRUIT STATIONS** *(the evangelists),*
- **BOOT CAMP TRAINERS** *(home group leaders, friends who are strong for those they are leading toward Jesus),*
- **INFANTRY** *(the ministry of helps),*
- **AIRBORNE** *(the prayer warriors),*
- **SPECIAL FORCES** *(those who go into the hard situations and communities to rescue the lost and hurting),*
- **ARTILLERY** *(those who prophesy into situations and command change),*
- **SNIPERS** *(the missionaries who go to unchartered places to win territories),*
- **COMMUNICATIONS AND INTELLIGENCE** *(media department),*

- **MARCHING BAND** *(the worship team leads us into unity and purpose as we enter the throne room where the battle is won)*, and
- **THE FOOD HALL** *(the ministry of hospitality is such a valuable blessing to the kingdom).*

In these roles and functions, as we mature and are faithful, and as we walk in excellence, we will become mothers and fathers raising up sons and daughters to do the same. When everyone stands up in his or her role, the outcome is always victory. All this mobilization is brought together into unity through our common bond of love in Jesus.

We will become mothers and fathers raising up sons and daughters to do the same. When everyone stands up in his or her role, the outcome is always victory. All this mobilization is brought together into unity through our common bond of love in Jesus.

CONCLUSION

Remember that God never created you to stay in the hospital bed of the church. And He never made you to become a professional student who always pursues knowledge but never graduates. Once healing and equipping is well underway in your life, it's time to prepare your heart and walk with God for the next season of serving and being raised up.

Obviously, each of these three departments are metaphorical, but they do represent phases of stewarding and facilitating people, and of church mission focus. Many companies have training courses at facilities in specific locations that all new employees travel to so they can be trained in the culture, protocols, and processes of the company. As they are placed in positions, then they can represent the company brand and culture, being consistent to the corporate standard. These three facets of the church do this and equip believers so that they are not easily sabotaged and deceived by the enemy.

May we pursue healing and equipping and take ownership of our place in the family God has created. As we do this, the church is raised up and the kingdom is strengthened in our cities.

Discipleship on a personal level through this process creates generational legacy in the church, fulfilling the mandate Jesus gave to us before He left earth. The church Jesus has established has a clear plan and an intentional focus: to build lasting legacy through discipleship.

CHAPTER 07
LEGACY AND THE *EKKLESIA*

Jesus established the church to be a hospital, a classroom, and an army. It is the place where we receive healing and impartation before we are sent out into the world to make disciples of the nations. Legacy is passed on through the church, through mothers and fathers investing in daughters and sons. The church is the avenue of God that is fulfilling His dream of having a family who look and act like Him, who carry His DNA, and who bring kingdom change to our culture.

While we continue to look at the legacy that God is building in and through His church, there are two somewhat overlooked details that are vital to understand: the role of the apostle and the true meaning of the *ekklesia* of God. It is to these two ideas that we now look to more fully grasp how God is building a legacy through His people, the church.

THE IMPORTANCE OF THE APOSTLE

As modern believers, most of us do not understand the potency and intentionality of what an apostle truly represented to the society and culture of Jesus's time. I find it amazing when I read Scripture and see the correlation between Jesus being the King and Him calling His seasoned disciples *apostles*. This was more than just a vague idea; it was the establishing of an identity that would have been threatening to the kingdom, culture, and system of the demonically influenced world. It's important to understand the historical context of the word *apostle* to grasp the message being communicated by adopting this word in Christianity.

Phoenicia was an ancient civilization that preceded Rome and built its empire mainly around seaport trading. The Phoenicians established and ran the major trade lines in the Mediterranean until they were defeated by the Greeks who, in time, were defeated by the Romans. The word *apostle* comes from the Greek word *apostolos*, which was a naval term that described an admiral and his fleet that were sent to create new colonies, which was a practice taken from the Phoenicians. The *apostolos* was sent out to establish new territories on behalf of the king. It is also why this word is interpreted as a "sent one."

Roman occupied Israel would have understood the term *apostolos* to mean the role of the governing person who comes in and takes over territories but does so as he brings in the culture of the new occupiers. The *apostolos* would override and transform the current culture into the empire culture from which he was sent. This tactic was well established by the Roman Empire, so much so that there are archaeological sites hundreds of miles from Rome that are exactly like Rome with Roman style and Roman influence.

The Romans adopted and implemented a position in their military called an *apostle*. Rome perfected this new form of conquering. Formerly, a nation expanded by coming in and wiping out all the inhabitants of the city they were invading. If this did not happen, then the invading party would have to repeatedly subdue the territory to maintain control over it, destabilizing the occupation, and ultimately creating a redundant long-term threat to the legacy and stability of an empire. The culture, the architecture, the economy, the customs, and even the food would be influenced by the invading culture.

In the time of Jesus, Pontus Pilate was an apostle. He was a governor, but so much more than a governor. He was sent from Rome to govern and oversee the Romanizing of the conquered region. If the Roman Empire did that, then the people would adopt the ways of Rome and they were far less likely to revolt in the future. Those who were conquered would be assimilated into Roman culture, thus losing their own culture and becoming Romans themselves.

This would ensure that the territory would stay conquered, embraced mostly willingly by the native population who had been retrained to think and interact with society like Romans. It's hard to fight something a conquered people have come to enjoy and benefit from. This was the goal of Rome when conquering and expanding their empire—not contain prisoners of a conquered population but rather have willing participants of a reformed society.

Rome would have the apostle they sent reshape every detail of society to create Rome in the new land. This would have been well understood by occupied Israel when Jesus used this term in the first century.

> *When believers heard the term **apostle**, they understood that it was conveying the idea of a new way of living and thinking that was going to be established.*

The highest compliment to any ruling apostle was for Caesar to visit their location and say it feels just like Rome. By using this term, Jesus was conveying the idea that God should be able to walk the earth and feel His kingdom being established by His apostles who are bringing His kingdom to earth.

Understanding this brings a much clearer picture so we can see what Jesus was portraying when calling Himself a King and using the word *apostles* to describe His followers. It's no wonder the kings and the local leaders of the time were afraid of Him and concerned about Him. They were getting reports that He was multiplying food, He was healing the sick, He was raising the dead, and He was aiming to establish a kingdom they didn't know and could not control. And He was clearly showing that God didn't need a very big army to do it.

The rulers of the day could see their positions of power being overthrown. The fear they were sensing was because Jesus was representing another kingdom that they were told was here to take over. The religious and political leaders had to be shaking in their boots because they were sensing that a revolt was on the horizon, that they were going to have to face this new movement in their territory. When Jesus used the word *apostolos*, He knew exactly what He was doing. But He also used *apostle* to let us know how the kingdom was going to operate.

What are the apostles, as Jesus redefined the term? They are seasoned individuals with unique and rare traits that can be entrusted to oversee and lead a highly organized operation. They are much like a general, but the purpose a kingdom apostle serves is to lead and empower people to go in and transform a culture so that it looks like heaven in the area that they have been entrusted.

This starts to bring perspective to the Lord's Prayer as Jesus taught His team how to pray: "Your kingdom come. Your will be done on earth as it is in heaven" (Matthew 6:10). Jesus wasn't giving us a mantra that alluded to some glorious event in the future. That was the prayer that He was actively praying: "Your kingdom come. Your will be done." It looked like a picture of a Roman apostle invading a territory and teaching everyone this new way of life.

What then is an apostle's primary focus? It should be raising up an army that represents the kingdom of God for the purpose of transforming the culture, making it look like the kingdom that we come from, which is heaven. The purpose for the modern church is to transform the worldly culture into a kingdom culture empowering the church to do the work of the ministry during the week.

THE IMPORTANCE OF THE *EKKLESIA*

When Jesus told His disciples that He would build His church and the gates of hell wouldn't prevail against it, what did He mean (see Matthew 16:13–20)? The *ekklesia*—the Greek word that is often translated as *church*—is an assembly or a type of governing body of believers that is led by an apostle.

In biblical times, the *ekklesia* was a term used for the body that gathered and sat at the city gate and who would determine what was allowed in and out of the city. They would also make judgements about what was unjust. So, when Jesus said, "I will build My *ekklesia*," He was talking about a body of believers under the authority of someone functioning in the model of the apostolic. Or, to put it in other words, He was referring to active participants furthering the dream of the king in their territory. They all acted in responsibility to what was happening in their society with the intention of establishing and expanding the kingdom.

Jesus chose the word *ekklesia* to describe His church because it was a word people could relate to culturally; it was a structure of governance that wasn't the model of the synagogue. Like the use of the reference to the apostle, Jesus did not necessarily mean a carbon copy of the secular model; rather, Jesus was saying that He was going to build His kingdom community version of this.

The *ekklesia* mission mandate has always been about raising people who have heavenly authority. The church was never meant to be a hub where people could blend in and accomplish very little, always needing counseling and remaining broken. The mandate looks like the saved being established in the Word and the Spirit, and then raised by seasoned fathers and mothers to establish and expand the kingdom Jesus gave so much for.

From this perspective, we gain clarity that it wasn't just a mystical term when Jesus referenced the keys of the kingdom, saying, "Assuredly, I say to you, whatever you bind on earth will be bound in heaven, and whatever you loose on earth will be loosed in heaven" (Matthew 16:18). Rather, Jesus was raising up a body of believers who would be pioneers of regions led by apostles, prophets, evangelists, pastors, and teachers.

When authentic apostolic leadership is properly functioning, the other four roles found in the prophet, pastor, teacher, and evangelist get stronger and, as a result, equip the body of believers at higher levels to establish the kingdom of God on earth. But when other apostolic roles try to function on their own, they lose their true purpose for what we're trying to accomplish in the big picture. These leadership gifts were designed to be submitted to and led by the apostle. If this is not happening in the church today, then these roles can become perverted where the focus shifts to empowering the gift instead of the Holy Spirit.

Healthy apostles keep the *ekklesia* on mission focus. Like when Caesar would visit his apostles at their outposts, so God is looking to visit our churches and see the establishment of His kingdom. Jesus is looking for the reward of His suffering.

To understand an important reason why the current church looks the way it does in this nation is because we can't have theology or culture that eliminates the apostle and expect to still fulfill the Great Commission. The apostle, the general, who understands and grasps the big-picture mission and mandate from heaven, has been rejected by much of the modern church. He has been rejected from leading the most important aspects of the foundation and building that Jesus commissioned. This alteration in leadership structure has completely changed the mission and discipleship focus of the local church, ultimately producing a different type of believer than Jesus originally intended.

The church has built sheep pens. We have raised up sheep that we keep within the walls rather than equipping our church communities to infiltrate businesses, social circles, and every single facet of society and lead them to Jesus, thus transforming the wider culture. God is waking up the church again, a people who will become His legislative body in the earth. They will be those who determine what is and is not allowed in the regions God has given to them so that society gets transformed to look like heaven.

> *The church has built sheep pens.*
> *We have raised up sheep that we keep within the walls.*

My genuine concern with the current state of the church is that it's a long distance from its original purpose and design. Much of the church has turned into an incestuous inward-facing country club rather than a military strategic assault on darkness focused on establishing heaven in a territory. Paul reminds us that "we are citizens of heaven, where the Lord Jesus Christ lives. And we are eagerly waiting for him to return as our Savior. He will take our weak mortal bodies and change them into glorious bodies like his own, using the same power with which he will bring everything under his control" (Philippians 3:20–21 NLT).

If this is the case, then how do we respond to this crisis?

THE RESPONSE OF THE CHURCH

It would be wise to address the sovereignty of God in relationship to the responsibility of the church. People tend to believe that because God is sovereign, then it relieves us of the responsibility of what we've been asked to do.

> *The church has the assignment to disembody and*
> *disenfranchise darkness and establish heaven's kingdom*
> *culture here and make the enemy Jesus's footstool.*

In Psalm 110:1, King David looks into the future, sees Jesus, and says, "The LORD said to my Lord, 'Sit at My right hand, till I make Your enemies Your footstool.'" The Father speaks to Jesus after the cross, after the resurrection and the ascension, and He calls Jesus to come and sit down until He makes His enemies His footstool. Who and what is the Father going to use to make Jesus's enemies

His footstool? If Jesus has now sat down at the Father's right hand, then it's the church, the *ekklesia*, who is going to make His enemies His footstool. We have a responsibility to respond to this call!

Yes, God the Father has, in His sovereignty, ultimate authority, but He doesn't exert control over humankind. Where there is control, then freewill would not exist because there would be no choice on whether or not we serve Him. And if there's no choice, then love cannot exist, for love cannot exist without a choice.

This is why there were two trees in the Garden of Eden. God, in His sovereignty, chose to give humanity dominion over the earth and partner with Him in stewarding it. Yes, God the Father has ultimate authority over heaven and earth. That authority was given to Jesus and then passed on to us (see Matthew 28:18–20). But that authority has been given to us for a purpose, which is to do exactly what Jesus said to do. This is why Luke writes of Jesus: "how God anointed Jesus of Nazareth with the Holy Spirit and with power, who went about doing good and healing all who were oppressed by the devil, for God was with Him" (Acts 10:38).

One of the things that has caused the modern church to move toward buying into withdrawing from instead of advancing the kingdom and waiting until Jesus comes back is a branch of teaching on the sovereignty of God. In that sovereignty, God chose to give humans dominion over the earth. He chose to partner with us to see culture transform so that what we have prayed for comes to pass—on earth, as in heaven. It didn't say this will happen in the future. It literally could be translated, "Kingdom of God come now, will of God be done now." It's a demand.

God is waking up a remnant to these truths. And I'm relieved because God never needed a majority to deliver a nation. He usually just uses the one person who says yes to Him.

A RETURN TO THE ORIGINAL MANDATE

Deception and distraction have become the church's greatest dilution and deterrent from walking out the mission that Jesus gave to us. And this is why Isaiah 61 is the most complete chapter in the Bible about the purpose for which Jesus came. In it, we begin to understand and partner with the true DNA and mission of the *ekklesia*. Of the over three hundred prophecies we know that Jesus fulfilled, Jesus chose to quote Isaiah 61 as His purpose for coming in Luke 4.

There's a picture of apostles, prophets, pastors, teachers, and evangelists raising up an army to go in and deliver cities and to deal with the trauma and the dysfunction that the previous leadership has put on the generations. This demonstrates why Isaiah 61 has always been one of the most important chapters in the Bible to understand as a believer. It paints a complete picture of what Christ was saying in Luke 4; it is the door for the rest of this to be fulfilled. Now that Jesus has come, the rest of that chapter can be fulfilled.

Apostles need to be honored once again in the churches and then a healthy reestablishing of the kingdom can begin to advance, retaking our cities with heaven's strategies and mandates, making space for all the gifts in the room. Jesus is saying, "I'm not here to relaunch another version of a synagogue structure. Apostles will pioneer and plant and oversee pastors, prophets, teachers, and evangelists, who will facilitate this original kingdom structure. The mission is to convert regions, to disciple all nations."

In conclusion, my question for you is, are our churches fitting this profile? And if not, then where and how have we wandered? Pastor-led focus oftentimes becomes hospital focused. Teacher-led focus often becomes academy focused. But apostle-led focus tends to produce a strategic advancing church, facilitating the hospital and the classroom, while at the same time mobilizing the army. Care, teaching, and impartation must lead to participation once a person is mature and healthy.

Participation must be in unity and in rank with what the local lead role is getting directives and strategies from heaven for the local church to partner with. This is so darkness is driven out of a region and kingdom culture is not only established but has normalized heaven's climate, culture, and atmosphere in the area, to churches and governments, believers and unbelievers, schools and social circles. This creates a space for the true *ekklesia* that Jesus established to come forth and function.

We are called to smash the gates of hell. Let's get back on mission. God wants His sons and daughters back. He wants them raised up and trained rightly, so we can commission well-equipped warriors with His vision who love well, thus establishing His kingdom on earth as it is in heaven. This is how we partner with God and build a legacy through the *ekklesia* of God.

CHAPTER 08

HOW PAUL STEWARDED THE EARLY CHURCH

So far, I have painted the picture of God's heart and dream entrusted to humankind from Adam to Abraham. Then from Jesus to the disciples, and from the disciples to the church, to you and to me. This is a phenomenal lineage of heritage that we are invited to steward well.

As part of the living line of heritage, it's important that we learn from church history. The church has had significant history throughout the centuries since Jesus ascended to heaven. Some of it has gone incredibly well with nations that have been changed because of the authentic gospel legacy being stewarded and impacted through generations that have come into the light of the gospel and relationship with God. And yet some of our history has wandered awfully far off course, contradicting and producing a counterproductive outcome in periods of history.

As a result of these fumbled segments of history, darkness has advanced on the earth, and the church has not achieved its assignment. Ultimately, this has come at the cost of souls that deserved to find the grace and mercy of the gospel that ensures believers salvation and relationship with God, and ultimately the assurance of eternity in heaven. The harvest remains great and the workers truly remain few, but I believe the heart of God is longing for a generation that will yield and covenant themselves to fulfill His heart's cry—for the return of His lost sons and daughters.

WE ARE NOT DIFFERENT

The church, like the sheep that Jesus often described in His time on earth, so easily wanders away from the shepherd. In Ephesians 4, God gave gifts to His church, which ultimately means that God blessed the church with those who would lead, equip, guide, and guard the bride.

The modern church has evolved into numerous denominations and sects, each differing from the other in some way. And while in some cases new movements that break away from old denominations that have settled in traditions and ritualistic religion may be necessary, it must be said that we do not need to keep reinventing the wheel.

We do not need formulas and franchises; we need to return to the old paths of God. His model and ways work.

In this chapter, I will focus on and examine how the apostle Paul stewarded the early church. This is a revealing and insightful detail that gives us perspective of how the Holy Spirit clearly was looking to guide the church into purpose, identity, structure, mission, and legacy. Although the early church, some two thousand years ago, was pioneering a raw developing culture responding to the Great Commission and the legacy of Jesus, we can find deep revelation and insights as we are able to reflect and compare their model, journey, and process with ours today.

While we may have more technology, and while we might be in a very different culture, and trends and times and formulas may have changed—the core construct of the human condition, basic needs and traits, along with human nature, remains the same. The Scriptures tell us that all of us like sheep have gone astray, each one of us has turned to his own way, and many times during Jesus's ministry, He referred to people as sheep and Himself as a shepherd (see Isaiah 53; John 10).

The church today is not stewarding a different humanity; in fact, the church today must deal with the same sin condition, brokenness, and human nature that it did in the early church. If we look at the secular sin culture in that time, there were the same issues at large. And equally, the same giftings, talent, and potential is available if stewarded well. It's easy to compartmentalize and differentiate between then and now, but it's the same human condition that we inherited from Adam. The only difference in the social culture and environment, if anything, is that we are more advantaged with technology and the modernization of convenience if utilized to advance the kingdom.

If you have ever had a chance to be around a sheep farm or herds of sheep, then you will know that sheep are an erratic and easily spooked animal that wanders and gets itself in trouble, if given the chance. And so, it takes the framework of a well-fenced pasture, or the guidance of an attentive shepherd, to ensure that the sheep are able to live a life of purpose and peace.

If one sheep wanders, then most of the sheep in the pasture will wander too. If one sheep gets spooked or frightened, that fear is contagious and spreads through the flock. While we might consider ourselves sophisticated and advanced, the inherent characteristics as human beings transcend time and seasons of the earth. So, as we study the early church and how it stewarded the Great Commission, we will notice that like sheep, the church requires being reminded, guided, and directed constantly back to the culture and the principles, values, and mission of the kingdom of God. And some of this needs to be discussed by stepping back from comfortable culture and egos to pursue the core answer to the question, are we on mission, or are we comfortable with large, entertained congregations?

NAVIGATING THE CHURCH

Being a son and daughter of God is not about making a decision for Christ in a church service and living the rest of our life entitled, repeating knowledge without personal transformation; it's about representing and reflecting who He is in our lives in our church and in our community because we have encountered the King. And we publicly live unashamed of His culture in our churches without watering anything down.

Let's examine the early church, starting with the apostle Paul, who started out as a zealous terrorist for the Sanhedrin, whose job was to kill Christians and persecute the church as it became a threat to Jewish faith. He would ultimately have a life-altering encounter with Jesus, realizing that he was wrong about everything, and that Jesus was the one whom he had been looking for his whole life.

There is a time where he is completely undone, and spends time being reformed, unlearning religion and being humbled that God would grant him mercy after slaughtering God's people.

Not only did Paul receive mercy, but he would ultimately spend several years being immersed in what the Scriptures were pointing to: Jesus. He would also spend that time pondering that God was entrusting him to eventually be a key lead role, one that would write a huge portion of the New Testament. Needless to say, while Paul was born into religion and zealous ritual to the point of a murderous life, he was deeply humbled and reset into a genuine perception of the kingdom.

Unlike today, with all the different church and denominational cultural influences that can blur our perception and expectations of what healthy kingdom culture looks like, Paul had little to no reference. He said he didn't consult with flesh and blood (see Galatians 1:16), meaning he didn't go and replicate an existing model from other people; rather, he went to God and got a vivid download on God's culture and agenda.

I mean, wouldn't you want to do that? After following the popular Jewish Sanhedrin model his whole life, to the point where he thought he was doing God a service by persecuting and killing Christians, then coming to an abrupt confrontation with Jesus Himself, it makes sense that he concluded he didn't know anything and needed to ensure that in this next season he really grasped God's heart and intent.

Paul didn't get his convictions from attending a nationwide popular church culture conference and replicating the franchise instructions hoping for big-brand success in his regions of responsibility. Paul seems to emerge some twelve to fourteen years later, and, when he emerges, he is a differently cultured individual. From that point on, he had a huge influence in the church. And while he specifically seemed to be called to the Gentiles, it did not deter him from speaking at times to Jewish believers.

Paul, a transformed son who becomes an apostle, led the early church with a fresh and unfiltered focus. His values and mission culture give us a model to follow and use as a mirror to reflect against how the church of our day is doing comparatively. The apostle that Paul was anointed to be, along with the other apostles who had been appointed, was commissioned to shape culture and direct the mission of the kingdom that he represented in the territory where he was appointed.

Paul's whole job was to steer and direct people, namely, the church, to represent heaven. And like he expressed in Romans 12:1, he was to no longer reflect, represent, or think like the world, but to be transformed by the renewal of his mind through the washing of the Word. Unfortunately, with human characteristics and the consequences of sin, we find ourselves with a wandering tendency much like sheep.

And so the apostles would have to lead by example. They would have to teach the Word, explain the concepts of the kingdom, and empower people to find the kingdom's purpose. Encourage, rebuke, exhort, and lead.

We can see the great focus for all the apostles like Paul, for the church was for their well-being, their safety, their nurture, and their care. But equally, we see a zealous watchfulness and assertive correction when they were wandering or exhibiting a tolerance of sin. In truth, while there must always be love and encouragement from leaders and spiritual oversight, these elements are not often the best way to address sin. Sin, whether blatant or naive, is missing the mark, and it causes us to miss God's best intention for our lives. Sin is usually a willful or mental stronghold that is a rebel to righteousness, purity, and fruitfulness. So, sin or tolerance of sin in the church is the enemy of the Great Commission.

Most often, wandering does not start with scandalous sin but rather subtle compromise. And it will, if left unchallenged, degenerate into a compounding compromise that removes the potency of the church's power.

Remember the Scriptures warn us to not give a place or foothold to the devil (see Ephesians 4:27).

So, apostles are like those who are defending the purity of drinking water. If water in a glass looks clear, but there is just one drop of water from a toilet added to the glass, we would want someone to warn us before we drank it, right? Well, that's the watchman duty apostles have for the church. It's not bigoted; it's love and stewardship—although in a complacent culture it's often treated like bigotry.

We cannot effectively shepherd those we are caring for if we just want to give out positive affirmations, which is ultimately a hateful task that appears kind and peaceful. The Scriptures tell us that if we refuse to discipline our child, we hate him or her (see Proverbs 13:24). We can see with Jesus, that when He came to the seven churches in the book of Revelation and said affirming and kind words, He equally challenged compromise, tolerance, and sin in each one (see Revelation 2–3). This is kingdom culture.

God is a jealous God; He is not going to sit by quietly with the elephant of sin in the room and emulate a positive parent. Like I discovered and embraced early in my life, as we read in Hebrews 12, whom the Lord loves, He chastens and scourges every son whom He receives. If we were without chastening, then we were not sons but orphans.

There's nothing written in Scripture about being able to receive information that qualifies sonship, but only the ability to receive correction. If this is a qualification for an individual, it's easy to understand that this is also a qualification for the church. It's not the great things that we are already good at that bring us value; it's our ability to be corrected on the things that can destroy us and assure our future. And once confronted, will we become bitter and resentful of the leadership voices sent to us? Or will we act on it and adjust, becoming like gold refined in the fire, vessels fit and ready for God's use in our regions?

AN APOSTLE TO THE CHURCH IN JERUSALEM

After Paul spent what scholars believe was twelve to fourteen years of preparation after he was blinded by Jesus on the road to Damascus, he was zealous for the true things of God. He was passionate about grace and freedom and God's intent that all should be saved through Jesus Christ. We even see that his boldness extended to dealing with leadership issues. In Galatians 2, he dealt with hypocrisy in Peter. Specifically, Peter had levels of racism and spiritual elitism coupled with an unhealthy double standard. Peter was eating with the Gentiles, but then, when Jews came along, he would disown the Gentiles and exclusively fellowship with the Jews.

Paul told us he confronted Peter to his face, not in some behind-the-scenes chat. Why? Many would writhe with this type of disrespect and public humiliation in today's world and post-public criticism on their social media gathering emotional responses from such an act. But the explanation is simple, "those who sin publicly need to be corrected publicly" (1 Timothy 5:20). If a leader is leading in sin, he or she is ultimately modeling a culture that an entire community is replicating. If it's not dealt with publicly, then an entire generation can be corrupted and stunted from ever walking in true purpose. This is love for the church. This portion of Galatians goes on to say that the other Jews and even Barnabas were enticed to follow Peter's example (see Galatians 2:11–13).

The balanced caveat here needs to be that public correction needs to be done in love that is partnered with uncompromising truth, which is what Paul did with Peter. His language, "I withstood Peter to his face," would indicate that Peter put up a fight, but Paul didn't back down. Paul had become zealous for the church.

Why am I talking about correction as a pillar of the early church and in a book about legacy? It's because legacy is passing down an unseen but tangible gift and, if that gift is marred or tainted, the vision is ruined and can't be completed as designed. Having a full gospel is of utmost importance.

Compromise in leaders produces a trickle-down effect where there will be compromise and hypocrisy in the congregation. Today, confrontation has become something that is looked down upon and treated as unloving and culturally insensitive. But we clearly see the same issue was in place because most people don't like being confronted and told that they're wrong; many of us have an ego that will not bow to humility. Many people are not lovers of truth, but lovers of convenience, comfort, and their own image. Paul dealt with this on a regular basis, as shown in his letter to the Galatians: "have I therefore become your enemy because I tell you the truth?" (Galatians 4:16).

Jesus loves the church and is jealous for her, and He gave the church the gift of the apostles to steward it, direct it, and guide it, which includes love, teaching, and confrontation. Nowhere is compromise mentioned. Part of effective stewardship is confrontation when things are off track.

Paul, operating as an apostle, has taken all his previous zeal as an assassin and has repurposed his focus with new eyes of love and is now jealous for the church.

If we truly hope to have a move of God in our generation, then we must be okay and ready to embrace things being set in order. In a world where anything goes, no boundaries and with little honor for leaders and dignitaries, this is a challenge to accept. But it is the way of the kingdom.

AN APOSTLE TO THE GENTILES

As the early church progressed from the gathering in Jerusalem to a thriving body of believers full of new converts, we see the church move into the dispersion of the various endeavors that came out to plant in the wider world. Churches birthed in cities such as Antioch, Corinth, Ephesus, and Galatia.

As these churches were established and grew, parental caregiving letters began to be written by apostles to these churches. Travel and communication were far more cumbersome and lengthier than it is today, and so the apostles would receive word of the condition of the churches, and, if they were not living in those cities at the time or able to visit, letters were sent to guide the congregation. Those letters are a significant part of the New Testament today as inspired by the Holy Spirit. They still can guide us.

The epistles were mostly written by the apostle Paul to various branches of the early church. It's interesting to note that at that time there weren't thousands of denominations—he would simply write to the church of the city. This is also true when Jesus addresses the churches of the seven cities in Revelation (see 2–3).

These epistles are mostly messages that start with a qualification of who wrote the letter, a greeting to the leadership or spiritual sons and daughters who were there, followed by a blessing usually involving grace and peace. Then we read messages of exhortation, encouragement, and doctrine that would help form and frame beliefs, give encouragement, and bring blessings. Importantly, there are specific messages that would confront the broken culture of that territory or compromise in that local church. Equally, Paul would often deliver correction.

Paul addresses publicly in a letter that would be read to the whole church, condemning and confronting what had been reported to him, that a man who had taken his father's wife as a lover was somehow still a part of the church. The Apostle Paul doesn't just disagree with this; he condemns it, judges it, and even hands this person over to Satan, with the intention and hope that he might repent (see 1 Corinthians 5:5). Like a doctor, Paul directly confronts a cancerous culture or compromise so it does not become an acceptable norm and spread into the lives of others. *What we refuse to confront will ultimately master us.*

Then we can see that Paul would often call out individuals who had caused him deep grief, pain, and had persecuted him. Or those who had damaged the church. In the church today, many people are afraid to talk about these issues, because there's been a misconstruing of the application of love and mercy and grace. In fact, there is a huge contingent of the modern church that has hidden behind the idea of God who ignores our sin. This simply is not true and has misled many. Paul called out "Alexander, the coppersmith" who did him much harm. Paul went on to say, "may he be repaid according to his works" (2 Timothy 4:14).

Many modern preachers would condemn this type of language because it seems like it doesn't follow the narrative of forgiveness, grace, and mercy. However, there has been a neutering all in the name of love, grace, and mercy, where certain issues are not allowed to be talked about. This has created a culture in much of the modern church where people who have been impacted by reckless behavior are not able to talk about issues through the lens of love and truth.

Paul addresses this when he says, "after the second or third warning, mark a divisive man" (Titus 3:10). This is someone causing division in the churches, someone who is a slanderer or gossip or who causes persecution of those leading—someone who has intentions or tendencies to bring divisions inside the community of the church. Again, and most importantly, notice that this wasn't a first-strike consequence, but this occurred after someone had been warned and pleaded with. Paul is clear about marking a divisive person.

What does it mean if we are to follow Scripture over popular culture? The clear application of this "marking a divisive man or woman" is that we make people aware that certain individuals are causing division. God is not the author of division, and division undermines the power of the church. The Scripture gives us clear insight into why this is important when it says, "Where the brethren dwell together in unity, there is the commanded blessing of God" (see Psalm 133).

There is a demonic assignment from hell to steal unity by introducing division. So, if there is a divisive person causing constant contention, or someone repeatedly or significantly trying to unjustly accuse the pastors or leadership outside of biblical pathways, steal people to another church, or create a culture of infighting and contention, that person is damaging the local body of Christ. And so, from this position, Paul clearly states, mark a divisive person. This means people are to be identified as dangerous for the well-being of a community if they do not repent from this type of behavior—because the well-being of the bride is so important to the outcome of the great harvest of souls.

This is not something we are trying to achieve or do but avoid; nonetheless it remains a healthy boundary that must be established. But we will find in most churches in the Western world today that if we say anything to warn people, the person doing the warning becomes the bigot, the oppressor, and the aggressor. But these warnings are clearly for the safety of the believers and the house of God.

Are we going to be politically correct and socially popular, or are we going to find the way of the kingdom and be in line with heaven?

PAUL'S LETTERS STILL APPLY

The early church had many encouraging letters and warm regards from Paul. But we constantly see the apostles, the diligent gardeners, pulling out weeds that would spring up, whether it was religion, hypocrisy, compromise, sin, or stagnancy. Paul again confronts the Galatians in this statement, "Oh foolish Galatians, who has bewitched you? You started in the Spirit, how have you ended up in the compromise of flesh?" (see Galatians 3:1–9). And again, "Some of you should be teachers by now, but you still require milk, the laying again of the foundations of the elementary teachings" (see Hebrews 5:12–14)

What we see here is a zealous shepherd who is not necessarily a pastor in the house, but someone who has a different perspective and overview. He was passionately watching for the safety, success, and growth of the church. He passionately pleads and contends and confronts the churches in order to direct her away from stagnant deterioration and toward maturity and fruitful growth. Apostles are not so much focused on popularity reports, but rather the welfare, DNA, and expansion of the church.

Like Paul, they must be willing to oversee and guide the navigation and direction of the church with doting parental care and yet equally the zealous and assertive command of a military general. They are people who ensure the moral and well-being of the church, encouraging the good and spurring on the upright. But also, apostles are fierce guardians for the purity and single heartedness of the church, confronting the compromised, exposing the false, and resisting the dilution of doctrine and obedience to the Great Commission.

My wife is one of the most gentle and caring women I know. But if you step between her and her babies, you're going to meet a lioness. Likewise, she notices things about our children that seem small in the moment, but she can recognize that if we don't address and correct it, it could hurt our children in the long run or even harm them physically. Our aim as parents is to train our children into adults. Not to just help them be children today, we are looking to the men they will be in the next twenty years. This is how the apostles viewed the growing body of believers. They, like a mother or a military general, can see that what gets overlooked today takes the movement off the path little by little and the outcome is not what it should be. So, they put in the daily work to keep things on track!

Through this lens we can understand Paul constantly teaching doctrine, encouraging and endorsing healthy churches, and confronting anything in social or church culture that if not identified and addressed would cause degeneration and sabotage the true purpose and power of the church. These apostles and guardians who walk as fathers in the faith for their generation, whose counsel, teaching, example, and confrontational correction serve as a plumbline for the church of every generation and century, as intended by God. So, we must take seriously the council, advice, and warnings that he issued because they still apply today.

Parents will always do and say what is best and most beneficial for their children, even if that means uncomfortable conversations and direct correction. Because good mothers and fathers understand that in the natural family model, children will go astray if left to their own devices, and also that children will wander from previously set boundaries and expectations until they are older and can have a more mature self-governance of good conduct.

Good parents are not buddies or best friends, but loving coaches who present loving environments that equally have high expectations. Paul, Peter, and many of the early church leaders and apostles were men and women of this caliber and character, so in love with Jesus that they lived to tend His people.

In John 21, Jesus restored Peter at the fish breakfast on the beach after He had arisen from the dead. During his betrayal, Peter had essentially betrayed Jesus and fled after making all his bold declarations of being with Jesus no matter what (see John 13:37). In that moment on the beach, while Jesus restored Peter, He asked him three times, "Peter, do you love Me?" to which every time Peter responded, Jesus replied with "feed My sheep" and "tend My lambs."

Fast forward from this moment to post ascension. Peter is living as a father of the early church. His focus can be seen in responding to the charge Jesus gave him on the beach that day.

Apostles and spiritual fathers and mothers are not political leadership figures who focus on keeping everyone entertained and happy. If parenting looked like this, the children being raised in this environment would undoubtedly have challenges and developmental struggles that most likely would present too late to be helped. No, these apostles must focus on the trajectory and well-being of the individual or church congregation.

THE AUDIT WE NEED

I have taken great care to highlight how the early church was led, overseen, and stewarded. It was under a constant watchful care of the God-given guardians of its progress. It was common for these apostolic guardians to audit the church and call the leaders and believers back to a pure and unadulterated gospel. So, if we can easily see this culture clearly displayed as a model God instituted for the early church, then we need to have a moment of sincere clarity and ask ourselves, what has happened to the modern church? Have we become laws unto ourselves without accountability?

Where are the prophets' and the apostles' voices that can direct the church around encouragement and confrontation? This isn't a subject we can sweep under the rug and just look the other way. The Scriptures accurately predicted the current generation we live in: "There will come a day, when men would no longer endure sound doctrine but rather heap for themselves teachers that would tickle their ears" (2 Timothy 3:2). This speaks to a replacement of apostles and fathers who will have uncomfortable conversations for the ultimate good of people, in exchange for motivational teachers and speakers who make people feel warm, comfortable, and empowered without any responsibility for their development.

The issue we have is that a real apostle and leader must choose between compromising to lower standards for more acceptance and popularity and holding the high standard of the purity of the gospel, even if it means being unpopular out of reverence and obedience to the Lord. And they will do this with the hope that those who follow will be developed into mature sons and daughters.

Paul clearly had a no-compromise stance, and I sincerely believe it is the right posture. I believe this because I am a father. I will hold a line so that my sons prosper in life. I don't necessarily need them to understand what I am doing as their father today. I need them to become adult men as successfully as I can. If we truly are the church that Jesus initiated, then there will be spiritual fathers and mothers and apostolic voices that watch over and care for our churches, voices that can speak into areas of our growth and development both on the encouragement and guidance aspects as well as the course-corrective conversations.

If not, then how have we ended up here? And are we truly walking out the identity that Jesus intended for us as a church? The question we are forced to ask ourselves is, if we can put all ego and pride aside, what letter would Paul write to our home church?

CHAPTER 09

WHY IS THE MODERN CHURCH FAILING?

THE SUCCESS OR FAILURE OF THE MODERN CHURCH must be measured by comparing its current progress against the mandate of Matthew 28:18–20. It can be safely concluded that the way we steward discipleship directly results in the failure or success of the church in the eyes of Jesus. We must assess our commitments toward Matthew 28's primary directive to go into all the world and make disciples of all the nations.

In the Introduction, I proposed the idea that if the perfect model of kingdom establishment, growth, and expansion was demonstrated by Jesus in the three and a half years of His ministry. This was shown in the focused simplicity of including and mentoring twelve men by example, and who were commanded to go into all the world and do the same with all the nations (or people groups). We must have missed something by not following the kingdom model closely enough.

If the eleven disciples each raised twelve disciples of their own, who in turn did the same, and every subsequent generation replicated the idea that fathers raise and shape sons and mothers the same to daughters, then the church should have populated most of the planet some two thousand years later. So why have we not?

OBEDIENCE OR POPULARITY?

In many ways, churches are physically bigger than they used to be, but does that mean we are authentically stewarding the kingdom well? All too often, one of the great tragedies in the life of a pastor is that he has served all his life, but in his older years there is no one healthy or mature enough to succeed him. There might be more people who attend his church, but are there sons to carry on the move of God? How are we getting to this point? And what can be done to turn it around?

Many of the larger churches in our generation are not truly realizing their kingdom purpose. They are essentially adult daycare and entertainment centers, where pop-culture worship and flattering motivational speaking are offered in exchange for attendance, excitement, and intrigue. One of the great tragedies of many of the churches in our generation is that popularity and influence have become more desirable than obedience to the authentic commission left by Jesus, our Commander-in-Chief. This is both shocking and insulting to many because there is a cultural disconnect between true kingdom culture and the modern church culture.

The fact that Jesus is King is not really grasped by many of our generation who use the phrase. One of God's names is *Jehovah Sabaoth*, which means "The Lord, Captain of the Hosts of Heaven." God is not a leader we voted into power; He has all authority on His own without our permission. He redeemed us from eternal death and eternal separation from Him, and He thus invited us and paid the price for us to be family and enter His kingdom and culture.

Many of us are desensitized to kingdom governmental authority because many Western nations are governed by elected democracy. And even that has a limited term of service. Furthermore, there is a culture even in the church of speaking slanderously against leadership. I am not suggesting we do not disagree or even speak out against evil, oppressive, or corrupt leadership—even that can be done with respect and dignity as sons and daughters who are walking in biblical protocols.

We can never lose this perspective of God's kingship and command. If we do, we will be effectively designing and building our own empires and leveraging our association based on popular models that are currently working and call it church, deceiving ourselves that we are great and that we have achieved "success." In doing this, we will abandon authentic obedience to God's instruction, more often without even realizing that we have left the path and missed His plan to extend His kingdom.

So, from that perspective, when Jesus gives us a command, it is never a suggestion. Rather, we must pay great attention to every word He has spoken and dedicate ourselves as loyal sons and daughters to bring Him honor through our obedience to that instruction. The Great Commission is by no means a multichoice interpretative suggestion, but a specific holistic command that cannot be dissected into electives. Will we choose obedience to God's commands over popularity in the culture?

ASSESSING OURSELVES FOR GROWTH

In the business world, I must conduct regular assessments of the departments that are operating within my organization. These assessments provide me with a clear and honest overview of the health, condition, efficiency, and profitability of the company I've set out to build. I will assess if departments and key staff are operating the company within the assignment and department briefs I designed and set in place. In order for this to be conducted accurately, all emotional bias must be removed. Truth must be the only objective. These assessments allow me to evaluate where instructions and guidance are working and where there is something that needs to be addressed.

As citizens of the kingdom of heaven, we must be prepared for spiritual assessments, being accountable to God's standards, instructions, and guidance in our churches, ministries, and culture. Through this filter, we ask ourselves, are we truly succeeding at obeying the Great Commission or are we entertaining, hyping up, and distracting those who come together each week and sit in well-polished, choreographed, and produced church services that only encourage but never challenge? Are we only seeking to keep people happy and excited but never correct, rebuke, or teach that sin must be repented of? Are we so immersed in a culture where the leaders stay at a distance from the congregation and never let the sheep get close to shepherds to be mentored through their challenges and struggles?

Compromised leaders don't want to get close to others because sheep are hard to care for and there is personal risk of betrayal, much like Jesus had with Judas. There's a risk of people not doing what they are taught or failing. The truth is that many leaders get hurt by reckless and wounded people. But true leaders cannot live with this outlook. This is why Jesus talked about the difference between a shepherd and a hireling in John 10.

A shepherd is committed to the well-being of his flock, while a hireling or an employee is only committed to his or her salary and benefits. A shepherd will commit all and risk even his reputation for God's kingdom, but a hireling is majorly focused on how he can personally benefit from the role and leverage his career. Both roles can even use the same language in their sermons and books, but their lifestyles and priorities will tell the real story.

> *"Wisdom is justified by her children," Jesus told us (Matthew 11:19), not by her statements, one-liners, or memes and famous quotes.*

We have compromised leaders who don't want to risk people leaving because of honest and truthful sermons. These leaders shy away from the Bible's truths that may offend or make people uncomfortable. Or they may even avoid certain topics because it would mean others would stop tithing to the church. But this type of culture is all based on leaders who are intimidated by fear and driven by the need for popularity and finances.

This is one of the reasons we hear Paul's heart when he stated in his letter to the church in Rome that "I am not ashamed of the gospel of Christ, for it is the power of God to salvation for everyone who believes, for the Jew first and also for the Greek. For in it the righteousness of God is revealed from faith to faith" (1:16–17). These leaders forfeit the true fruit of the gospel by being ashamed of its fullness.

The Holy Spirit once spoke to me about this passage: "Andrew," He said, "when people become ashamed of My gospel, then My available power is removed from their reach." This made so much sense to me. I've experienced many churches that have watered down or backed away from an aspect of the Scriptures, gospel, or kingdom absolutes, and thus witnessed a church culture but not a strong presence of God.

"Andrew," He said, "when people become ashamed of My gospel, then My available power is removed from their reach."

The Scripture also tells us, "For the time will come when they will not endure sound doctrine, but according to their own desires, because they have itching ears, they will heap up for themselves teachers; and they will turn their ears away from the truth, and be turned aside to fables" (2 Timothy 4:3–4). I believe we are living in a time like never before where the truth has become globally unpopular, where people become easily hostile when offended, and where people speak evil of leaders (see 2 Peter 2:10).

We find ourselves living in a time where people have more options than ever before. A pastor may preach forty minutes a week in a local church, but his or her congregation is being heavily influenced by media, social media, entertainment, and all forms of podcasts and YouTube at every other point. Leadership is a kingdom relationship. In the secular culture of the world, we find that if relationships don't work, then people go online and find a new relationship. The truth is that we live in a generation in which commitment has been attacked like never before.

If a pastor tells his congregation some truth that is offensive, those people will claim to have received deep emotional trauma and will immediately look to dispose of that relationship and utilize other options for church community. All of this to serve self-preservation instead of being lovers of the truth. But in the kingdom of God, relationships are not disposable. If we have created a culture of divorcing relationships that speak truth to us, then we have departed from a healthy community and love.

Love is not just about the emotionally charged good times. And love is not just about covering up issues and problems because we don't want anyone to feel uncomfortable. "Love covers a multitude of sins" (1 Peter 4:8) only *after* those sins have been addressed. It does not ignore and act like it was never seen. Love rejoices in the truth, no matter how much the truth hurts.

The only way we should present truth in the kingdom is through the vehicle of love. And yet, in no way is love foolish. Love does not empower, support, or endure abuse from long-term abusers. While relationships are not disposable in the kingdom, we must recognize the requirements on this unique leadership relationship structure.

Jesus had masses who loved His sermons. They loved it when He multiplied loaves and fishes and fed the thousands.

But those same people were offended and walked away when Jesus started to discuss the personal price of discipleship.

When Jesus said that His followers would have to eat His flesh and drink His blood if they were going to have a part in Him, many left (see John 6:52–57). That was a price people couldn't swallow. There are many people who love blessings and encouragement, but few are lovers of truth, being transformed and matured by it.

Jesus told us, "You shall know the truth, and the truth shall make you free" (John 8:32). But that truth is most likely going to insult our flesh and our old unrefined nature. Because of that, we face two types of leaders: those who want to be right with God and those who want the applause and popularity of the people.

When I first entered ministry, a mentor told me there are two types of ministers: The first type is like Moses who went up Mount Sinai to a place of intimacy with God and came down to the congregation of Israel, thus representing God to His people. The second type of leader is like Aaron the high priest. He was supposed to walk in a priestly role, but when Moses was on the mountain and the children of Israel began to descend into revelry (see Exodus 32:6), the people began to worship false gods. Aaron built them an idol of a calf covered in gold and gave them what their hearts wanted instead of the truth. Aaron lowered himself from the standard he should have held and represented the people's sin back to God.

My mentor told me, "You will need to choose which type of minister you want to emulate." And that is the challenge to each one of us today. Do we want to be like Moses and represent God to the people? Or do we want to be like Aaron and give the people the sinful desires of their hearts?

There is a famous quote by Plato that I have cherished. He said, "No one is more hated than he who speaks the truth." You see, truth demands that everything hidden and dysfunctional is brought into the light and addressed with an honest perspective. The truth, which is God's Spirit, is at war with the flesh, deception, and lies. If fathers and mothers intend to raise sons and daughters who honor the King and influence the earth, building the kingdom of God, then truth must be the chisel and hammer that fashions and shapes champions, not cowards.

We have to have an honest assessment of our current condition as the church. Are we raising sons and daughters who will be able to stand in darker days than we are standing in? Or are we raising entertained, entitled orphans who have little substance, who do not know how to stand in adversity, and have little to no character or kingdom ethics? These are hard questions to ask.

While the church may look big numerically, it has become weak spiritually and compromised on an authentic execution of obedience to what we were instructed to do.

So, if we are going to participate in pure kingdom legacy, then we must unsubscribe to the pursuit of popularity, entertainment, and the empire-building culture in the church today. And we must return to the model Jesus perfectly demonstrated.

My wife and I have three sons, and while they are young and in our care, they have an inexperienced perspective of the world. We are present to set boundaries, set guidelines, have fun, create teaching moments, and lead by example. God's given us the responsibility of stewarding and forming them. Left to their own devices, my boys would only eat ice cream and damage their health, not to mention that they could seriously hurt themselves. It is our job as parents to uphold standards, not just do as we say but lead with a lifestyle that says follow me. We lead them while they are small, even if that means meltdowns at the dinner table due to uneaten vegetables or a want that is not immediately given. While it might not make us popular in their eyes in the moment, it makes them great in the story of their lives.

In essence, what I am getting at is that churches that only major on feeding their people ice cream, never consuming nourishing foods, will ensure bad spiritual health and create a culture of rebels and orphans who can do whatever they want and will treat God with contempt. The result of these lives is a tragic story of defeat and ruin.

Quotes in sermons and social-media one-liners mostly create an audience that call out "Wow" and "Amazing" in the middle of well-polished sermons. But I am concerned that those same people would not endure a message that corrects and confronts in loving truth. We have become a generation who loves knowledge because it makes us feel powerful instead of convicting messages that cause us to cry out to God for mercy and forgiveness. Enjoying a moment of revelation and explosions of wisdom in the room is great, but these same people going away completely unchanged is not. It leaves room to further deceive people that they are in right relationship to God because they have moments of someone else's revelation in a meeting, but it does not birth a transformation in them.

There is only ever the wide road and the narrow road, the high and difficult road or the low and easy road. And only one can be compliant with God's plan. Church leaders must choose to recognize the fight for the next generation and commit to showing up through loving truth, or they will destroy their destiny through a compromised gospel and a weak leadership model. In order to achieve reformation, we must recognize and identify destructive culture and reject it so we can embrace the authentic culture that Jesus is establishing.

THE OUTCOME OF INEFFECTIVE LEADERSHIP

In pursuing God's paths, I have observed in my life and studies church movements that were birthed at great costs. Denominations founded out of reformations that were revolutionary against church stagnancy, compromise, corruption, and comfort. These movements and denominations were like fires in a dark night that brought clarity and purity and singleness of heart to the world.

While millions of souls were saved and stewarded well, decades and centuries later there are well-funded buildings but no presence of the Holy Spirit. There are congregants but few authentic sons and daughters. There are theological believers full of intellectualism and head knowledge but few intimate lovers and followers of Jesus. What a shame and loss of legacy to the original fiery founders of these movements.

Stewarding the spiritual DNA entrusted to us, as the succeeding generations, is something I have heard the Holy Spirit talk to me about often. But I have not heard many other people talk about this. So, let's investigate this tragedy and look at why these birthed dreams dissolve into the sands of time?

What do I mean by stewarding spiritual DNA? When God raises a generation to walk rightly with Him, it attracts the next generation to gather around and observe what God is doing. All of that combined wealth of experience, personal journeys of sacrifice, and paying prices to obtain and carry the anointing draws in the next generation. Spiritual reproduction, or legacy, is a natural byproduct of authentic godly movements. God's intention is always for reproduction. Otherwise, why would He have made everything living with the ability to create "after its own kind" within itself?

And here is where we start the breadcrumb trail of explaining the DNA breakdown. We have the original man or woman of God who initiates a "movement," but small (and sometimes large) digressions begin to dilute what started out as potent. As it gets transferred to the next generation, it does not stay consistent due to many factors.

In the natural realm, as well as the spiritual, we can see when a son or daughter is raised in a spoiled way. They display a sense of entitlement toward their natural and spiritual inheritance (in this case spiritual transference), a gift that cost them nothing to get. There is a lack of value toward what's been passed down to them. They have no respect for those who provided the inheritance and often do not consider those to whom they will one day need to provide an inheritance. This is because what has no cost will never be valued.

When a movement has been birthed through earnestly seeking God, that is without a doubt a difficult thing to do. If it has been birthed based on someone's name or a popular church brand or franchise, then the cost of leadership is undoubtedly much less. However, when a church is born with blood, sweat, and tears in obedience to the call of God, the leadership team will pay a price to walk and stand in that atmosphere.

But over time, the church seats fill up and things become somewhat easier. It is in this place that pastors, leaders, fathers, and mothers can forget that for the upcoming generation to truly succeed, they must pay the same price and display the same commitment. They have to do this to qualify for inheritance. It may look different, but a price must be paid. They must allow the Holy Spirit to show them how to build on the foundation of the legacy that was passed on to them.

In most cases, this is simply not what happens. Eli didn't train his sons to steward the position of leadership that he held. They were raised as spoiled children, without the fear of God in their lives. The reverence toward God's house and leadership role was not present in their hearts. Eli and his sons stayed in the temple, but a healthy spiritual DNA did not pass on to them. Instead, Eli was so casual with the training of his sons that they became rebels and backslid on every level, which eventually cost them their lives. If we as fathers or mothers are soft handed, spoiling our children, and do not train our children to fear the Lord and walk through their own process of being fashioned and scourged, then we are sabotaging their future. Not only that, but to keep the peace, we are destroying kingdom legacy passing down through our lines.

Anyone can come into a church and get around leadership, even serve their way into roles like armor-bearing or the leadership team, and not truly obtain the heart of what God is doing or His culture and heritage in the lives of their leaders. They can be so busy fitting in and trying to be accepted that they become performers and parrots. Anyone can repeat the teachings, culture, and statements they have heard under leadership, but that doesn't change people. It's a cheap counterfeit that will look good for a season, but it is full of compromise. It is head knowledge without heart transformation. It's the heritage of positions and titles without kingdom sonship identity. Perhaps their hearts are genuine, but they're not properly trained and, left to their own devices, tainted.

Additionally, another reason that DNA is diluted is because sons or daughters get a promotion too soon. They get an opportunity before they have conquered character and sin issues, and this sends an incorrect subliminal message that there are no standards in the kingdom. When fathers are lenient on children, or don't encourage their children to go deep in God and build personal maturity through their own process rather than shading underneath the father's covering, the DNA dilutes to varying measures. Those sons and daughters grow and enter their time to lead and then replicate the problem and give the next generation promotion and inheritance early. As a result, more compromise is made, further compounding the problem.

And so within three to four generations of the first leader that pioneered a church or movement, with compromise like this introduced into the culture that erodes the potency of one generation to the next, what was fought for has devolved into the very opposite of what was originally established. This is why we must be intentional with the stewarding of generational legacy.

CHAPTER 10

FALTERING CHURCH MODELS

To steward the legacy that Jesus passed on to us and we are to pass on to the next generation, we have to understand where we are currently at as the church of Jesus Christ. We need to honestly assess what we are doing if we are to have hope for change. Without being honest with our current condition, we can't know how to get where God is calling us to go. Jesus has given us the Great Commission to make disciples of all nations, but much of our current church culture distracts from this end. Let's look at some reasons why the church is failing to fulfill the mandate Jesus gave to us, to father and mother the next generation.

FAST-FOOD CHRISTIANITY

The fast-food industry has really painted a picture of what the modern church has slowly adapted to over the years. Fast-food restaurants became popular in mass producing simple meals that often don't have great nutritional value and serve people so rapidly that they could walk into the restaurant and eat quickly and walk right back out in a matter of minutes. This has had an appeal to many, and it is a relatively successful business model given that the fast-paced lifestyle of most people wants to get food and eat quickly and move on to the next activity, task, or event.

But fast food didn't stop there—they made fast food even faster when they created the drive through, in which people don't even need to get out of their cars to order and receive food. They can simply drive through on the side of the building, speak into a microphone, and proceed to the window for payment and collection of their meal. Then they can quickly consume these in their vehicle while rushing to the next event.

This type of convenience has caused people's mentality to be slowly reshaped from one of making something of value from scratch that takes time and attention, like a home-cooked meal on a weeknight that involves a couple of hours to bring together, to a mentality of collecting a much lower quality meal from a restaurant while out on an errand. In this process, families lost the gathering and the discussion in the kitchen while a meal was prepared. This is an interaction of helping to prepare and cook that brought about learned skills into the children's lives, as well as sitting down around a respectful family table sharing a meal together and bonding in a beautiful way.

This isn't just about groceries and family meals; this is a picture of a society losing the fabric of foundational values that build a better and stronger world focused on quality time and food or products being worth the wait.

> *Instead of patience, we have learned impatience, all in the name of progress and efficiency.*

Instead of allowing time and experience to fashion our lives, we find ways to speed up the process, and, once we do, we add a drive-through shortcut to get there even faster.

My point? Jesus took thirty years to prepare Himself for His ministry of just over three years. Likewise, John the Baptist took thirty years to prepare himself for three months of ministry. Moses took forty years in a desert preparing himself for ministry, having to unlearn everything he was taught in the previous forty years. As a matter of fact, we can see this trend with so many great men and women of God in Scripture—David, Joseph, and many more.

There is a kingdom cultural trend here that should not be ignored. But somehow the modern church believes that a cheeseburger brought together in a loveless kitchen and served in seconds is somehow more valuable than a home-cooked meal that took time.

Why are we sending kids to Bible school and three years later they are emerging with all the cocky arrogance and confidence of Joseph after his dreams, and wondering why five years later most of these zealous students who were ordained ministers are no longer in ministry, let alone walking in strong faith? And many have even deconstructed their faith. When will we learn that quality takes time? Longevity takes commitment in adversity, not entitlement amid accommodating comfort or influential associations.

If we want to see the next generation rise into their full potential, it's going to take longer for their development than they or we realize.

It's not a classroom that will qualify sons and daughters; it's multiple battles and adversities and afflictions where they choose not to give up.

Fast-food Christianity has failed us. It's time to return to the old paths of God's ways and allow God to prepare us in *His* time, not in humanity's classroom or through our connections. This is how we are losing legacy. It must be stopped and the kingdom taken back on earth. For legacy to continue, we must develop patience and know that true growth in God's kingdom takes time and perseverance.

ACTIVATION CULTURE

This is one of the most disturbing factors that is doing more damage to the church body on earth right now than good. Activation culture is a massively destructive trend sweeping popular circles, and most of us do not even recognize the issues and fallout that will result from it. It's done with good intentions but poor foresight. Let me explain.

It is like babies being sent into the battlefield.

Imagine a ferocious battlefield where two armies are aggressively in combat with each other. Weapons are drawn, soldiers are being killed, and what is known as the "fog of war" has moved in over the combat zone. Imagine a baby there with nothing on except a diaper carrying a small sword and growling like a lion cub, moving confidently into the center of the battlefield. Wouldn't that cause any normal person significant concern? Anyone with common sense watching this knows the baby is about to get injured or killed. Why? Because the baby does not belong there. They are out of place and not mature, trained, armed, or experienced for that environment or task.

But the tragic truth is that this is exactly what it looks like in the Spirit realm when looking at what much of the church is doing with "activation" culture. They are taking people who have a low level of maturity, minimal character, little submission to and personal intimacy with God, and instead of majoring on people's personal development toward being qualified, these same people are being prematurely launched into ministry. This activation culture usually produces rebellious, unsubmitted, and arrogant individuals who have no value system for the process of fashioning and preparation found in Hebrews 12:3–11.

Many times, this can come across that the activated individuals behave like free agents with a full deputized authority from a minister who has released them into a "high-level ministry authority." These people create the biggest messes in local churches and create a nightmare for authentic leaders. They get an apparent title with no price or process to get there, which gives them entitlement and a false sense of ownership to a role, function, and title. They devalue and even disdain the older, more-experienced generation of fathers and mothers, because in their process they got to where they are without needing these fathers or mothers.

Here's a few examples of the instances we had to address when my wife and I were leading a local church, situations we found more common than not. We experienced "activated" individuals with little life experience, who have probably never held down a solid full-time job for more than a few months, don't have a clean bedroom, and who struggle with basic life skills—these are the ones I'm referring to. They don't press into faith in God for finances and work hard like everyone else in the body of Christ; instead, they put their faith in everyone around them by using guilt and marketing techniques to crowdfund their lifestyle of so-called "ministry" of not working and doing a little bit of evangelism and supernatural miracles each week. (To be clear, I'm not referring to legitimate ministries that are doing significant kingdom work and that rely on the sowing of partners.)

These activated individuals have been to well-known Bible schools for a few years and have been released to conquer the world and many act like they don't need to submit to local authority. They have graduated with puffed-up chests instead of humble hearts and believe they know more than local seasoned pastors. This is also an example of the dilution of leadership issues. These "activated" people are trained to think that they are the solution to the world's problems, all the while they are devoid of character, proper training, and true maturity.

My wife and I have had to shut down the lone wolves during our worship services. The glory of God is so potent that anyone who has any sensitivity to God is captivated by Him and lost in His presence to the point where He is the only one who matters in the room. But not to these individuals. They walk around boldly like they cannot even sense His presence the first time they ever visited our church. And without approaching leadership, they believed they have a right to start laying hands on anyone and everyone in our church. We shut this type of behavior down quickly because we believe in protecting people from novices who have no known character.

In many cases, these same individuals have major character issues, sexual compromise, and lack of financial integrity. That's not someone I want ministering to me or anyone I know. The real problem is that so-called fathers and mothers want to have bragging rights of how many sons and daughters they have launched into ministry at any cost, to the point that these fathers and mothers are defying scriptural commands to attain these bragging rights.

Specifically, Paul wrote to Timothy about leadership qualifications: he is "not a novice, lest being puffed up with pride he fall into the same condemnation as the devil" (1 Timothy 3:6). Much of the church has ignored crucial kingdom commands around key pillars of faith and wisdom. And so, these so-called sons and daughters are rising and are unruly and rebellious, entitled and extremely flawed.

I would suggest all believers study this passage:

> THIS IS A FAITHFUL SAYING: If a man desires the position of a bishop, he desires a good work. A bishop then must be blameless, the husband of one wife, temperate, sober-minded, of good behavior, hospitable, able to teach; not given to wine, not violent, not greedy for money, but gentle, not quarrelsome, not covetous; one who rules his own house well, having his children in submission with all reverence (for if a man does not know how to rule his own house, how

will he take care of the church of God?); not a novice, lest being puffed up with pride he fall into the same condemnation as the devil. Moreover he must have a good testimony among those who are outside, lest he fall into reproach and the snare of the devil.

LIKEWISE DEACONS MUST BE REVERENT, not double-tongued, not given too much wine, not greedy for money, holding the mystery of the faith with a pure conscience. But let these also first be tested; then let them serve as deacons, being found blameless. Likewise, their wives must be reverent, not slanderers, temperate, faithful in all things. Let deacons be the husbands of one wife, ruling their children and their own houses well. For those who have served well as deacons obtain for themselves a good standing and great boldness in the faith which is in Christ Jesus. (1 Timothy 3:1–13)

The truly deep tragedy I have witnessed more times than I want to admit is that these people usually burn out when their character cannot keep them where their gift and non-discerning leaders so easily took them. They either give up or radically backslide. In some cases, I have even seen them completely defeated in sin and a compromised lifestyle. But because there is no fear of the Lord, they continue using ministry for financial gain and support so they don't have to take on the responsibilities that come with maturity.

> *Why do we believe we can do greater things than Jesus by spending less time preparing for service?*

We want a drive-through, fast-food anointing and commission to be somebody, whatever "being somebody" is supposed to mean. Joseph spent years of preparation in slavery, servitude, false accusation, and prison before he even came close to being used by God on a greater scale. Moses spent forty years being trained as an elite military leader and royal in Egypt's upper echelon and then forty more years herding sheep in the desert wilderness before he was activated by God to step into his greater calling of leading Israel out of Egypt.

David spent all his childhood seeking God under a tree, cultivating a relationship with God while he tended his father's sheep, then killing a lion and a bear while no one was watching. Then he killed Goliath, endured the persecution of King Saul, and was the object of a fourteen-year manhunt before he eventually became king. John the Baptist was anointed at conception to be the one who would prepare the way for the Messiah, but what most people do not pay attention to is that John spent approximately thirty years in preparation for his calling, which would only last three months. But those three months were potent and effective.

Jesus was more qualified to minister than all the scribes at the age of twelve. Even though He was teaching the religious scholars when His parents took Him to Jerusalem, He still submitted to the timing and maturing that was required for full effectiveness of His ministry. Jesus prepared for thirty years as a carpenter, not a priest in the temple. He walked in humility and did not use His gifts to gain notoriety before His appointed time. He submitted to being baptized by His cousin John in the river Jordan, then He passed the testing of temptation by the devil in the wilderness immediately after. He came out of the wilderness endued with power from heaven, preaching and demonstrating the kingdom, because His time had come!

Of all these great heroes recorded in the Bible, not one of them had a three-month or three-year part-time Bible school education. Most Bible schools are four to five hours a day. And many people think that Bible school for a two- to three-year period is the same as discipleship. But Bible school is not discipleship; it is teaching in a classroom, not a lifestyle to be emulated.

Even Jesus's disciples were discipled in a lifestyle, not in a school. They were with Jesus twenty-four hours a day, learning almost all facets of life and interaction with Jesus, with people, and about His relationship with the Father. All this was taking place as they traveled all over the region. It's easy to recognize that much more is gained in a lifestyle of discipleship than a classroom or church-pew setting for a few hours a week. One cannot compare the disciples' three and a half years with Jesus, for twenty-four hours a day, to a three-year Bible school.

We easily forget that if the devil cannot stop us committing to God and our call, then he will try to push us where we are meant to go before we are ready for it. This is the danger around premature "activation." And when this is modeled in a public ministry or church setting, it tragically results in a skewed image and example of kingdom discipleship of being raised to the upcoming generation.

If the devil cannot stop us committing to God and our call, then he will try to push us where we are meant to go before we are ready for it. This is the danger around premature "activation."

Equally toxic to this cultural trait is that these leaders who activate and release these so-called sons and daughters into ministry can be seen in the absolute lack of authentic fathering of these children once they are commissioned. There is almost no accountability or transparency required by these fathers once their sons are sent out. And once activated, these prematurely commissioned ministers can do whatever they want without consequence or submission to senior authority. This creates chaos in the church culture. The image of sons being raised up is again blurred to the younger generation, setting demoralized standards and expectations.

I'm not trying to establish a concept of control here, but accountability. The person quickly raised up and activated will not possess value or honor the character and integrity required in the authentic development process, and, as a result, will not value the father who raised him. This will never result in individuals who hold accountability and submission to godly authority in high esteem in their life. Instead, this creates a rebel culture.

WORSHIP EXPERIENCES

A huge symptom of a sick and diabolical church is that people think nothing is wrong or out of place for their favorite worship leader or band to sell expensive tickets for people to come and experience the "privilege" of being able to sit and be entertained by their popular worship songs. The people in the crowd hold up their phones like lighters and sway to their favorite song, take selfies with the crowd, while worship celebrities are performing. Where in any kingdom model was this type of big business and celebrity worship demonstrated in the Scriptures? Oh yeah, only one, Lucifer's story of demise.

Many of these groups generate multimillions of dollars each time they tour. And the tragic thing is that these worship teams and tours are run more like a business model than a ministry. The team members are usually not selected because of purity but rather because of skills and talent. Because talent sells albums and fills stadiums, the crowds and trusting Christian audience are naive to the real narrative and culture that goes on behind the scenes in most of these groups. Without wanting to be critical, the truth needs to be told about this corrupt industry. It's time the fear of the Lord returned to the church and to those holding themselves as God's ministers.

I've known too much of what goes on behind the scenes in many of these worship ministries, and someone needs to blow the whistle on this corruption. The only reason these ministries get away with this level of monetization is because the church has become a consumer of entertainment. When I first started visiting the United States before moving here, I went into a vision while in prayer where I saw a lifelike statue of a preacher behind a pulpit pointing as he made a statement. The figure was gold and looked like an Oscar award. The crowd gathered around this golden statue of the preacher and appeared to almost worship the figure. Although lifeless, the preacher was empowered by the people. A toxic codependency was created where the people worshiped and idolized the preacher, yet the preacher was coveting and pulling fame and money from the people. God spoke to me and made it clear that He was angry with what had become of the modern American church and the displayed model was an insult to Him.

Unfortunately, the power and notoriety that is given to novices with little maturity who grow in experience of how to run in this circle creates an absolute corruption of purity and kingdom culture. These worship experiences create an excessive amount of funds for the entertainers and makes way for a talented entertainer to have an angelic presence on stage. Yet, as soon as they step off stage and return to their multimillion-dollar luxury home or hotels paid for by the faithfully entertained, these entertainers can be any type of person they want. Sexually promiscuous behavior, alcohol, pornography, and even drug use can be present, and the faithfully indiscriminate have no idea. This is far more common than we realize. We would never drink from a dirty cup or eat from an unclean plate, so why would we allow perversion to minister to us?

In any part of kingdom culture that we observe, experience, or are entertained by worship, this is a perversion and corruption that is an abomination to heaven. The same corruption that caused Lucifer to fall—why should we even consider accepting it?

There are well-known people in the worship celebrity world who make millions of dollars on a tour and are sleeping around while on tour, snorting cocaine, and then apparently worshiping on stage in front of thousands. They are not worshiping at all; rather, they have monetized the gospel, and if Jesus was here in person today, He would trash their stage and equipment in front of their faithfully entertained crowds just like He did the money changers and merchants in the temple.

I know these are heavy statements—I'm not here to persecute or dishonor anyone, but people are not addressing this compromise culture that is discipling the modern church, and it must change. Don't get me wrong: there are pure worship leaders and ministries that tour, and everything is done with honor and humility before God. I have a friend, a globally well-known worship leader, and I am so blessed by his purity and humility in the way he leads, models, and stewards his gift and anointing.

I don't write this to create a witch hunt; however, I will tell you that a lot of big brand Christian worship is not pure anymore. We must return to the true heart and purity of worship.

CHURCHES BUILT ON HYPE

Paul said in Romans 1:16–17, "For I am not ashamed of the gospel of Christ, for it is the power of God to salvation for everyone who believes, for the Jew first and also for the Greek. For in it the righteousness of God is revealed from faith to faith." Jesus also told us that if we were ashamed of Him before others, then He would be ashamed of us before the Father (see Luke 9:26).

What happens when leaders and pastors choose popularity and comfort rather than an unashamed loyalty to the realities of heaven and the truth of God's words, laws, and commands—ultimately, His culture? What happens when we become ashamed of aspects of God's standards, culture, and Word? Well, the answer is simple yet tragic: we are left with a beautiful building, a congregation that knows the songs, protocol, church lingo, and dress code, and a feeling of fulfillment that they have done their duty with God. But tragically, their form of godliness is all that remains after God's presence leaves the building. And there is an awkward emptiness watching people doing church when Jesus isn't in the room.

Here we see the real reason why people need to create more and more exciting and entertaining church programs and curriculums. This is the distraction built into the entertainment culture in much of the modern church. It's the distraction that stops people from facing their actual real selves in the atmosphere of the potent presence of God or the presentation of God's Word unfiltered.

But churches with multimillion-dollar choreographed services, superstar worship sets, dynamic motivational speaking rather than convicting preaching, results in a hype culture rather than a conviction, redemption, salvation, and restoration atmosphere. We don't need churches creating concert experiences and hype culture to entertain people. This culture significantly reduces someone's ability to be able to submit to and couple themselves with true discipleship.

Why do I say this? Because first impressions really matter. New believers who get saved into these atmospheres have expectations and impressions set that this hype culture is the pinnacle of the church, of the kingdom of God, and even has Jesus's approval. We need open heavens in churches where heaven truly comes, which isn't just a church culture statement.

This chapter was not to be exhaustive, but only to give a few examples of how the church is failing today. But it is not meant to end there. In assessing where we are, we can more clearly see the path we need to take to get to the place Jesus has invited us to go. In order to fulfill the legacy that Jesus has passed on to us, we have to acknowledge our weaknesses and do our part to rise up and be pure in heart, faithful mothers and fathers, faithful sons and daughters, who trust God's timing for all things.

CHAPTER 11
COMPROMISED FATHERING ROLES

When assessing where we are as the church, it is important to look at how fathering and mothering roles have been compromised, as well as how orphans are celebrated as sons and daughters. Fulfilling the Great Commission and discipling the nations means that fathers and mothers cannot tolerate compromise in their hearts if true sons and daughters are to be raised up. Once again, we must recognize where we are so we can change where we are going. An honest assessment can give us great hope for the future. So, let's look at some ways that fathers and mothers have compromised their roles in the body of Christ today.

CELEBRITY-STYLE PASTORS

Lavish examples of celebrity leaders create questionable motives for aspiring leaders.

Unfortunately, the success of the modern-church model has been our greatest failure.

It has made way for ministries, churches, and worship leaders to be embraced as celebrity idols, which has made way for the monetization and perversion of the gospel. This has led to money and fame becoming huge and perverting motivators for aspiring ministers who want to climb the ladder of notoriety and success.

Unfortunately, as I have personally witnessed, these successful established ministries throw money around flippantly in front of young interns and aspiring ministry disciples, assistants, and team members. I've seen luxury stores shut down so ministers and their teams can privately shop, where five- and ten-thousand-dollar watches are purchased by these ministers using the giving of the people. These watches are then given to young associates who could never dream to buy these types of items, all the while buying loyalty from these young people. And the list goes on and on—private jets, big money, and checks flashed around.

We've hit the point where the world mocks us as Christians. Reality shows like *Pastors of XYZ City* and streaming platform programs about the behind the scenes of megachurches or mocking televangelists who display nothing of God's kingdom. Being prosperous is not bad; however, portraying the gospel as a source of monetary gain is not of God's kingdom and is a snare to the body of Christ.

Celebrity-style ministers and leaders create groupies, not sons and daughters, who feed from the scraps of their tables.

And this lust- and greed-driven impression brands these groupies with a corrupt model of the kingdom that isn't pure or righteous at its core. If these groupies ever rise to notoriety, it is almost certain that they will become fraudulent leaders themselves, unless the Holy Spirit is able to heal and teach them the better way.

The question is obvious: how can these so-called fathers and mothers live, lead, and set examples like this and not think that it's going to create twisted, perverted, and corrupted motivations for aspiring ministers? Instead of creating sons and daughters, it creates followers who are hungry for the same lifestyle of excessive luxury and power that has been flaunted to them.

The model that this devastating example copies into these impressionable young men and women is a treachery to any purity of heart toward serving the kingdom of God. And without even realizing it, it creates a self-seeking ambition that builds the personal kingdoms and empires of people rather than the kingdom of God. In essence, this is a satanic culture with the false label of "Christian." This is a counterfeit imposter trojan horse of the enemy. It's a form of godliness that denies His power (and Spirit culture of the kingdom of God).

This creates a questionable motivation to rise in promotion, and to do so prematurely. It allows the inception of a materialistic lifestyle that isn't healthy, conceiving the seeds of lust and ambition for fame and power, instead of pure service to Jesus. Tragically, like Jesus said to the Pharisees, this is discipleship that produces sons that are twice the sons of hell than these fraudulent leaders themselves, as perversion and compromise only ever multiply and increase.

YOU HAVE MANY TEACHERS

Sophisticated marketing and statistics are great in many areas of life, but unfortunately, we have taken a hold of these tools and used them to find the most successful and popular response in the church. We have discovered that parenting as a buddy rather than an authority figure makes people who want acceptance but not growth feel safe, because growth requires discipline and coaching. We realized that people are drawn to teaching without correction, knowledge without accountability. Many people love teachers but not many love fathers. A teacher's focus is to fill us with knowledge, whereas a father's focus is to shape a son through relationship, affirmation, training, coaching, and correction.

When we read, "For though you might have ten thousand instructors in Christ, yet you do not have many fathers; for in Christ Jesus I have begotten you through the gospel" (1 Corinthians 4:15), what we are really reading is, "You have a lot of people you have strategically *subscribed* to, filling you with entertaining knowledge, but you have very limited fathers who will correct and train you into maturity."

We are operating in a high level yet subtle manipulation when we isolate ourselves and say that teaching voices are fathering or mothering us. That's a huge cultural and personal deception if we are truly seeking the kingdom model of discipleship. This is in essence the ultimate picture of a deceived fatherless generation that has enough knowledge onboard to not even notice the problem.

THE COUNTRY CLUB

This might seem like a strange correlation to the compromise of fathers and mothers, but it is related. A country club is established with a set of guidelines and practices that all members agree on and adhere to. No one is there to rock the boat because each person wants to enjoy the benefits of being a member. Unfortunately, many of our modern churches have taken on a similar model.

In a country club, people are most often there to network and have the benefits of association. There is a sense of privilege that comes with a club membership, where truth is conditional. For example, this is seen in fathers who cover sons in ways they shouldn't. There is a place for love covering sins; however, there is a mentality now that if you're in the club then I don't address the issue because it makes you look bad and therefore it makes me look bad. This is a perverted kind of privilege that is hiding sin issues and never bringing correction into true freedom. Another shape it takes is empowering associated ministers to carry on in a negative state without any true care for their souls. If you're in the club, then I don't rock the boat.

These environments carried on without any tested repentance cause more damage than good. Who do you suppose is held responsible for the damage to the trusting sheep on the other side of these situations? I'm not in any way shaming leaders and ministers, but if a minister walks in gross sin that would cause people to not trust their leadership, then they need to publicly repent and humble themselves. I have witnessed these shameful cover-ups and gloss-overs from some of the most well-known ministries in the world, when, in truth, they should have dealt with these leaders in a biblical way.

Some leaders believe that once they reach a certain level of success, they are no longer accountable to the same laws and benchmarks of holiness that the Bible lays out. They become so familiar with ministry, the anointing, and being the important person in the room that they forget the basic precepts of the kingdom. A true son or daughter should be trained better, and a true father or mother should not compromise standards for appearance and comfort.

These clubs of compromise look after their own interests and preserve the reputations of those who are a part of the group, no matter how vile the secret sins and abominations committed. These clubs are loyal to their own, have a cup of coffee and have no real accountability, but they tell the world that there is. Then they release these frauds back to their trusting followers, unchanged to repeat more of the same.

Internal realities will always express external patterns. These clubs endorse these ministers, but essentially, they are enablers to orphans dressed up as sons and daughters. It's a "look the other way and tolerate sin and compromise in the name of grace" culture. God has not called us to be a country club, but a group of individuals who relate in intimacy with God and with one another.

Let's now turn our attention to how orphans are celebrated as sons and daughters.

NETWORK OVER KNEELING

The luxury and celebrity lifestyle emulated by these leaders creates a frantic ambition that dismisses the patience of waiting on God's process. It introduces a frantic and hasty ambition to get to the top of success as fast as possible, whatever the cost. This causes people to bypass kneeling and seeking God, thus trusting in Him to establish them in the right time. Instead, it causes people who begin to network and utilize their circles and relationships to climb to their perception of success.

Success, or even the idea of success, can be achieved with enough hard work, favor, networking, and determination. But was that God's path for our destiny, or just our own lust, willpower, or desire? The challenge I have for us is that when we get to the level or place of "success" that we desire, did God give it to us, or did we strive for it ourselves in sheer willpower?

You see, success that God didn't plan for us is simply a tragic failure and a neglect of His perfect will for our life.

Networking will never supersede kneeling.

NOVICES GIVEN INFLUENCE

In 1 Timothy 3, Paul outlines the benchmark traits of a true kingdom leader, standards that put into question a lot of the church's culture today. These are standards we would be wise to verify in the life of those who lead us so we can be sure that they are in fact healthy, humble, Spirit-filled, mature, and sincere people. After all, the people who attend their churches, listen to them preach, and who are counseled by them about how to live are entrusting their journeys, lives, marriages, and families to the standard that these people live, not just what they say.

There is one detail here in this passage that I want to draw your attention to. Timothy writes that a leader must "not [be] a novice, lest being puffed up with pride he fall into the same condemnation as the devil" (1 Timothy 3:6). A novice should not be raised up into positions of leadership. Because of elevation of position and status, pride could enter this novice and he could get ensnared into the same sin that defiled and condemned the devil. This is not a casual suggestion; this is strong instruction.

Like activation culture but on a leadership level, these aspiring believers are given positions before they are ready for it. Gifts are often apparent far before maturity and character are. So, leaders will tend to give the extra points or bias to the gifted because they are focused on the giftings, talents, and charisma of the individual. It's incredibly deceiving.

And often at first, their gift carries them so well that no one notices. It's like building a house without foundational blocks—the walls and the roof go up so quickly that everything looks like it's going well, but the most crucial aspect of their preparation is missing and almost no one notices. Our gifts are so amazing, but they are called gifts because we were given them, we didn't fashion and create them—God gave them to us, and so they are His. We may hone and steward them, but just because our gift seems impressive does not qualify us.

Our gift can get us into the room of promotion, but it is only developed character, discretion, and integrity that will keep us there.

Unfortunately, these novices around undiscerning father figures who do not hold a standard will get promoted and raised up before they are truly kingdom qualified or ready. And when they do, they will lead like a person who got millions of dollars for free. Tragically, most of these people will abuse their position in some way, significantly damage or destroy others' lives and spiritual walks with God, and possibly shipwreck themselves.

Let me give you an example. When we led our first decade of church in the United States, we discovered that it was common for a musician or singer to be up on the stage in the worship team of many churches within a few weeks of attending the church. It seems many pastors were more focused on the gift of the individual rather than assessing how much purity that person was walking in, if he had addictions, personal issues, sexual compromise, or a long list of unhealthy traits that we wouldn't want to influence our family.

The tragedy is that many of these pastors are not even considering that. When they put someone up on that stage, they are putting them on the holy altar of God. So, when they put these gifted novices up on stage, it causes the congregation to trust these new-to-the-church people as mature and healthy, which plays with the trust of leadership in people's minds. Not only this, but it sends a loud-yet-unspoken message to the entire church that this person is approved by the leadership, meaning that anything they do on stage or in private life is likely on par with church standards.

This has created the most disastrous situations in churches. For instance, a guitar player came into a church and was put on the worship team and given a position without any real relationship because his gift was amazing. Well, a year later, he had used that position and seduced and slept with several women in the church. Other examples that need to be taken seriously include instances like megachurches raising up gifted speakers, preachers, or musicians. And next thing we know, they are getting drunk in nightclubs, voicing radical activist statements that are contrary to what the kingdom and church believe, or they build a monetized career peddling the gospel for financial gain.

I don't want to traumatize anybody, but we really need to rethink who our heroes are in the kingdom of God. I've seen ministries that travel the world hosting big ministry events, and after the events the crew and team are all sleeping with each other behind the scenes all the while their families are at home sleeping soundly. This isn't kingdom, my friends, this is demonic. How did it get to this place in apparent leadership or influential ministry? Novices being raised up, that's how! And it needs to stop.

The next tragedy that has become more prevalent in today's church is well-known pastors or worship leaders deconstructing their faith in front of the world.

This is the picture of someone who never really had a firm foundation, climbed the ladder of leadership using their gifts and not the Spirit, got hurt along the way, saw problems in the culture but were compromised themselves and got disillusioned and started to dismantle their faith.

This is a sad reality and is the fallout of a generation of churches where gifts have been used and promoted more than souls cared for in the church. We must stop raising up gifts ahead of people's healing and maturity in Christ. I feel deeply for these novices who got position and got lost in it, and I pray for these to meet the real Jesus rather than the "industry of worship or ministry" in the church they have been immersed into and likely hurt by. I'm not attacking anyone, but rather screaming that we need to wake up.

What is the answer to all of this? Maturity takes time, it takes patience, it takes the adversity of life to fashion strength, resolve, purity of heart, and resilience in intimacy with the Father, Jesus, and the Holy Spirit. It takes passing tests and making good decisions, all the while sitting at the feet of the wise leaders who won't raise us when we think we are ready, but only once the Holy Spirit moves and confirms the time is right, the preparation has been completed, and trustworthiness is in place.

Do we really believe that these examples above are okay with God? People don't need opinions from novices; they need counsel from the mature and wise. We don't need orphans but true sons and daughters.

ENTITLED CHILDREN WHO DO NOT PAY THE PRICE

In Proverbs 29:21, we are told, "He who pampers his servant from childhood will have him as a son in the end." If you remember, Jesus only started referring to His disciples as friends near the end of His training with them. Until that point, they were His servants or apprentices. They were expected to serve His ministry and the people around who came to Jesus. They each had tasks—even Judas, who was the treasurer. They were all waiters the day Jesus multiplied food and handed it out to the crowds.

If an individual is allowed to have proximity without personal cost and interaction of serving actively and consistently, then they will not understand the excessive cost and preparation, posture of heart, and serving that the father or mother walk in to facilitate the environment and relationship they now enjoy. They will begin to associate ministry as being great, respected, and served, because they will begin to ride the coattails of their teacher and father, thinking that the respect due to their leader is now theirs.

> *Serving has an amazing way of branding humility and perspective into a person.*

If a son serves throughout his younger years while in his active training season, he will become a servant leader, just like Jesus was. However, if he is raised with ease and never has personal cost or requirements to be in proximity with a father, to become accustomed to a lifestyle of serving, then he will quickly become entitled and will never pay the real price to graduate to higher levels. Instead, he will always find ways to avoid or delegate the difficult work, always being served but never serving. Eventually he may navigate his way to a more significant role, but now he is toxic and dangerous; his path cost him little, thus creating a narcissistic and dangerous individual who will create an environment that may be called church but is far from kingdom culture.

This travesty breeds high mortality rates in aspiring sons and daughters. But we must strive for a servant-hearted culture in which the fruit of discipleship remains and reflects servant leaders, not entitled ones.

ASSOCIATION VERSUS APPRENTICESHIP

If you ever want to be a great swimmer, then you are going to have to jump into the water. Standing on the beach or next to a pool gets you close to the water, but you can never be a competitive swimmer unless you immerse yourself daily into that water and submit yourself to that commitment. Standing on the beach cannot teach us to keep swimming when everything hurts, it cannot teach us to regulate our breathing when we're feeling fatigued. Only daily practice can do that.

The same is true with discipleship. Many believers trust that watching online teachings, whether that is YouTube, podcasts, or even reading books, is discipleship.

This is a great mistake that has deceived many. While it can be and often is a great teaching tool, the consumption of information is not the same as discipleship.

We cannot stand at a distance and watch a master builder construct a home each day and say we were trained by him. Now maybe we saw a few aspects of his progress, we may have even brought him sandwiches and cold lemonade on a hot day and had some endearing conversations, but we were not trained by him. We were merely an observer, one who was associated with him but not intricately trained by him.

When I finished school, I worked for a master carpenter as an apprentice. Even though I was young, strong, and enthusiastic, looking back all those years ago it's amazing to realize how I really didn't know anything at all. I aspired to be a great carpenter one day, but watching was not enough—I had to serve a master carpenter, working with and for him task by task, day by day. I would be given tasks, and some I would mess up miserably and some I completed well. Some tasks took me far too long, while others I finished in a good time. But it took the example and accountability of the master carpenter training me to invite me into the learning and development process. Simply being associated with him would cause a twisted and failed attempt to train me; it took an apprenticeship with a master carpenter.

The church must grasp this concept. Association and gathering of observed training without personal interaction and accountability will result in a failed development of a would-be son or daughter. And aspiring sons and daughters must embrace the fact that learning at a distance is not the same as discipleship. We must be immersed.

PARROTING VERSUS OWNERSHIP

Why is it that there are people who can talk, act, and even preach and lead with such a convincing representation of the kingdom of God at times and yet they end up living a double life? They are one person at church, in public, or on platforms, but someone different in private life, living a countercultural lifestyle, making bad decisions, and compromising in many areas.

This all comes down to the heart. In school, children are taught to learn, rehearse, and repeat knowledge. But a student repeating information does not mean that they have grasped its true meaning, purpose, or power; it does not mean that they are a master or a professional just because they have learned to repeat a professional's story. Here we find the exact issue in the modern church.

Language can be learned in many ways, but only Spirit can be imparted by Spirit. This is what I am going to refer to as the language of a son or daughter but heart mentality of an orphan. In truth, this can catch us off guard sometimes because we are used to thinking that people only speak out of authenticity. But sadly, this is not the case. Yes, out of the abundance of the heart the mouth speaks, Jesus told us. But the mind can say almost anything and not truly grasp what it said.

Have you ever been around someone's pet parrot? Parrots can learn to mimic noises and words. They say the same words that they hear their owners repeat. But the parrot has no real grasp on what those words mean; rather, they repeat familiar sounds, songs, and words like a rhythm. Discipleship and being raised up does not mean learning to mimic a leader's words. This is the problem in much of the modern church culture—people learn to copy a local church or ministry culture, but they do not often get to a point of conviction.

We are not called to mimic our environment, which is called environmental adaptation. Octopus, squid, and cuttlefish are cephalopods, which are among a small number of creatures on the planet that can change their skin colors to match and blend into its environment. Another well-known creature that has this ability is the chameleon. The motivation of these intriguing creatures to change their skin colors can either be to hide and camouflage themselves into their surroundings so as not to be seen, or to create bright colors or patterns to stand out or promote their presence. Sometimes it's fear of being hunted by other predators, while in other cases it is used to blend in and not be seen when hunting prey.

Sadly, many churchgoers become just like these cephalopods—they learn the language of the house but not the heart of the house.

People blend in rather than surrender.

They hide in plain sight, often afraid of their own shadow, loaded down with the shame of private struggles, but publicly they wear a smile with all the encouraging and positive church and "Christianese" words that keep everyone thinking that all is well. Everything is about appearance and saying the right things in the right way to get approval and acceptance. It's being seen but not transparent.

Essentially, this creates a culture where people learn how to quote language from their minds but end up privately having a compromised lifestyle. They become so focused on saying the right words and cultural references that they overlook the extreme value and urgency for ownership of these principles in their hearts. This problem ends up promoting the orphan who can repeat culture the most convincingly, but not true sons and daughters of God.

LONE WOLVES AND UNSUBMITTED ORPHANS

Another huge dysfunction in the modern church is that it has become self-directed around culture, convictions, submissions, and standards. There has become a trend toward people making decisions because we have become a feeling-based and emotionally led generation. Statements like, "I feel like God wants this or that for me," have become all too common. And while it sounds spiritual, it is a self-revealing statement. "I feel like" is an opening statement that has been summarized from a soulish and emotional receptor. It's a lazy language to say, "I want."

This, in and of itself, is counterfeit to a submitted son or daughter who has taken time to be with God and has come out of a posture of seeking with a clear directive. This lifestyle will never say, "I feel like God is saying," but rather, "I spent time with God and He showed me this," or, "God has spoken to me clearly on what I need to do."

This blind spot has been tolerated in much of the church. I have heard many well-established ministry leaders and "influencers" state that they didn't have a spiritual father or mother, but that they were fathered or mothered by sermons or podcasts from certain individuals who were significant generals or leaders. It sounds glamorous, doesn't it? But it is not a true statement.

Can anyone at this time in history say, "The Apostle Paul is my spiritual father?" Of course not—that would be madness and delusional at best. Now the Apostle Paul has had great influence in billions of lives over the last two thousand years, but the amount that Paul fathered was a tiny fraction of that number—he could only father those he was personally present with.

So, what's missing? Relationships. Media, podcasts, and CDs are all teaching material, but it is an impersonal one-way street. It is a transfer of information without a relationship of intimacy. Discipleship is a specific relationship in which a mentor has a unique insight into the protégé's life. It is not just the issuing of information and ministry tips; it is the fine tuning and fashioning of the soul. It is not a teaching series; it is an intimate and uncomfortable private one-on-one conversation where a younger person wanting to grow in God is developed for greatness. There is nothing more terrifying to an orphan-hearted individual than having to be vulnerable with spiritual authority.

Pride is the bodyguard of shame.

"Pride is the bodyguard of shame," the Holy Spirit said to me many years ago. This is why orphans hate correction or vulnerability. There is so much brokenness in their lives and hearts that pride has appeared to bring false security and confidence. The problem is that this is the enemy of true discipleship and will see authority as the enemy of its comfort.

The lone wolf or orphan will hide in large churches, camouflaged in pews, and will claim discipleship from teaching that can be controlled. This is the ultimate symptom and intention of orphan wounds as intended by the enemy. This person will likely have little growth and realization of any legacy if he or she remains in this state.

These people will major on giftings and minor on character. If they gain influence, they will be quick to claim the title father or mother but will have never been fathered or mothered, thus claiming to be something that they never submitted to.

More than ever before, we need to focus on reformation, not revival.

It is important that we dissect what is happening in the modern church so that we can begin to pull apart what is not of God's kingdom and breathe life into what is of His kingdom. Being faithful to the legacy that God has passed on to us depends on it.

CHAPTER 12

THE GOOD AND THE BAD: FATHERS AND MOTHERS

SINCE THE BEGINNING OF TIME, it has been the dream of every good father and mother to pass on life experience, heritage, skills, wisdom, and traditions to their children. Passing on the baton of legacy is a naturally inbuilt instinct that resides in the heart of every parent. Stable parents understand that a child is advantaged to succeed in life if they can build on the foundation of existing heritage rather than having to learn everything from scratch.

As a parent, I want to be able to help my children avoid the pain and mistakes I've made so that those mistakes do not disadvantage them through years of setbacks and struggle, like I had to walk through. They will still need to make their own mistakes, and they will still learn many things I could never teach them through their own struggles. I'm not here to protect them from their own learning process, but, if they are wise, they can learn from my mistakes.

If passed on and well stewarded by the next generation, the transfer of legacy catapults them to outrun the previous generation, extending generational success. But this is dependent on the heart of the fathers and mothers, because they set the environment in which this can occur.

It has often been said that if a good male role model is around a young boy, the chances of that boy having a successful future are exponentially increased. But equally important to note is that if an abusive or an absentee male role model is in a young boy's life, the chances of a healthy future are challenging but not absolute. In fact, statistics show that fatherlessness effects the rates of youths in prison, youth suicides, adolescent chemical/substance abuse, high school dropouts, and more. In a similar way, great moves of God that died often had to do with corruption in the lead role. Good leaders produce healthy movements, while corrupt leaders will produce tragedy in movements.

A father is not just a leader but a baton-bearer, one who must mentor the next generation in the wisdom he has learned, coaching sons to succeed where he has failed and to be wise to walk with God in all areas. And he will show successful paths that God has led him down, which will save time and setbacks for those he fathers. A father is a leader who is not afraid to both affirm and confront, to complement and correct; whose focus is to raise and produce leaders with the heart of both a lion and a lamb, a warrior and a lover.

> *A bad father or mother is not necessarily the opposite of these attributes, but the absence of them.*

It is one who affirms but does not confront or correct; one who offers an absence of true love. A father's own cowardly incapacity to confront a son is an expression of the epitome of devaluation and unbelief in the son. As Proverbs reminds us, if we don't correct our children, then we are not demonstrating the love that will shape them for their future (see Proverbs 13:24).

This facet of truth is not always easy to process or even apparent. But too often a parent will withhold boundaries, correction, and discipline from a child in order to keep the peace or treat them like a friend. But we must agree that a diet of sugar and the absence of vegetables will not produce a healthy person. A parent who wishes to please his child with sugar is ultimately grooming her for an unhealthy and probably short life. Requiring vegetables in a diet is a demonstration of love.

I want to briefly walk through some biblical examples of fathers so that together we can observe some good and bad characteristics of what fathers (and mothers) pass on. Let's first look at Elijah and Elisha.

ELIJAH AND ELISHA: THE DOUBLE PORTION

Elijah selected Elisha by the leading of the Spirit of God to be his protégé, not strategically for his own liking or advantage. Elijah threw his mantle over Elisha as he was passing by as a cultural act of choosing him while Elisha was plowing in the field of his family farm with the oxen (see 1 Kings 19:19).

This act in Jewish culture most of us probably will not understand. The act of a rabbi or teacher throwing his robe over the shoulders of a young man meant that everything the young man saw the older man walking in—the anointing he was carrying—the young man could walk in and carry also. He was saying, "Come walk with me, serve me, and I will serve you with mentorship and impartation." That day Elisha decided to leave all to follow Elijah.

Elisha served Elijah for about six years. I'm speculating here, but from Scripture it seems that Elijah was not easy to keep up with and did not focus on his protégé's comfort. He did not focus on being a fun and likable father—Elijah focused on walking out his calling and obedience before the Lord. It was Elisha's opportunity to keep up and learn along the journey.

Elisha learned to walk in wisdom, discretion, and relationship with God. He was learning to walk as a genuine prophet of the Lord. Like Jesus, Elijah gave his disciple the opportunity to quit and leave, but Elisha remained in pursuit until the day Elijah was supernaturally taken up by what Elisha described as a chariot of fire. As Elijah was taken up toward heaven, his mantle dropped down and Elisha received the double portion that his mentor had carried (see 2 Kings 2:13).

While Elijah probably could have been a lot more relationally hospitable to Elisha, Elisha did not allow the challenging relationship to deter him. He understood that his future was connected to this father. Elisha pursued Elijah against a lot of odds, finally ending up with a double portion of his master's anointing. This was a successful passing on of legacy.

ELISHA TO GEHAZI: THE FAILED TRANSFER

As Elisha's ministry unfolded, he became a father as Elijah had been to him. He had a protégé named Gehazi. In that time, this role would have been defined as a servant—he would serve the father to gain the privilege of proximity and the classroom of relationship. The servant would gain the shaping and influence of the teacher, leader, prophet, or father whom he was following. However, there appears to have been a breakdown in either the fathering of Elisha or the stewardship of Gehazi.

In 2 Kings 5, we read the account of Naaman, the commander of the Syrian army. He was a notable and prestigious man, but he had leprosy. This was arguably the most feared and repulsive infectious disease of the day. Naaman heard about the miraculous power that Elisha walked in, so he sought him out, believing that Elisha could cure his leprosy. The story recounts that Elisha told Naaman to dip seven times in the Jordan, which was known to be dirty with waste, and he came out healed after obeying that humbling command.

After this miracle, Naaman was so deeply impacted by the healing that changed his life, family, and future that he offered Elisha a gift, and probably a generous one. In this case, Elisha did not receive the gift, which is most likely because the Lord prompted him not to receive anything. However, in 2 Kings 5:20, Gehazi becomes greedy and pursues Naaman. He lies and alludes to the fact that Elisha changed his mind, that now he would take the gift that Naaman had offered. And so Gehazi takes silver, clothes, and gifts from him. But Elisha's spirit observed the act of deception and greed. And the resulting judgment was that Gehazi inherited the leprosy that Naaman had been freed from instead of Elisha's mantle.

This is a deep tragedy because the baton was never passed on. Consequentially, Elisha never had a spiritual son who inherited his anointing. And so Elijah's spiritual lineage and legacy died with Elisha. The proof of this is found in an interesting way.

Years later, after Elisha had passed away and his bones were buried in a cave, we see that instead of his mantle and anointing being carried by another, it stayed in his dead body. The Bible tells us, "Then Elisha died, and they buried him. And the raiding bands from Moab invaded the land in the spring of the year. So it was, as they were burying a man, that suddenly they spied a band of raiders; and they put the man in the tomb of Elisha; and when the man was let down and touched the bones of Elisha, he revived and stood on his feet" (2 Kings 13:20–21).

Elisha's bones were still carrying the anointing, which raised a soldier's body from the dead when he was thrown into the tomb and touched Elisha's bones.

The tragedy of a great leader is one that fails to pass on his or her mantle to the next generation. Who was the next major prophet to lead? And how many years did the land suffer for the absence of transferred legacy?

Success without a successor is a failed legacy.

ELI, HOPHNI, AND PHINEHAS: NEPOTISM AND PASSIVITY

The story of Eli the high priest and father of Hophni and Phinehas is a two-part story. It is a tragic account of corruption and nepotism-natured empowerment. There's an aspect of Eli's sinful sons who were willfully corrupt and recklessly familiar and abusive of sacred things. But the second half of this situation is a father who is in the highest role of the temple and did not hold his sons to the standards of God. By being passive, he empowered them to continue in their sinful lifestyle.

In 1 Samuel 3:14, we read reflectively of Eli, "And therefore I have sworn to the house of Eli that the iniquity of Eli's house shall not be atoned for by sacrifice or offering forever." What a deeply tragic and distressing state Eli's failed legacy arrived at. There was a complete discontinuation of lineage with his two sons. That is the epitome of failed legacy. In fact, the story led a chain reaction of overwhelming loss, grief, and tragedy. But how did it happen?

Eli's sons, Hophni and Phinehas, were irreverent and corrupt men. They were guilty of multiple abuses. Their father had trained them in the holy matters of priestly duties. However, they had no reverence or fear of the Lord, which raises the question, were they only instructed in matters around the mechanical duties and not the holiness and fear of the Lord? Did Eli present a casual kingdom in the temple so that they never showed any reverence to the elements, offerings, and people around this role?

The areas in which they crossed boundaries and angered the Lord were all significant. As high priest, Eli gave the roles to his family even though he would have known that his own sons were not qualified. This is the epitome of nepotism in that a father in a place of great responsibility would designate those who were close to him, even though they were wicked, over those who had pure hearts. Surely a father would be aware of the flaws, weaknesses, and sin conditions of his children.

He would equally be aware of their strengths and attributes. But not Eli—these qualifications or disqualifications did not seem to count. Family equaled status.

Hophni and Phinehas did not even know the Lord. As priests, they were supposed to represent God to the people, but instead they presented around the people's offerings as mafia-type bullies. This disdain for the holiness of God insulted and angered God Himself. Instead of respecting the order of the sacrifice, which in the case mentioned was boiling the meat of the people's offering in the temple pots, Eli's sons would demand and force the people to hand over their meat so that they could roast the meat instead of boiling it. They misused their trusted position to force the people to give their offerings in an extortionary way.

The next tragic flaw in these two sons' lives was their greed for the offerings. The custom was that once the meat of the offering was boiling in the pots, a priest would take a fleshhook, which probably looked like a three-pronged meat hook that butchers use, and whatever meat came out of the pot on the hooks was the food for the priests, while the rest was holy to the Lord. But not Hophni and Phinehas. They took all the meat for themselves and cooked it however they wanted to. This again was an abomination to the Lord.

The next great evil culture these two consistently displayed was that they slept with the women who served at the door of the temple, otherwise known as the door into the tent of meeting, which was a holy place. They used their prominent, respected positions to take sexual advantage of and seduce the women who probably looked up to them like they were God's own representatives.

How did these two corrupt sons get into this position? And once there, how did they stay in these roles? It is as if Eli's love for his sons blinded him to overlook the blatant face-value issue that was present. In that time, the cities were smaller and people talked. I'm sure word got around that Hophni and Phinehas were corrupt and hurt the hearts of many genuine and sincere temple goers who experienced the extortion of their offerings intended for the Lord. At some point, we can conclude that Eli would have heard these reports. But it's as if he reacted years later with this corruption already well established.

The reality is that Eli must have intentionally overlooked their wickedness and empowered their behaviors for years. One cannot be high priest for years and not notice the offerings being diverted from the pots to the roasting grill and not realize that something was going on. One cannot be a high priest and not hear about the girls in the temple sleeping with your sons. And if a spiritual man, you would discern this and hear from the Lord about it.

In 1 Samuel 3, we read that Eli's eyes had grown dim. While it is referring to his natural eyes, this is a picture of his spiritual condition. Eli didn't hear from God. When God needed to speak, he spoke to young Samuel in the temple and not to Eli. When God needed to speak judgment to Eli about his sons, He didn't speak directly to him but needed to have a man of God come into the city with the message. It's safe to conclude that Eli was passive in upholding the standards of holiness, at least toward his sons.

The great failure in this example is that we find a man not willing to confront his sons, hold them to a standard, or walk in any integral leadership. At the very least, a good high priest would have fired the priests who abused and desecrated the holy temple grounds. But we only see Eli slapping them on the wrist. Nepotism is the toxic culture of the leader who chooses to give positions close to him regardless of their qualifications or purity level, rather than to those who qualify.

The end of the story is found in 1 Samuel 4. News comes from the battlefield that both of Eli's sons were killed and the ark of God's covenant had been captured by the Philistines. When Eli hears this, he violently falls back in grief into his chair and breaks his neck. Ninety-eight years old and blind. At the same time, Phinehas's wife went into labor from the trauma of the news that her husband had died and the ark had been captured. She too dies while giving birth to her son, naming him Ichabod, which means the glory of the Lord has departed.

This is the end to a devastating story in which legacy was destroyed. First Samuel 2:31 says, "Behold, the days are coming that I will cut off your arm and the arm of your father's house, so that there will not be an old man in your house." All of this could have been avoided if Eli had said no, stood up to his sons, or, even better yet, not have given them position because of proximity.

Nepotism is a dark evil in that it gives family or favored friends biased positions. Even though Eli's eyes were dim, what father does not at least have an idea that his family members are corrupting the workplace, not to mention the temple of God? Eli's spiritual eyes and discernment was failing horribly. It's not that Eli didn't know about the wickedness his sons were committing; it was that he chose not to see and acknowledge it, and therefore he would never need to confront it.

As the story plays out, we see that judgement falls and a clear prophetic message begins to resound. The sons are slain in battle—because Eli refused to discipline his sons, his legacy was cut off. The ark was captured in battle—because of sin, the covenant glory of God was removed. Eli hears of it and collapses to his death in shock, snapping his own neck, which is prophetic symbolism of the head being severed from the body.

Phinehas's wife dies in childbirth, naming the child Ichabod—what was trying to be born, died, and the Lord in a second way confirmed that He was pulling away from His people due to gross tolerance of sin. Isn't it amazing how tolerance and unhealthy grace in a father make way for severe tragedy in the children and the decimation of a legacy?

DAVID AND ABSALOM:
TOLERANCE, EMPOWERMENT, AND PASSIVITY

While King David did many amazing things in his life, fathering was not his greatest strength. He had two failures in father figures: A natural father in Jesse who overlooked him when Samuel came to anoint the next king of Israel, and a spiritual father in Saul who competed with him and tried to destroy him. But what I want to share with you is an example of David as a father so that we can learn another aspect of what it means to be a father.

Absalom, the third son born to King David, in many ways was a troubled youth. He planned vengeance against his eldest brother Amnon for the rape of his sister Tamar (Amnon's half-sister), which was an act of justice in his own eyes (see 2 Samuel 13). Scripture tells us that David did nothing about this situation, so Absalom assumed the role of judge and executioner, bypassing the king's judgment of the matter, and moved straight to vengeance. Like Cain before him, Absalom created the perfect situation in which he would strike down the man who had wronged his sister. As his father, David should have addressed the issues more directly in Absalom, but it was smoothed over instead.

Absalom was the favorite son of Israel, as far as his good looks went. It seems that he rode in favor of his good looks instead of developing discipline in his character. Why did King David allow him to develop thinking like that? Let's examine why David did not deal with Absalom like he should have.

We must remember that this is the same King David who killed the lion and the bear, slayed the Philistine giant Goliath of Gath, and who killed tens of thousands of enemies on the battlefield with ferocious tenacity. But in this role, David was passive with his own house and his own sons. Why the disparity?

I wonder if David's failure with Bathsheba and the death of her firstborn son stripped away his authority and he never regained it. I have watched many men who are powerful and authoritative in the marketplace, in war, or in ministry, who are like broken little boys in their own houses. And in this case, either David's inability or his refusal to confront Absalom's character issues and blatant rebellion was the ultimate destruction and death of Absalom.

This created a license for Absalom to do anything he wanted. He burned down fields, subverted David's counselors, and began to sit at the city gate, telling everyone that David did not have time for them anymore. Absalom started to set himself up in the place of David. There was no true repentance, only face-value apologies with nothing to back up a changed attitude in Absalom. If anything, it enforced his reasoning to keep operating as a free agent and make himself king in the eyes of the people.

Solomon, the son who eventually succeeded David as king, wrote Proverbs 13:24: "He who spares the rod hates his son, but he who loves him disciplines him promptly." I propose that as Solomon wrote this deep truth from the spirit of wisdom, he lamented his fallen brother Absalom.

David had tolerated Amnon's rape of Tamar instead of swiftly dealing justice. David had been passive in dealing with Absalom, who orchestrated the vengeful death of Amnon. He had been weak instead of strong when Absalom burned crops in a riotous manipulative protest, and he had done nothing to confront Absalom for forty years as he set up a subversive governing office at the city gates and drew people away from his father, eventually building an army and revolting against his own father.

It's important to recognize that Absalom had lost significant respect for his father. For the most part, the kingdom subjects revered David's valiant history and authority. Absalom, however, had crossed so many boundaries without discipline that he did not respect David's authority at all.

What we refuse to confront, we will ultimately empower.

This statement is crucial in parenting. If we ignore dysfunction, bad character, and sin, then it will grow into a force that is destructive and pours grief out in the end. A loving environment is important in parenting, but we see from David that being overly gracious and avoiding dealing with issues does not make those issues go away; rather, it gives them power to get stronger. Many believe that God is always happy, which is incorrect. God is always joyful, yes, but He certainly experiences anger, frustration, and regret at times. Love is the underlayment of every encounter we have as parents and leaders—it supports honest conversations while addressing issues; it does not sweep them under the rug.

The healthy presence of boundaries and consequences creates peace in our children's hearts and stability in their lives. The absence of these creates chaos and strife. It is a saddening reality that many great names in the church today struggle to walk in one of their most important roles as father or mother to their own children.

Don't aim to save the world at the cost of your own children— that's a complete loss and failed legacy.

David understood that God was a God of discipline, correction, and even judgment, which he experienced in several notable moments in his own life. But David failed to lead as a father in the way that God had led him. And so, we see in the case of Absalom, a failed legacy. If Absalom was disciplined well, who could he have become?

JESUS: THE EVERLASTING FATHER

One Scripture that got me to stop and think about fathering in the life of Jesus was Isaiah 9:6–7: "For unto us a Child is born, unto us a Son is given; and the government will be upon His shoulder. And His name will be called Wonderful, Counselor, Mighty God, Everlasting Father, Prince of Peace. Of the increase of His government and peace there will be no end...."

I knew Jesus was a Son, I knew He was Wonderful, Counselor, Almighty God, and I even knew Him as the Prince of Peace. I've always recognized that when He returns, all governments and authority would bow down and submit to Him. But I had not fully grasped that God the Father was foretelling through Isaiah the prophet that in Jesus's nature He would be an Everlasting Father. The Holy Spirit began revealing glimpses to me of this deep relationship between Jesus and His Father.

We know that Jesus wasn't married and had no children, so how can He be an Everlasting Father? As I began to ponder this, the Holy Spirit began to unpack it for me. Firstly, Jesus is the perfect Son of a perfect Father. He was so submitted and close to the Father that He went as far as to say that He was the perfect representation of the Father, making the statement: "He who has seen Me has seen the Father" (John 14:9). And again stating, "I only say what I hear My Father saying and I only do what I see Him doing" (see John 12:49).

Jesus had such a perfect relationship with the Father that He became a father Himself.

Jesus had such a perfect relationship with the Father that He became a father Himself, which is explained in the phrase, "You become what you behold." We begin to look like what we worship. Jesus didn't just speak the wisdom of the Father; He represented Him in both words as well as behavioral and relational actions. Jesus was a Son perfectly submitted to a Father, which is so paternal that He too is a father forever. It's important to note that Father God is paternal with heaven's paternal values and standards.

You become what you behold.

To understand Jesus's culture, we have to stop seeing Him as a classroom teacher who did miracles in the marketplace. Rather, we must see that Jesus was a teacher, yes—they called Him rabbi, which means teacher—but we need to understand that the rabbi was a fathering role with the intention to duplicate knowledge, wisdom, and skill. It was to transfer the mantle of stewarding the office, role, or position. It wasn't just the transfer of knowledge; it was the shaping of the soul, emotions, value system, character, giftings, and commitments to excellence.

There was a nurturing focus in Jesus over His disciples that looked like someone who would water, tend, and nourish a seed from germination to fruitful harvest. He was a father to the twelve, and He remains to have a fatherly nature even to this day. Although there is one true Father, Jesus reflects Him well and always will.

Jesus is the perfect model for a son who looks, talks, acts, and values like his father.

In the Great Commission, Jesus is ordaining a legacy of sons to become fathers, who, in turn, raise more sons in His model.

PAUL AND TIMOTHY: A TRUE SON IN THE FAITH

"Timothy, a true son in the faith"

We can also see valuable lessons from the way that Paul fathered Timothy. When opening his letter to him, Paul wrote to "Timothy, a true son in the faith" (1 Timothy 1:2). Paul addresses Titus in the same way (see Titus 1:4). But Demas, Paul said, "has deserted me because he loves the things of this life" (2 Timothy 4:10 NLT). What makes Timothy different from other spiritual sons who would have been around Paul?

Why did Paul have to say he was "a true son in the faith"? I believe it is because there are many who want the benefits of proximity but not the discipline, correction, or submission to the godly authority of a father.

It's interesting that Paul states in Philippians 2:22 about Timothy:

"But you know his proven character, that as a son with his father he served with me in the gospel."

Timothy didn't join an associative apostolic covering for an annual fee. He didn't get close enough to be validated but not close enough to be accountable and transparent. No, he got right alongside Paul and served him as a father. He was with him and took care of Paul's needs and embraced them as his own.

When Paul refers to Timothy "as a son with his father," he is referring to the Jewish culture of the time in which a son would serve and work for his dad in the family trade and become his apprentice until he himself became a master of that skill. There was always respect for the father who had taught him everything he had learned. Essentially, Paul was saying, "Timothy has served me and worked with me, and learned the message I am carrying and the culture of heaven I represent, so much so that now he has been sculpted by it and serves and sounds just like me."

Paul also refers to Timothy's "proven character." Timothy was not just a likable guy who agreed with everything Paul said. On a much deeper level, he had his character tested and proved so that he was qualified and matured to steward such a task. This is where most of the modern church has become drastically disconnected and distracted. The church today wants a short "discipleship class" and hasty empowerment, which is why genuine kingdom legacy has become an extremely rare occurrence.

Timothy's longevity in serving and walking with Paul resulted in his validation: "For I have no one like-minded, who will sincerely care for your state. For all seek their own, not the things which are of Christ Jesus" (Philippians 2:20–21). Paul did something well to have this result in Timothy's life and development as a spiritual son. He passed on his legacy to a true son in the faith.

CONCLUSION

If we pay attention to these stories in our biblical history, which span both the Old and New Testaments, we discover that both good and bad fathers exist. There are good mothers and there are bad mothers. Each of these—whether good or bad—influence the next generation. It is clear a bad father does not sentence a son to a bad future, but it is equally clear a good father does not assure a great son. However, these influences have massive impact on much of the next generation.

When fathers and mothers refuse to parent well, either consciously or unconsciously, they will ultimately produce children who are not coachable, unemployable adults, and unteachable believers who are not able to be discipled.

Parenting well at a family level catapults our children to be able to receive spiritual parenting later in their lives.

Fathering is not about creating the perfect environment for sons to grow. Rather, as clearly seen from the above examples, fathering well is a choice we make to steward those God has entrusted to us. God has called us to learn from those who have gone before us so we can raise up the next generation with a legacy they are proud of, one they can build upon.

CHAPTER 13

THE COUNTERCULTURE OF LEGACY, PART 1

The disconnect between parental roles and children is a tactic of the enemy. To every culture, nature, and strategy that God's kingdom has, the enemy tries to get people to partner with a counterculture to undermine God's agenda. While discipleship and the raising of physical and spiritual sons creates legacy, the opposite counter assault to this divine strategy of legacy is used by the devil. God creates life, but the devil enacts death and destruction.

The destruction that the enemy comes in with to separate the generations is nothing new. However, in the current secular culture, it is widely considered progressive or modern. If people don't like their marriage, they get a divorce. If their job is challenging, they get a new one. If their family is difficult, then they cut them off. If they have an unwanted pregnancy, they simply terminate it. If they're threatened by up-and-coming people in their sphere of influence, then they find ways to undermine them, cut them down, or just cut them out.

Division and destruction are the enemy's way to completely divide legacy from action. Let's look at some biblical history and modern examples so we can clearly see some patterns that, when made plain, will help us get to the point where we can create and sustain legacy. The broken succession of legacy is destruction on a scale that we cannot quantify. Much like when a baby is terminated in the womb, an entire life and destiny is cut off, the ripple effect of who that baby would have been, who he or she would have impacted, and every generation that would have come from his or her lineage will never be. There is fallout that occurs when legacy is cut off and when the normalizing of the practice seriously destroys God's foundations.

The enemy has used this tactic many times to try and destroy a generation and stop the raising up of God's deliverers. In the beginning, the devil came to cut off God's legacy through Adam and Eve. And then Exodus shares with us the account of Pharaoh destroying all the male children; the same in the Gospels with Herod when Jesus was born. This acted as a demonic tactical sweep to try and kill Moses and Jesus in their generations. Pharaoh and Herod exercised their authority to try and exterminate the move of God that was being birthed. Only a parent can abort something, and we need to recognize how legacy is cut off from the top.

SATAN'S STRATEGY

When God cursed the serpent in Genesis 3, He was not cursing an animal; He was cursing Lucifer, the fallen cherubim who had deceived Eve and then Adam by default. We know it was Lucifer God cursing because He begins to talk about the devil's seed and the woman's seed being at war with each other.

Satan understands that God's entire strategy is wrapped up in both natural and spiritual bloodlines of legacy. He understands that if he destroys generational relationships, then he destroys the potency of destiny and legacy in each person removed from that equation.

This is why it's so important that believers understand what abortion is about—both abortion clinics, as well as spiritual generational abortion. Satan wants to destroy the next generation who are ripe with potential in the plan and destiny of God.

Pharaoh

In Exodus 1:15–22, we read that Pharaoh wanted to kill all the male children under two years old. Pharaoh was the reigning ruler over all of Egypt, which at the time was the greatest empire on the earth. He was provoked to murdering a generation because their multiplication inside of Egypt's empire started to threaten the Pharaohs, and so the Egyptians began to oppress Israel and enslave them. It was most likely a slow-moving and stealthy change of atmosphere for the Hebrews. I imagine that because of the famine, they were enticed to Egypt by necessity, kept there for comfort, and distracted by that comfort until they woke up one day as slaves.

> *Enticed to Egypt by necessity, kept there for comfort, and distracted by that comfort until they woke up one day as slaves.*

Pharoah's motivation was to kill numbers of the Israelites so they didn't multiply and overpower the Egyptians. But as we know, there was a demonic agenda behind this plan to assassinate Moses, who would become the future deliverer, that Pharoah may not have even known about.

The Herods

Like the traits we saw with Pharoah, we fast forward to the nation of Israel and the time of Jesus where we see the ruling Herods during Roman occupation. There are actually six Herods mentioned in the New Testament. They were all related, and none of them were good people.

Herod the Great ruled from 37 BC – 4 BC and was the Herod mentioned in Matthew who ordered the murder of all the babies and toddlers in Bethlehem after being alerted via a visit from the wise men on their way to find the baby Jesus. This Herod was Jewish and was named by Rome as the King of the Jews. Scripture tells us that he was looking to destroy any threat to his kingship. The entire lineage of Herod was absolutely perverted, ruthless, evil, and twisted. History records that he accomplished many things for Rome and Judea, but he was also seen as extreme. He murdered several of his own children, a wife, and countless others in pursuit of retaining his position.

Herod Antipas ruled from 4 BC – 39 AD. He married his brother's wife, killed John the Baptist, and participated in the trial of Jesus. Herod Philip ruled from 4 BC – 34 AD. He ruled the area north and east of Galilee. He married his niece Salome, who was the daughter of Herodias, who married her husband's brother (Herod Antipas). Salome danced for Herod Antipas and requested John the Baptist's head as payment.

Herod Agrippa I ruled from 37 AD – 44 AD. He was the grandson of Herod the Great. He is the one who imprisoned Peter (who supernaturally escaped) and executed James. The people worshiped him like a god, but when he did not give God the glory, he was eaten by worms and died (see Acts 12:21–23) And finally, Herod Agrippa II ruled in the AD 50s. He facilitated the trial of the Apostle Paul in Caesarea.

Fathers are supposed to represent protection, love, identity, provision, empowerment, teaching, leadership, legacy, security, role models, and mentors. I mention the Herods because it shows the legacy of Herod the Great and how his line continued to oppress the legacy of Jesus and Christians in the territory. His own bloodline suffered the consequences of his treachery. Herod means "hero like," but they all lived the opposite as tyrannical leaders and oppressors.

KING SAUL

King Saul attempted to kill David, the one anointed to be the new king of Israel. The people of the day celebrated David over Saul because David's feats had exceeded Saul's significantly. You can read more about this in my book *The Spirit of Cain*. In essence, Saul, the father and guardian of a nation, sought to kill David, a son of the nation. Saul lost his kingship in God's eyes because he did not follow God's directions, and then he wanted Samuel to help him save face in front of the people. As time went on, in the eyes of the people David was more esteemed than Saul. And this spirit of competition and destruction captured Saul, causing him to attempt to murder and hunt David for many years.

KING DAVID AND URIAH

Tragically, David repeated the sin of his previous king, Saul. But in this case, David fulfills the plot and kills Uriah, Bathsheba's husband, temporarily covering up the sin he had committed, at least in the people's eyes. In this, David, the father of the nation, kills a son of the nation for his own convenience and lust. This act cost David dearly and impacted the landscape of a good portion of the rest of his life.

*****

I'm using these biblical examples to show that this counterculture spirit takes the father role and perverts it into that of a tyrant, predator, and enemy. God models the role of a father and the enemy seeks to pervert fathers into legacy destroyers. He seeks to use any form of termination to stop God from moving. But even amid generational destruction and the constant interference of the early church, God still had His deliverers birthed and His message preached.

The church cannot expect to rule while in compromise or fear. We cannot allow an acceptance of this dark culture, whether that be in the natural or the spiritual realms. We must learn how to hold up the standards of the kingdom of God and rule in the authority of Christ, even amid such hostile spiritually wicked enemies. God always ensures that He has His people who haven't bowed in place on the earth; they may not be the obvious big-name representatives, but they are present.

Part of the power of this destruction being able to take root in our society is that so much of what is accepted in culture becomes common. We can clearly see that Saul tried to abort David as the next king of Israel. Our modern culture has deeply accepted abortion as a means to an end, and, unfortunately, it is so engrafted into the cultural psyche that it is no longer horrifying.

I'm taking us down this path because the modern church has a lot of examples of older ministers trying to abort the calls of younger ministers because they are threatened or don't want to put in the effort that a new believer needs to get grounded. This ties in our culture today whereby babies are murdered because they are an inconvenience to the parent. I need to tie in where this spirit of abortion comes from, which lends itself to a deeply disturbing cultural shift that is taking place—the return to full-blown demon worship. It's become a blatant affront to the gospel and the power of God's kingdom in the earth.

MOLOCH: THE DEMON GOD OF ABORTION

Who or what is Moloch? And why are we addressing it in a book about legacy? This strange name has as much relevance today as it did thousands of years ago—it did not fade away like a myth. And so, it's important to be aware of who he is so that we understand the dark forces at work in our world today. To understand Moloch more fully, we will journey back into the Old Testament era.

Satan rules through counterfeit deities, which are direct expressions of demonic principalities. In the Old Testament, there were three primary demonic idols known as Baal gods. Specifically, these three demon gods had individual characteristics, so we'll look at them all so we can see clearly who Moloch was and how it fits into the narrative of the counterculture to legacy.

The three demon Baal gods were all human-animal hybrids portrayed in physical form and represented in statues and pictures throughout history. The people groups who warred and plundered the children of Israel were known as worshipers of these demonic beings. Similar expressions of the demonic beings can also be seen in almost all the early Egyptian hieroglyphs. Many ancient cultures unashamedly sacrificed their children to these gods to curry favor with the demonic powers and to gain whatever the offeror was seeking. Many religions today still sacrifice food or alternative shrine offerings to false gods to produce this same favor.

Dagon is a half-man, half-fish demonic god, much like a mermaid. He represents fertility, multiplication, crop harvests, dew, and rain. Baphomet is the half-man, half-goat demonic god figure. It is the closest demonic figure to Satan, the deity that most modern satanists connect with. It also has an element around pedophilia. And then there is Moloch, who is half man, half bull. He represents child sacrifice and prosperity. He can also be known as an owl figure.

Moloch is the false God most often referred to in the Bible. Leviticus 18:21, Deuteronomy 12:31, 2 Kings 17:17, Psalm 106:37, and Jeremiah 7:31 and 19:5 all refer to the practice of the Israelites letting their children pass through "the fires of their gods," and it being an utter abomination to God. Moloch had the head of a bull, the body of a man, and a furnace for a belly, with its arms outstretched to receive an offering.

The heart of God that would send Jesus to die in our place would never require a sacrifice such as this. In Jeremiah 19:5, we are reminded, "They have built the high places of Baal to burn their sons in the fire as offerings to Baal—something I did not command or mention, nor did it enter my mind" (NIV). I bring this up because there are things that we bring into the modern culture that are not from

God and would never have occurred to God to ask them of us. But the culture asks for it and the demonic realm fosters it.

Let me make it clear that these demonic gods are not just statues made of wood, stone, or metal. These are real demonic principalities, powers, rulers of wickedness, and spiritual hosts of wickedness, as described in Ephesians 6:12. And these have been worshiped throughout history. These are the diabolical spirits that incite the most debased forms of hell, expressing itself in, though, and toward humanity, who is made in the image of God. The most depraved spirits cause people to be influenced into partnering with these demonic powers and satanic culture. The reason we need to dissect this is because we need to see the origin of how divine legacy is perverted. It is sneaking into our culture today and will eventually come out and be accepted publicly.

One of the most blatant and concerning examples of this spirit in the modern world is abortion. It is nothing less than convenience killing. It is called prochoice or family planning, but it's not prochoice at all—the baby wants to live and its choice to do so is stripped away.

Some parents choose to terminate the lives of unborn babies, all for the purpose of a more convenient life. Now there are medical situations in which an incredibly painful decision must be made in which there are life-threatening scenarios. Of course, I am not talking about these instances, and only God knows the pain people must go through in these cases. But I am referring to the act of intentionally ending an unborn child's life at any point of the pregnancy for the sake of convenience.

I believe that from the moment of conception, human life is formed. It's not a few cells or chemicals—it's a person. To terminate this person, no matter how early in the pregnancy, is to kill a human being. But the secular culture has determined that it's a person's right to that decision. This is an unconscious cultural pollution that's found its way into discipleship culture where modern churches serve themselves and their own desires instead of loving and serving others at the expense of themselves.

We live in a period in which fancy words are issued to dull down the true effect of what is happening. Statements like prochoice means the apparent right to murder. Terminating a pregnancy means killing the baby. Many phrases have been dumbed down and renamed to lessen the blow of reality in our modern and advanced society.

In Bible times, the worship of the pagan demon-god would cast babies into the fire as an act to sacrifice the child in hopes to gain a better life, better crops, and a blessing from the demon. In modern times, however, people get a medical procedure to terminate the pregnancy with the reasoning that a baby is not convenient at this time. This all happens at a sanitized hospital, with modern medical doctors in a surgery room. Then the aborted fetus or, more truthfully, the baby, is then taken to the disposal furnace and incinerated as medical waste. When described in these horrific details we cringe, don't we? But how easy this procedure is carried out every day in our nation.

Our generation is no different than the cultures that sacrificed to Moloch. Now, our generation does not sacrifice at temples to physical idols, but we do sacrifice—we sacrifice to the god of self-convenience and gratification. It's still the same demon-god. This is the epitome of incarnate evil. This principality has been worshiped by pagans and satanists for centuries, and now our modern culture openly accepts it.

If you have ever had an abortion, please know that Jesus is more than willing to forgive you if you repent and ask for His forgiveness. This segment of the book is not here to condemn you or make you feel guilty for past mistakes. Shame and guilt do not define you moving forward. Only Christ's death and resurrection defines you.

SPIRITUAL APPLICATION OF ABORTION

I have taken the effort to build a portrait of this destructive spirit, this horrendous and diabolical satanic practice that is accepted in our modern culture and that has been around in the earth from the very beginning. If we look at it for what it really is, then we see that Satan is a murderer and hates humanity, and he has craftily taught people to do his dirty work for him. But I want to apply this culture of abortion to the spiritual application surrounding fathering and mothering, around discipleship.

Rogue Fathers and Mothers

I want to show how this spirit translates as more than just an abortion of someone or something. We are not dwelling on negative subjects here, but studying culture, history, and stories that we have become familiar with to better grasp the point of what is happening in our day. It is my desire that we become aware of what not to build into our relationships, whether you are a father or son, a mother or a daughter. Some of these facets people are afraid to talk about, but the body of Christ is owed honesty. And so, I'm going to explain these areas and scenarios of spiritual abortion.

Saul: After David saved Saul's life, and that of all Israel, by slaying Goliath, the people started to admire David and Saul became jealous as a result. He saw David as a threat and no longer as a son. Saul revolted against him, trying to kill him, which was an act of abortion to remove a competitor. This is a clear biblical example that we can look to for a father who aborted a son relationship.

Darth Vader: You probably know the classic villain in the *Star Wars* science-fiction saga, who wears a black mask, cape, and suit, and breaths through a machine with deep filtered breaths. His backstory is an apprentice named Anakin Skywalker who was incredibly gifted. He was trained under a skilled master, but his fear and ambition were leveraged against him by an archnemesis of the Jedi who seduced him with gratifying power rather than the discipline of process. During this dark seduction, he abandoned the accountability and requirement of his Jedi mentors and rejected what he deemed to be the limitations of their boundaries that insulted his ego. Instead, he embraced the indulgence of having unlimited and unrestrained power without price or restraint.

As he crossed over to the dark side, his name is changed from Anakin Skywalker to Darth Vader. He then proceeded to treacherously kill almost all of the Jedi. As the story played out, we see that he ruled in a harsh and brutal manner. Although this is a fictitious story, it reflects a human condition of a misguided would-be son apprentice who becomes a rogue father who destroys rather than builds up. Because every rogue father has a broken son origin story.

Dictators

Many countries today have political structures that lean toward democracy, a somewhat free political governance in which the population of a country can vote for who they want to lead them. And that normally has reasonable term lengths. But dictators are a different form of leadership. Usually using military enforcement, and usually taken office by a measure of force, a dictator is an absolute authority that will normally become a tyrant oppressor of a nation.

In almost all cases, dictators will live lavish lives of luxury while the people they rule over usually live in fear. There is a dark sense of empowerment to any leader when they know that they can do whatever they want and not be held accountable or be removed from office, which births some evil, oppressive conditions and corruption.

The result of this is that injustice becomes normal, and thus people lose hope. Evil dictators cause a land to be under the curse of an angry child who was given unlimited power. It is the opposite of a father of a nation who genuinely loves his country and has a heart to nurture and protect his people.

Woe to the Shepherds

When I was in my early twenties, I was in the fallout of a really difficult time of life, having experienced a spiritually abusive situation in the church I grew up in that left me traumatized. This was compounded by a broken home in the middle of that time. Needless to say, I was broken.

One morning, I remember opening my Bible to Ezekiel 34 and reading it. It was as if I had never read it before, even though I had, and it was as though Jesus Himself was speaking to me in real time. I can vividly remember weeping significantly as I read through the entire chapter. I would recommend you read the entire chapter within the context of this section of this book.

In Ezekiel 34, God speaks against church ministers who have not cared for the sheep, fed them, or healed their wounds and bruises, but instead they have taken care of themselves. This is another example of rogue fathers, those who have prominence and position and forget why and for who they are there, who are the very people that they are charged to care for.

The redeeming part of this passage that reveals God's deep anger around this level of abuse is that God says because they have not cared for the sheep, He will come and heal them, feed them, and be their God. He will be the one who will lead them into green pastures and restore them to Himself.

Abortion is an abomination to the Lord. Do not allow it in your heart or mind, and do not tolerate it in any of your relationships. Make no mistake, this is a demonic spirit. And we must take it as seriously as a Jezebel or Absalom spirit.

It's easy for churches to label abortion clinics as operating in a spirit of Moloch, but can we give the same sober assessment to spiritual leaders who squash and abort raising sons and daughters? It is the same spirit at work. This is the enemy's counterculture of trying to subvert godly legacy being passed on to the next generation.

CHAPTER 14

THE COUNTERCULTURE OF LEGACY, PART 2

INSECURE MOTHERS AND FATHERS

The reason people often miss that sons need fathers isn't because they need someone with a title or position, but because they need a person who has walked out life under a father and been a faithful son. They need someone who has encountered trials, pain, and persecution in life, made good decisions and bad decisions, and who has grown in time into a father themselves with good fruit and a sweet spirit.

Sons and daughters don't need an exciting influence; they need stable experience that can walk with them and guide them through life's journey.

That's the perfect scenario of a seasoned and mature father. Unfortunately, there are those who posture as fathers and mothers and have not been healthy sons or daughters themselves, those who have not walked out the process of kingdom preparation in their own lives in a healthy way. Once they get influence and status, they naturally begin to influence and even father young people who are aspiring to carry what they carry. But these influential leaders who bypassed true kingdom discipleship now find themselves fathering sons and mothering daughters.

Because their process was bypassed, however, many of these fathers and mothers are lacking the maturity they need in areas like personal identity and security, which can cause a toxic leader to emerge. Usually, they are insecure in their own self and can end up either squashing, competing, or emotionally abusing their followers.

This isn't something that can be fixed quickly or easily, but a good start is that these leaders find and adopt a spiritual father who can cover them where they are, humble themselves, and begin to invite guidance and input from more seasoned fathers. I strongly recommend young people who are aspiring to be fathered or mothered to never follow a leader who isn't submitted to and following another father or mother more seasoned and mature than themselves.

Insecurity is the result of an absence of identity. Introduce those who are insecure and have a lack of identity into leadership positions, and it's going to amplify insecurity and abusive culture. When a father cannot lead out of dignity and identity, he becomes tense and insecure while trying to influence those in his sphere. This leads to a toxic and abusive culture that can be found in either absentee or narcissistic control characteristics. Nothing in these traits will establish healthy kingdom legacy, and so we must recognize it as countercultural to God's dream of legacy.

MORAL FAILURE

When a disciple commits to follow a father or a mother, there is trust of the whole package, and this trust must be held in the highest sacred stewardship by fathers and mothers. Jesus said, "If anyone causes one of these little ones who believe in Me to sin, it would be better for him if a millstone were hung around his neck, and he were drowned in the depth of the sea" (Matthew 18:6).

Like many of you, I have sadly witnessed leaders who walk in significant moral failure. This can be beyond devastating, as trust and confidence in the purity of that leader is destroyed in an ugly reality of compromise. Everything that the disciple learned from this father's teaching can come into question as the reality of the failure comes out. I have watched young trusting men walk away from God and speed wobble into sin in the wake of their father having betrayed the values and standards that they had trustingly adopted from the father's teaching and earlier example. This can destroy destiny and spiritual legacy with treachery that makes God weep.

In the natural world, when a mother consumes any level of alcohol or drugs during pregnancy, the substance can make its way into the womb and damage the growth of the baby, stunting and endangering its development, potential, and health. The same is true of spiritual discipleship—the womb is the incubation of trust and endearment found in discipleship. When moral failure comes, it touches a son deep in his soul in a way that others do not, because proximity and trust of personal discipleship produces a vulnerable intimacy that isn't common.

If not managed with wisdom and walking out healing, the disciple will start to reject teachings and values, and, worse still, backslide as the deep pain of parental betrayal breaks his heart and soul. This deeply grieves the heart of God. This is the image of "strike the shepherd and scatter the sheep" (see Matthew 26:31).

I have had to deal with significant moral failure and betrayal by both natural and spiritual fathers. The impact it had in different seasons of my life was enormous. It carries levels of trauma and treachery, the likes of which I wouldn't wish on anyone. And in the case of my spiritual father, he came out fighting, lying, and attacking everyone around him instead of taking ownership for his actions and failures. It was a violation of innocence and trust.

While God had to remove me from these relationships, God stepped in as the Ezekiel 34 Good Shepherd and brought me into relationships with healthy fathers who have taken up the baton of discipleship in my life. We should never allow our story of pain to push us away from the kingdom culture of legacy.

I had a children's book as a kid that the Holy Spirit powerfully used in revelation later as a young man. The *Berenstain Bears* book called *A Day with Dad*. In the book, the young bear has various adventures in the outdoors with his dad. In each activity, the dad bear boldly explains he knows what and how to do things, and as he begins to demonstrate disaster ensues—canoes sink, bikes crash, bats chase him out of a cave. And in each case, the young son learns from his dad's mistakes and proceeds to do the activity without the painful lessons he just watched his dad encounter.

God was teaching me that a good son can grow even in the midst of a father who makes big mistakes. Sometimes we can learn just as much from the mistakes of others; we just need to make sure that we never disdain them in the process.

REJECTION

Rejection is the devaluing and shunning disapproval that leaves an individual wounded with the pain of not being wanted or worthy. In a family dynamic, a mother carries a nurturing role whereas a father will often carry a security- and identity-giving role. The approval of both parents from these different dynamics is incredibly important. There is a validation and approval that only a father can bring.

Understanding this will help clearly establish why the rejection or disapproval of a father is a devastating soul wound in a person's life. If left unhealed, and the individual climbs the social ladder around church or ministry, then the individual could navigate his or her way to being a lead role or father figure and could devastate a wide range of people. Many unhealed leaders find themselves in position to fulfill an internal narrative that says, "See, I showed you," or, "I proved it to myself." But accomplishment cannot resolve or disprove the pain of rejection in a wounded soul.

And ultimately, in a leadership scenario, if this individual gains a position and starts to gather interns or followers who are pursuing mentorship, it is almost certain that this unhealed father will operate in the culture and nature of rejection with these the way that he was led. That is, of course, unless there is significant healing that takes place. A father walking in a culture of rejection will inflict untold damage and cause abusive culture to be in place for the next generation.

DISAPPROVING FATHERS AND MOTHERS

Many today talk about the orphan spirit and identity issues found in wounded people, but not many are talking about the generation of would-be sons and daughters who have been damaged by tyrant fathers and mothers.

An orphan is an orphan because of a missing, dysfunctional, or abusive parent. It's easy for a would-be generation of fathers to point at an orphan generation, not realizing that they hold the responsibility for that generation. It is the job of fathers and mothers to pursue sons and daughters, and then continue to empower them and pour love into them.

Although we live in a generation full of orphans, we must understand that boys become sons when a father validates them and girls become daughters when they receive validation. While the concept of the orphan spirit is real, there are instances where it is not through the sin of the child that this condition exists but through the sin of a previous generation of parents, spiritual leaders not doing their job and, in fact, abandoning their God-given duty.

DIFFICULT SONS

Not all sons are easy to work with, and not all son's journeys go smoothly. Along the way, fathers must deal with sons who make poor decisions and help clean up the mess where possible. In other cases, some sons fight against their fathers in rebellion or stubborn pride, disregarding advice and correction and ignoring guidance. They live at a distance until they are forced to come closer for various reasons, only to withdraw once they apparently resume control of their lives. This can create a difficult burden for fathers to have to cope with.

However, if these boundaries are not understood by both father and son in the relationship, and difficult sons continue to live recklessly and erratically, and a father is not stable, mature, and able to navigate with wisdom, boundaries, and understanding, then a father may get to the point of being frustrated. In this place of frustration, confrontation, repentance, and healing cannot occur. This usually happens because the rules of the relationship have been neglected and grace has been abused.

If this occurs and a father becomes exasperated by the unhealthy and dishonoring cycle of one or more of these various immature traits that waste the father's time and energy, then a father may begin to shun or reject a son. Even to a wounded son with orphan traits, this can be devastating. It is also why they must clearly understand the requirements and boundaries of this type of relationship before entering it.

If a son is going to choose rebellion and independence over discipleship, and invite all kinds of instability, chaos, and tension into a father's world, it's better that the son understand that his actions are breaking covenant requirements. It is not the father's rejection. If this happens, it's because the son chose to walk away via his actions and nothing else. But it must be emphasized that spiritual fathers cannot hastily jump into fathering relationships and then reject sons when things become difficult or bad decisions are made. Fathers are there to walk people through life, and we all know that life can be messy at times.

This doesn't mean that fathers must just live with bad behavior, but it does mean that fathers cannot spiritually abort the difficult son in life due to these reasons. Jesus's disciple Peter was awkward, messy, and impetuous at times, but Jesus held boundaries with Peter and loved him with grace and opportunity. Because Jesus believed and saw the gold in Peter, Peter made it.

> *If Jesus hadn't championed Peter's destiny,*
> *then Peter's destiny would have died with his failures.*

Difficult sons are not easy to deal with, and while some choose a different path, others have treasure in them that can change the world if stewarded well. A father or mother is in a uniquely intimate role that encompasses nurture, care, and protection, among many other attributes. The ultimate violation of a biological parent, spiritual parent, or pastoral role is that this sacred role of protection, nurture, and entrustment of legacy is abandoned and exchanged for a temporary indulgence in a selfish pursuit of defending either their own perceived seat or power. Or it is left in a state of irresponsibility to care and cultivate others.

Abortion is ultimately an abandonment of responsibility to pursue selfish values. Jesus didn't abort Judas even though Judas's heart and actions were beyond wicked. Judas broke the relationship, Jesus didn't. And even then, I truly believe that if Judas had run up to Calvary while Jesus hung there dying, and like the thief he cried out for forgiveness and mercy, Jesus would have graciously and mercifully forgiven him. Jesus never aborted Judas's ability to grow and have opportunity.

Parents, pastors, ministers, and leaders, we must learn from this. How do we walk with the broken and the healthy, discerning who we are called to father or mother, and not abort anyone during the rest of our lives? If the relationship breaks, let's not allow it to be from our contribution. Jesus was happy for His disciples to do more and greater things than He did. He did not try to cancel and nullify anyone because someone's growth and success never threatened Him. The foundation He laid caused others to excel.

Almost all God-fearing Christians understand that abortion is murder and an atrocity to God. Most understand the extreme evil that this represents. But do we understand that spiritual abortion is just as evil? It's just not recognized the same because it looks different and there is no blood spilled. This needs to be recognized for what it is and our thinking changed so we can heal and grow the legacy Jesus launched. Abortion is the termination of life through the most vulnerable phase of life. Conception is the moment life is created, but pregnancy or gestation is the vulnerable phase in which a mother carries the life of the baby within her for nine months. In this period, the baby's life is tender and completely dependent on the mother for every facet of life.

When it comes to spiritual discipleship and sonship, fathers and mothers must be aware that a son is not born—a son is made. He is made through process in discipleship. There is a significantly important phase in the earlier stages of discipleship, in which a father is birthing in partnership with Holy Spirit a follower into a disciple, the disciple will progress in time, and, through the tests of God, he will mature into a son. A spiritual son does not just simply appear; there is a pregnancy, infant, toddler, juvenile, teen, young adult, mature adult, and finally a seasoned adult.

During the pregnancy phase in a discipleship scenario, a father is building a relational bridge of endearment and trust between himself and the disciple that the disciple must equally contribute to. But in this phase, the relationship is volatile and not yet stable, and, for this reason, fathers and mothers must select disciples wisely in partnership with the Holy Spirit. The young follower is entering a world of a mature and stable father's environment, and yet the follower will lack the personal maturity and framework on how to steward the honor of having a father invest into his life and destiny. In this vulnerable state, a son behaving recklessly or impetuously can cause great damage. Ultimately, a father can turn on a son at any stage of life, and in the same way a son can act treacherously also in any stage of life.

This is not just a matter of new thinking; it's also an issue of being healed of all rejection and past wounds so we do not project others' growth or promotion as a threat against our own progress. A true healed father or mother is established and approved in the success and promotion of their sons and daughters. We must learn this.

CONCLUSION

In the last two chapters, I have just outlined several causes that can significantly contribute to a spiritual and emotional environment where abortion can occur. When one of these elements or environments is on the rise in a generation or culture, we will also see a rise in spiritual abortion, resulting in a wounded and orphaned generation.

When we see abortion on the rise, our hope is that every time this counterfeit culture is gathering in a generation, a deliverer generation is being raised up. God is not silent when this is occurring; He is never caught off guard. Whenever Moloch is being worshiped in a culture, know that God is raising deliverers. This has to be more than a declaration; the church has become far too flippant with our great statements, so we must now commit to the significant investment of time and effort to transform and purify our fathering and discipleship culture.

The dark spirit of abortion is a complete contradiction of the spirit of sonship and discipleship legacy. There is no room in the kingdom for the spirit of abortion to function. While sons can sabotage or disqualify themselves from access to a particular father by breaking the agreed boundaries of the relationship, there is absolutely no excuse or acceptable reason for a father to abort a disciple in the process of discipleship. While disciples can become unteachable, if there is going to be a breaking of relationship, do not let it come from the fathering role.

The answer to avoid the evil expression of hell's culture anywhere near kingdom discipleship relationships is for fathers and mothers to walk out a deep healing process in their own journey before they ever assume to take on the responsibility of a young believer hoping to receive guidance along their own journey. Especially in the early years, disciples are not always easy to manage and lead, as they have a way of pressing buttons in fathers during this awkward phase where they are full of zeal and dysfunction. Healed fathers raise healthy and whole sons, while wounded orphans who become leaders and influencers wound and abort young hopeful protégés.

The spirit of adoption is the counter to the spirit of abortion. Ultimately, the Spirit of God is the one who adopts us, but in the same spirit fathers and mothers can adopt disciples that become sons and daughters in the faith. Never underestimate the power of a father calling a disciple authentically by the name *son*. The healing, security, and empowerment that this can instill in a disciple is life changing and pours love into the environment. God calls us by the spirit of adoption, and we can steward sons and daughters in our world with the same heart.

> BUT WHEN THE FULLNESS OF THE TIME HAD COME, God sent forth His Son, born of a woman, born under the law, to redeem those who were under the law, that we might receive the adoption as sons. And because you are sons, God has sent forth the Spirit of His Son into your hearts, crying out, "Abba, Father!" Therefore you are no longer a slave but a son, and if a son, then an heir of God through Christ. (Galatians 4:4–7)

Jesus came to redeem us through the spirit of sonship, not through orphanhood or slavery. God's heart is the spirit of adoption and not abortion.

There is a deliverer generation arising, and it must be fathered by healed sons who mature into fathers.

WHY IS LEGACY FAILING?

SECTION III

A BUILDING IS MADE UP OF MANY BRICKS. *So in order for that building to be structurally sound, each brick must be integrally crafted. Progressing further into this next section, you will notice that the book's focus moves from the church and on toward a more personal perspective. Legacy is not just corporate; it is personal as well.*

> *This segment is going to discuss the good and bad sides of relational legacy. Like the previous section, there is going to be some continued challenging conversations, as well as some beautiful examples of discipleship and legacy at a personal and relational level. We are going to be borrowing from the past so that we can understand the present and move into the future.*

Prepare your heart as we walk towards a developing image of what healthy relational discipleship looks like.

> *I say prepare your heart, as sometimes in order to embrace the new, we need to see that in certain cases, the way we have gone about things in life and community has not always necessarily been the most beneficial or efficient paths. So we must prepare our hearts to relearn the old ways of God, or better put God's perfect way of doing things to best align with his will and heart.*

CHAPTER 15

THE GOOD AND THE BAD: SONS AND DAUGHTERS

Generational legacy is crucial on two key components: the fathering and mothering generation, as well as the son's and daughter's generation who will serve, steward, and receive the inheritance and extend the lineage of heaven's legacy that has been passed on to them. We have discussed the need for good fathers and mothers, as well as the results of bad fathers and mothers. But equally important are the ones who receive and those who extend the fathering generation. These sons become fathers and these daughters become mothers.

THE QUALITY OF THE SOIL

While good fathers are important, they are not the only crucial ingredient in this amazing heritage transfer of God's blessing, power, and wisdom. You see, the power of seed always reveals the quality of the soil. What I mean by this is that while fathers and mothers can have the best quality seed to sow into the soil of hearts, the quality and preparation of the soil will determine what happens to the seed. It will determine whether it grows and replicates or starves and struggles to manifest any fruit.

The seed can possess the most pure and powerful genetic DNA, but if it is sown on a stony patch of ground, the chances of anything good coming out of the effort and investment are minimal. This is the exact point Jesus was conveying when He told the Parable of the Sower in Matthew 13. The seeds were all the same, but it was the soil that received the seed that differed and thus caused different yields.

Good sons can come from difficult environments and difficult leadership. King David is a great example of this. He grew up overlooked. His own father, Jesse, could not see his potential when Samuel came to their house to anoint the next king of Israel. Jesse didn't even bother to call David to the lineup when all David's other brothers were presented to Samuel for selection. Can you imagine David's heart when he realized that he was an afterthought?

And then there is David's spiritual and kingly authority and father figure, Saul, whose life David saved in the valley of Elah when Goliath stood there challenging all of Israel. In that time, the first to die after such a challenge like the one Goliath proposed would have been the king because he would have been the first to stand up and fight for the people. However, David saved Saul's life that day. But as history reveals, Saul became threatened by David's exploits, favor, and anointing and initiated a fourteen-year manhunt for David. And yet, with all that bad leadership and fathering, David emerges as a good son, a man after God's own heart.

Equally true, no wrong-hearted son can emerge as a good son, even from good environments and leadership. This is because of the law of what is in you will define and magnify how you steward your environment. Judas is the perfect example of this. He had the perfect leadership and spiritual father in Jesus, and yet his evil heart was not changed but rather amplified to the point that he turned on and tried to monetize his proximity to Jesus.

Absalom had a father who had one of the most intimate relationships with God, and yet Absalom was a terrible son. His heart was evil, his principles were compromised, and his character was broken. And yet he used his father's title, position, and name to leverage his own sadistic uprising and attempted rebellion. He used his proximity to his father to divert David's loyal subjects toward himself and create an insecurity that David did not have time for them, nor was he interested in their needs. Absalom presented himself as their solution. His life was a tragic failure because his heart was wicked and corrupt.

To understand why not-so-great sons can come from great environments, let me give you this example from money. Many people say that money is the root of all evil and thus completely misquote the Bible. However, the correct quote is, "The *love* of money is a root of all kinds of evil" (1 Timothy 6:10). Money magnifies what is in a person. Give a good person a million dollars and good things will be stewarded through his or her life. Give a bad (or ill-equipped) person a million dollars and all the evil he or she could previously not afford will now begin to manifest in his or her life. Many people don't even know what is in them until more money comes into their hands.

If you are faithful with a little, then you will be entrusted with much (see Luke 16:10). Money in the hands of an unhealthy heart will amplify ego and pride and license sins and evil desires to be achieved. Likewise, the quality of the soil of your heart will determine what you do with what is sown into your life by fathers and mothers.

PROXIMITY IS NOT ENOUGH

Many sons and daughters believe proximity will afford them approval and opportunity from their parents. They believe being close enough will bring validation and impartation. The problem is that once the anointing starts to get released in your life, it will do one of two things: it will either empower you or destroy you. When people have unhealthy and wrong hearts, the second side of the anointing can destroy a person.

Proximity to a leader, to a father or a mother, is not enough. It certainly wasn't for Judas or for Absalom. The lack of proximity of Absalom to King David was what he used to get promoted. Through his last name and his good looks, he inherited a position. He got away with literal murder and insubordination.

Many would-be sons love the experience of a father's acceptance and protection, but they drift away from staying close in relationship, trying to protect themselves from the pain of their dysfunction, mistrust, mistakes, issues, or wounds being touched by a father. Because of this, they slowly distance themselves from intimacy in this type of relationship.

I've watched this happen with many individuals. Sons want desperately to be seen, accepted, affirmed, and believed in by fathers. There will be a discussion where they talk through a difficult or painful issue, which usually causes a drawing closer in the relationship. But then slowly there is a drifting away, until finally there is a relational disconnection that takes place over time.

After a noticeable distance, the son comes out of drifting away and opens up with accusations pitched as offenses at the father role. Or, if humility is present, he will talk with honesty about sin, torment, and bondage. It will come to light that the son will have been experiencing mental mind games of accusation against the father that he was not able to control or cast down.

This will be talked through and, if the father is healthy and secure, grace will be applied and truth levied at the son so that there can be a breaking and a working through of these unhealthy strongholds. In this case, there will be tears, hugs, restoration, and joy. But if the son does not address these issues and walk through healing in his heart with the Holy Spirit to rebuild the once-wounded broken soul areas, this cycle will begin once again. And although there was nothing but grace and love shown to the son, if he remains unhealed, the son will enjoy the shallow restoration of intimacy for a short season, but over time, whether that be weeks, months, or years, he will drift again. And in time, he will slowly but surely back away from proximity.

Each time this cycle repeats, it strengthens this stronghold. If it is not dealt with, at some point it will become far too convincing and established for the son to fight anymore, and there will come a tragic moment where the would-be son breaks the relationship and disconnects. He chooses rather to get promotion or "freedom" by going the easier route, unsubmitted, than staying under covering. This usually involves those around who gained respect for the son because of his apparent appearance of proximity to the leader who gave him credibility. These people will usually get influenced and led by such a disconnected son and a church split will begin, creating nothing but fallout and destruction, even if things look exciting and refreshing in the short term.

There are individuals who have the language of sons but the hearts of orphans. They want all the benefits, appearances, licenses, and inheritances of sons but do not want to commit to honor or submit to godly authority and guidance in every season of life. As they do this, voices of accusation, mistrust, and even scandal accumulate in their minds, affirming their distance. These would-be sons become lone wolves, and the fathers they once relished being close to now seem like a toxic threat because these sons refused to push through their emotional wounds.

HOW PRIVILEGE GOES WRONG

Entitlement, unhealthy privilege, and a blurred heart comes to a son or daughter mismanaging and misinterpreting the honor and access poured into him or her by spiritual parents. When such a rich caliber of honor, service, parenting, and training has been poured into a son or daughter over a long period of time, unquestioned honor and loyalty is an entry level response.

Such a healthy privilege to be led, served, and raised by godly leadership should be answered with double honor for life, which includes healthy submission and a never-ending consideration for the parents' well-being. It is not wise to damage by dishonor the individual through whom such a rich foundation has been laid into a son or daughter's life. Such damage will occur even in the unspoken silence that raises a question of integrity toward the ones who have sown nothing but quality into the individual's life.

Absalom, using the title of his royal family name, went away from where he should have been and set up shop at the city gates and stayed there long enough until the people began to love and trust him more than his father. He perverted and diverted God's ordained rivers of trust and submission from King David toward himself. The people were David's subjects who were appointed by God, but gradually Absalom began to see them as his own. A false sense of confidence grew within his heart, and Absalom started something. This always occurs in the name of "a righteous cause." Absalom had done nothing of himself to draw respect. He manipulated the name and position his father's throne had given him. He operated in entitlement through association. Absalom did the wrong thing while attempting to have the appearance of displaying the purest intentions.

Only fools would dishonor and compete against their spiritual parents and then ask for their blessing. It is clearly against the Bible's admonition to honor our father and mother. It is like Saul going against God's instructions regarding King Agag in 1 Samuel 15. Saul asked Samuel to make him look good in front of the people, even though he blatantly disobeyed God's and Samuel's direct instructions.

What astounds me almost more than anything else here is that there are sons and daughters who have been given privileged access to some of the richest and wisest teaching and guidance I have ever witnessed. It is obvious that there are leaders who have generously poured their lives into the younger generations around them, and every time the sons or daughters open their mouths, we can freely observe the jewels that have come from their spiritual leaders. These have enriched their lives. Isn't it amazing how people value themselves based on what has not cost them? How could some turn around with such a rich heritage, understanding, and foundation and sow one of the most devastating seeds into their own destinies by turning against the ones who have shown them the way?

We need a generation that develops what they have received. We need those who are reaching maturity, not just going from place to place and conference to conference trying to obtain the next spiritual stimulant. We need a generation that is exercising what has been placed in them and given to them through fathers and mothers. The idea of receiving impartation is so that it can then be rooted in the son's or daughter's life, cultivated and matured by a spiritual parent, thus showing them how to take an impartation and solidify it into an inheritance.

ADVERSITY CREATES GREATNESS

Modern culture tells us that if it feels good, then that's the road to take; but if it doesn't feel good, then we should choose a different path. But the Bible is full of examples showing that adversity is the way of training. Even Jesus learned through the things that He suffered (see Hebrews 5:8).

History shows us that it's those who have come up against great odds who accomplish the most. They see what is possible instead of making excuses and refusing to show up. Proverbs 26:13 tells us that the slacker says there is a lion in the road so he or she can't fulfill what needs to be done. Good sons see adversity, but they are pressing in against it. They understand that every mountain in God's way has to move, and that the enemy would love to take them out by portraying a false reality about the father training them.

Jesus was on point when He said to the Pharisees that their Father is the devil (see John 8:44)! We need to not just ride out adversity or training; we must know who the Father is to us and embrace the process. Because we'll never be a good father unless we learn to be a son in our mentality, posture, and actions.

We need to take the Bible's admonition seriously: "Honor your father and your mother, that your days may be long upon the land which the LORD your God is giving you" (Exodus 20:12). And Paul tells us in Ephesians 6:1–3: "Children, obey your parents in the Lord, for this is right. 'Honor your father and mother,' which is the first commandment with promise: 'that it may be well with you and you may live long on the earth.'" *The way we treat those God gives us to spiritually parent will determine what our future looks like.* The sons who see the invitation and opportunity, and act right in the position, see the outcome.

Elisha

Elisha committed himself to Elijah and never looked back. So much of our culture today is looking for the best option. Elijah had the anointing, but he probably did not seem to be the best "option." Sons, you need to keep an eye out for those who are calling you into their circle. What might seem like a father in God passing by is him seeing if you're fit to respond to his invitation.

Elisha recognized the invitation and burned the bridges that would allow him to get back to his old life. Elisha as a son was completely committed. He obtained a double portion of Elijah's anointing because he kept his eyes on the prize of his calling. He fully recognized, and did not despise, that becoming who he was called to be was directly connected to letting go of the past and hanging on through the training.

Peter

From the Scriptures, we can assume that Peter was the oldest disciple. We know he was married because Matthew, Mark, and Luke all record that Jesus healed his mother-in-law. He also paid the temple tax in Matthew 17 and was a seasoned sailor. Peter had lived a whole life before Jesus called him to follow Him. Peter is a great example of not letting obstacles stop you from becoming a son.

Peter wanted Jesus. He wanted to leave all he knew to follow Jesus. He wanted to be called out on the waters to Jesus in a miraculous way. He wanted to cut the guy's ear off in the garden and defend Jesus. He didn't want to believe that he would deny Jesus three times. And when he utterly blew it, sinking in the waves, denying Jesus, and going back to the boat, he was still the first disciple to run to the tomb and to leap into the open seas when he saw Jesus on the shore after His resurrection. We learn from Peter that age or baggage is not an obstacle to becoming a son of a father.

Timothy

We've seen that Paul was able to promote Timothy as his son because they were of the same spirit. Timothy valued what Paul valued. Many fathers crave sons to raise up, but they can't because that son does not hold the same values, does not trust the father, and cannot see the line of submission. Timothy came from a strong mother and grandmother in the faith. But he needed a father also.

Sons, remember to identify who the fathers are around you and commit yourself to the vision that they carry. Daughters, identify who the mothers are around you and commit yourself to their vision as well. Let their passion become your passion, their heart your heart. This is the making of being entrusted with whole territories, as Timothy eventually was.

These men carried the DNA of their spiritual fathers and accomplished more than what they saw their fathers do. And this is what God is asking of us in John 14:12: to receive what Jesus is giving to us—the legacy of taking what was inherited through life training and expanding the kingdom of God. As we do this, we will become sons and daughters ourselves, thus passing on the legacy to the next generation.

CHAPTER 16

DISCONNECTED GENERATIONS

History often holds lessons and reveals cycles and patterns. This generation does not look back often enough, and we need to regain the key of looking back to gain insight so we can move forward. We will go through some concepts and historical context in order to provide us with a framework to address generational disconnection and give us perspective to embrace and empower legacy.

THREE TYPES OF DISCONNECTION

"In those days they shall say no more: 'The fathers have eaten sour grapes, and the children's teeth are set on edge'" (Jeremiah 31:29). While this statement is spoken to Israel, there's a deep sentiment to it that we can learn from. If a parent eats sour grapes and it causes her offspring to be born with defects and deformities, then we are not really talking about grapes, are we? We are talking about sin, offense, and dysfunction being passed from mother to daughter, from father to son. If a dad is unhealthy, he creates a culture that is an unnoticeable "normal" environment in which children are cultivated to operate and thrive in without question.

Let's look at the three types of disconnection that are passed on from parents to their children.

Absentee or Disconnected Relationship
When parents are absent or busy, or maybe were never there in the first place, it creates a dangerous dynamic in the next generation. The absence of a mother figure starves children of nurture and care. And the absence of a father figure denies a

culture the security and the affirmation of identity that is unique to the masculine role. The removal of these two crucial foundations creates an untamed, unhealthy wild survivor mentality that screams orphan.

> *This disconnection mostly produces people who do not trust, value, or respect authority or elders.*

This absence from parental authorities could be established in one of a few different ways, such as a departed or removed parent who has completely abandoned their role in that child's life. A father who is married more to his career than the hearts of his children. Or a mother who is distracted or obsessed with things that divert her passion, attention, or focus from the family.

The absentee parent broadcasts a deafening message that the child is not important or valuable enough to spend time with them. It devalues the child. Neglect turns into pain, and then pain in that child establishes as rejection. Rejection drives those children into deep brokenness. And that reality, once realized, starts to build into sharp resentment, anger, and rage against parents and authority.

Abusive Environmental Culture

When a parent is angry, violent, or abusive in any form, it shapes a deep sense of trauma in the child that can tragically form a cyclical culture of abuse and dysfunction. Ultimately, most children who experience this environment will hate their parents and hate or undervalue themselves. This traumatic damage is a gateway to various avenues of addiction, sexual confusion, and identity crisis.

When abuse happens to a child from a parent, it has the opposite of the nurturing, care, protection, provision, affirmation, and love that should be communicated to a child. And when a child is dealing with an "anti-parent" culture and being subjected to abuse, it contorts the physiological state and traumatizes the soul and spirit. This causes a deep resentment and hatred to be established, thus separating generations.

Present but Toxic

When a parent is in close proximity to his or her children but has a deeply unhealthy, toxic culture, we find yet another vehicle for poisoning a generation. The innocent trust of a young child immersed into this environment will absorb and accept everything they encounter. The parents may be around in the house, but the culture is so bad that it creates deep issues of identity crisis and unhealthy emotions in the child. The sad detail around this is that the child, when younger, will not be able to identify where the confusion, hurt, and toxicity is coming from, but instead will replicate what he or she has learned.

RESTORING GENERATIONAL LEGACY

In the book of Malachi, we read: "Behold, I will send you Elijah the prophet before the coming of the great and dreadful day of the Lord. And he will turn the hearts of the fathers to the children, and the hearts of the children to their fathers, lest I come and strike the earth with a curse" (4:5–6).

When Malachi refers to Elijah, he is referring to the spirit of prophecy coming before the day of the Lord. I see the great urgency and value for the need to bring restoration to the generational connection described here. God is saying that the generational relationship and legacy has been broken. He is, after all, the God of Abraham, Isaac, and Jacob, the generational covenant God. He is the God who promised to bless the earth through Abraham and his descendants, the God who promised that He would crush the serpent's head through the seed of Eve.

God is the perfecter of unity, while Satan, on the other hand, is the dark force of division. He wants to drive nation against nation, ethnic group against ethnic group, and family against family. He wants to divide father and son, mother and daughter, and to cease the generational legacy that God the Father designed and authored.

The disturbing final statement in this passage is "lest I come and strike the earth with a curse." This is the last verse of the last chapter in the last book of the Old Testament. The final thing a person says before he or she leaves is always important, and this seems to be a sober warning for us as well. And in character to

God's value system, it's all built and focused on the family. The topic of generational disconnection is far more of an important topic than we originally thought.

What does it mean for the earth to be struck with a curse? Well, sadly that's a church that is generationally disconnected, where the younger generation is isolated from the wisdom, guidance, and affirmation of the mature generation. Because of this, they are not able to receive the inheritance of what the older generation has acquired. This ultimately leads to an ineffective stewarding of the gospel to the world. The world struck with a curse leads to orphans who think they are wise sons and daughters, with no healthy guidance or foundation.

In this case, history must become our teacher, or we will be doomed to repeat it. Let's look at history to see how this generational disconnection has impacted people, nations, and even the whole world.

THE DARK AGES

When the average person hears the term the *dark ages*, we often think of medieval knights, castles, and King Arthur. That period truly was a dark and godless era, but here is why. In that time, the Catholic Church was well established in Europe, and the pope, bishops, archbishops, and the clergy operated in such a way to show that God was busy and must be accessed through the church franchise only. The way that they achieved this was to keep the Bible and church services in Latin, inaccessible to the common person.

Seems simple enough, right? Well, the reality was that barely anyone spoke or read Latin at that time, except for the Catholic priests. The people would come into the church to meet God but would only hear a foreign language being proclaimed in the services, creating a disconnect between the people and God. There was no Google; the people had to trust the priest's word. The result was that they became disconnected from God, from any sentiment of right living and who God was and is. As a result of this, the culture in Europe became depraved in every way imaginable. Witchcraft gained momentum, and the spiritual and moral climate of the Western world became grossly dark.

This is the picture of a generation who has access and knowledge of the truth starving the next generation from it. The result is that a hideous cycle starts as the younger generation falls into a dark and difficult season where things become unhinged and degraded. Our hope is that things get so desperate that a generation turns to God. But even in this cycle, a generation loses all the platform it had and, in essence, has to start over like someone who fell down a ladder.

THE HITLER YOUTH

Let's fast forward and look at this past century. We see how this type of generational disconnection relates between generations over the period of a hundred years.

Adolf Hitler and the Nazis understood the power and influence of healthy parents and authority figures. I want to examine the period in German and Austrian culture before World War II unfolded. To understand this witness in history around this generational disconnection concept, we need to grasp all the aspects that contributed to this degeneration in healthy legacy and ultimately perverted and corrupted an entire nation's emerging generation.

Germany was in the fallout of a massive economic depression, due to the cost of defeat in World War I and the abdication of their kaiser, plus the manipulation of the banking system. The fallout was devastating, and most people did not have work and were in extreme hardship. Out of those ashes, Adolf Hitler had grown up, a perfect type of an antichrist or demonic father on a national level.

Hitler was an aspiring artist. His father was an extremely abusive alcoholic, which is an important detail to understand in Adolf's story. The beatings his father gave him and his mother were so bad that they were said to take him to the edge of his life. I believe that this was a deeply forming culture that Adolf grew up in that deranged his sense of value and ideals, and that fueled his hatred, resentment, and deep psychotic wheelhouse. His father was so damaged that the identity he gave Adolf was of zero value. And in return, a monster was born that hated his father. This helps us understand what happened next.

The German nation was heavily impacted and impoverished, both economically and socially. As the Nazi Party began to rise, it gained momentum by pointing the finger of blame for the economic hardship at the rich Jewish bankers and business owners who were employers and lenders to many who had seen hard times. Hitler's vehement hatred for his father translated into hatred for authority figures, which then transferred to those who were more financially established, thus creating a hatred toward banks and business owners.

During this time, the National Socialist Party was voted into power and things began to change. Adolf's party talked about change so much that it became a sentiment adopted by the nation, and antisemitism was established in that generation. Hitler's Nazi Party began to radically change many facets of society.

To turn the economy around as they saw fit, the Nazi Party launched a socialistic plan where everyone worked for the government and had a guaranteed salary. But for that to happen, both men and women had to be enrolled in work. The men were made to work mostly in factories, while the women worked in administrative roles. But then came the catch—the children were required to attend compulsory school and afterschool attendance, including weekend activities and summer camps. This separated the children from the nurture and fostering of the parental environment. And this is where the major shift took place.

Radio stations were owned by the government, so they started to broadcast indoctrination and propaganda. So, while the parents were busy working their jobs to survive, the Nazi Party began to romance the youth with exciting programs and community. The young men were given access to learn how to shoot guns at airfields on the weekends, ride motorbikes in clubs, and even fly gliders. The young girls were taught baking, sewing, and other domestic skills. It was like an advanced version of the Boy and Girl Scouts, with fun and attractive activities that the parents could not afford to offer. All these opportunities were largely unavailable to these children because their parents were heavily involved in day-to-day survival and unable to provide such luxuries. This lured the children away from seeing their parents as providers and caregivers and began to consolidate that the state was their father.

As time went on, the socialist leadership began to accelerate what they could get away with. They began to increase the disdain of the now officially named "Hitler youth" for their own parents. The statement that the Nazi socialists made to the youth of the nation was so evil we can hear Satan himself saying these words: "Your parents got us into this economic mess, allowed the Jews to become rich rulers, and blindly allowed your future to be endangered—don't listen to them anymore. They do not understand how to fix this mess, and they do not understand your generation. Only Hitler understands you and has a plan for your future." When that generation began to chant "Hail, Hitler," these brainwashed youth were in essence worshiping their savior.

As time went on, these youth were taken to mandatory summer camps where they were indoctrinated that the God of their parents was wrong, and that they should be promiscuous to create a perfect race of soldiers for Hitler's army to rebuild the nation. In a few short years, Hitler severed the sacred trust of children to parents. And when this was achieved, he postured himself as their provider, protector, and savior—a father of a generation of young people.

Once this idea was established, Hitler had a generation that would do anything he said. They would go on to torture and exterminate over six million Jews and other groups in the death camps, invade several surrounding nations, and try to conquer the world, along with many other horrific and demonic achievements. Although many groups have tried to erase this history, we can never forget this example of a generational disconnection that happened.

THE HIPPIE MOVEMENT

As a result of the war that Hitler had started, many soldiers fought and died in World War II on both sides of the battlefield. The men who survived came home, but most of the men who came home did not come back the same as they had left. Most of them had seen deeply traumatic horror on the battlefield that they did not know how to deal with or how to relate to the peacetime world.

They were troubled men, men surviving in a shell of who they used to be, trapped inside their existence with horrific dreams at night. Modern language calls it Post Traumatic Stress Disorder, or PTSD. These men came from a generation of not only being raised with authority and respect in the home, but also military order and respect. Add this to the PTSD that they harbored, at a time when they didn't know how to deal with personal torment, so everyone suppressed it.

These men came home from war fatigued, traumatized, and jaded. Then they married and had kids. The deep problem was that many of these men didn't know how to relate to their children due to all the damage they were carrying. They were strict, harsh, and had military level rules and expectations. The children born into this generation in the late 1940s and 1950s grew up insecure, disconnected, and with an oppressive unrelational standard of perfection. The disconnect was so great that once these children were old enough to choose for themselves, they mostly rejected the authority and religion of their parents' generation and went in the opposite direction. And this is what I call the pendulum effect.

These teenagers were rejecting the form and ceremony of their parents' whole way of life and became what we know now as the hippies, free spirits, or flower people. Can we just appreciate for a moment how far removed a battlefield was from the hippie movement of drugs, music, loose living, and delving into Eastern religions and other belief systems? There is a clear generational disconnect that took place between fathers and their sons.

A father not healed is a child who is disconnected.

THE SHEPHERDING MOVEMENT

Many hippies were saved, and the church grew out of the Jesus Movement. This was a great conversion movement, but it appeared to lack a lot of fathering nurture and direction. Some of those who were saved into the hippie movement became leaders, many of whom didn't have healthy covering themselves but were trying to lead the next generation. Out of this grew what has been termed the Shepherding movement.

A model emerged in the church in the 1970s and early 1980s, presenting a new way to steward and grow members of the church and disciples in the kingdom. At face value, this was a great concept that honored the Great Commission that Jesus instructed all believers to follow in Matthew 28:18–20. It emphasized discipleship as a major value system and placed a priority on the kingdom of God, which would expand the kingdom and the message of the gospel.

But as this new movement emerged, it went around the world and formed a church culture. For a season, it seemed to have a lot of numerical growth and excitement in many local churches. However, there was a big hole in the idea around who should be shepherding or fathering, and things quickly got out of hand as fast as this movement had emerged.

The system started to look like a multilevel marketing structure or syndicate. It quickly became a system of power, control, and abuse through people posing as leaders, fathers, and mothers who were not healthy or mature themselves. Many people got hurt. A lot of church circles held on for dear life to keep this system in place, while others let it go. Now, decades later, if the Shepherding movement is mentioned in most church circles, people cringe because it reminds them of abusive hierarchy and control.

But what happened in the years that followed was sad. People moved away from the model of discipleship altogether and it just became a corporate free-for-all, making way for church models that downplayed the potency of the gospel. This again showcases yet another pendulum effect where abuse happened from fathers and mothers. Sadly, the children grew up and resented healthy authority and are more described as free spirits submitted to no one in the church body. They are nothing more than orphans pretending to be sons. The Shepherding movement would have been the hippies who grew up and the hippies' children.

CONCLUSION

In these various case studies between the Hitler youth, the hippie movement, and the Shepherding movement, we can see an entire century of generational disconnection taking place. And the fallout has not changed the world for the better! Because of this, things must change.

How can the world see Jesus in us while we remain disconnected from the healthy, wiser, and older generation? If left unhealed, these generational disconnects will ripple through decades and centuries, causing sabotage to the heavenly plan of legacy. If this is not broken, each generation is orphaned and makes compounding messes from the last one. We must be the generation that breaks the curse of disconnection due to someone else's failure.

If you have been hurt, then do not allow yourself to use that instance to justify a lifetime and legacy of disconnection in your story. The blood of Jesus heals every wound and scar from previous generational toxicity, whether that be from a natural or a spiritual family or authority.

Out of every demonic spirit of the age comes the birthing of a move of God. The hippie movement gave birth to the Jesus People, which stirred up a massive move of salvation. It is almost the perfect environment for a reset from a generation or move that became stagnant and dropped their legacy into a fresh new wave of the kingdom being birthed.

It is important to discern the good with the not so good. We've looked at these examples to understand movements and how to steward fathering relationships, keeping the positive of what transitioned well while unpinning what didn't work. There's an adage that says that one should eat the meat and spit out the bones. We must do this without becoming hyper-critical or suspicious of what God is doing in our day. We must be able to trust the people God has sent to steward us without punishing them through the filter of past experiences. In short, we must keep ourselves from the pendulum effect and thus lean into the legacy of discipling nations through fathering and mothering.

CHAPTER 17

DEALING WITH PARENT AND LEADERSHIP WOUNDS

Generational disconnections are strategic splinters the enemy sows to divide generations from the intended flow of legacy. These disconnections are meant to sabotage with wounds and mistrust, creating a culture of independence. Wounds and disconnection cannot be allowed to remain a disempowerment against our lives. We must seek healing so we can progress toward legacy.

Every single one of us will have to face this reality in our lives. All of us likely have wounds from leadership. These wounds range from parents to pastors, coaches to bosses, and they even reach out to government and law enforcement personnel, as well those in positions of authority outside of direct relationship. You might be thinking, "I don't have any wounds from those in authority." That may be true, but in reading this chapter you may recognize that there are some wounds hindering your ability to receive or pass down legacy to the next generation.

Wounds not dealt with create generational curses, which is the opposite of legacy. Many of us have had first- or secondhand experiences of generational curses that have been passed down, such as alcoholism, perversion, or poverty. But maybe you have not yet considered what leadership wounds have been passed down to you.

Wounds can come through both good and bad intentions, as well as negligence and abuse. And to break these generational curses, to create purity while passing down legacy, we must address them. We may recognize the effects of abuses in how we react to specific situations but may not yet have recognized that these effects stem from the root of leadership wounds.

So, once you have recognized the hurt you have experienced, how do you deal with your wounds? How do you make sure you're passing on a legacy of blessing and not curses?

DEALING WITH WOUNDS

Because many of us have wounds, this may be a chapter you may want to revisit to keep yourself on course. You don't have to live with the effects of wounds, but you'll have to be ready to continually keep your heart clean from them because they are going to come at some point in your life. Even Jesus let us know that offenses will come, so it's in our best interest to be ready when they do come (see Luke 17:1–4).

What you'll be better equipped to do is recognize that you have wounds, acknowledge their effects on your life, and refuse to be blind to them. You'll be able to bring reality to the surface so that you can break agreements and bondages, allowing you to move forward in a healthy manner. And ideally, you'll become equipped to set others free because you are no longer living under the power of wounds.

But before we come to this place of maturity and helping others break free, we first need freedom ourselves. In pursuit of that, may I suggest that you pause reading for a moment and make some space for the Holy Spirit, asking Him to reveal to you if there are any of these wounds in your life. This is so you'll be able to connect with the rest of this chapter from a place of perspective.

What you'll most likely notice is that a lot of wounds can be traced back to wounds from your parents that stem into further wounds from leaders and authority figures. There is such an assignment on parental relationships because they are the first interaction of legacy in practice. In our formative years, parents are where we learn how to function. Ultimately, what we have learned through our upbringing spills over into every aspect of how we interact with the world around us, as well as our beliefs about who leaders are in our lives and what legacy is.

The enemy attacks our concepts of parents and leaders because it creates a misconception and muscle memory about who the Father is. And often, if we are wounded from those in leadership, it can affect our intimacy and trust with God the Father. The way that we learn to interact with natural parents or authority figures is often the same posture we take with God the Father. A wounding in this area often blurs the lines between natural parents and spiritual parents. Just because your past trauma gives you a perception does not mean that it is reality. This is why we must face the reality of some of our experiences, trauma, and wounds.

There's a powerful statement that is often said when dealing with our hearts, "This is just how I am." And honestly, most of the time that's just a cover for wounds and incorrect beliefs, thus reinforcing abuses we've suffered. Until we recognize the reality of wounds, we are going to be that little kid who just accepts our environment as how we are instead of getting healed and living from a place of wholeness.

Dysfunction that keeps popping up in our lives is a sign of a coping mechanism. We just think these things are normal for us, just how we are, but these are the result of unhealed wounds and will continue to hinder us, inhibiting actual success in walking out our gifts and calling.

A wound needs to be healed; it's not a habit that needs to be changed. This is why we must stop and unpack these wounds, because living with them instead of healing from them will be the nemesis of our ability to authentically and truly connect with God's legacy for our lives. Living unhealed will cause us to live untrusting and disengaged from God and suspicious and hostile to spiritual fathers and mothers God has sent to help us. We will end up fighting the fathering role that God has sent to enrich our lives. We'll see him as a threat rather than a blessing.

THE FRUIT OF WOUNDS

If any of the following experiences happened to you, then there is most likely a wound that needs to be addressed—you've experienced neglect, abandonment, verbal abuse, physical abuse, sexual abuse, emotional abuse, spiritual abuse, financial abuse, moral failure, hypocrisy, or overindulgent/controlling/narcissistic parents or guardians.

It may be that you've never heard of these before, or that you've spent years acknowledging them and their effects on your life. You may recognize that you're still experiencing the effects of these wounds to this day—you may still struggle with insecurity in making decisions because you suffered emotional abuse while being told you're stupid and will never make good decisions; or you may have suffered sexual abuse and believe that you are inherently bad, dirty, and a target.

On the flip side, perhaps you've always been unhealthily championed and believe that you can do no wrong because you were never corrected. The fruit or manifestations of wounds tend to reside on a scale of a pendulum. You were abused in some phase of your life, either in the formative years or later in life, and that could manifest as being terrified of everything or full-blown raging at everything. These are the fruit of the same wounds of abuse, just manifesting differently.

You may have dealt with all your previous wounds and landed in a church community with an unhealthy culture, and they took advantage of you. There are a variety of ways you can be taken advantage of within communities. That's abuse that causes wounds too. The caveat is that spiritual leaders will at times have to steer you in hearing and applying God's voice because the good, God-appointed shepherds are assigned to help you. Don't bite them. But there are countless stories (and maybe your experiences, too) where bad leaders have abused people and gotten away with it. Because of this, the concept of legacy is marred and rejected. Why would anyone believe in transferring legacy anymore?

What I want all of us to recognize is that our reaction to specific scenarios reveals our wounds. And when we become familiar with recognizing the fruit of wounds in our lives, then we are that much quicker to acknowledge them and return to sender every curse they are trying to bring with them. If you find in yourself triggers of insecurity, pride, emotional instability, inability to genuinely connect with other people, suspicion toward God's goodness and other people's love toward you, hatred, poverty and stinginess, self-preservation, a lack of trust, or lust, there is a good chance it's probably time to start asking the Holy Spirit about what wounds might be festering in your life and hindering you.

It would take another book to spell out the enormity of addressing wounds from abuse, but right here is the space where you do business with God, asking Him about what's hindering you, what open access there is in your life due to these wounds. And then take seriously what God shows you and go to war with it. If it is neglect, and you don't trust anyone, ask the Holy Spirit how to start trusting others. If it's pride, and you think you're always on the cutting edge of what God is doing, ask Him to reveal humility to you so you can be connected to others instead of rejecting them.

The symptoms are all there. God wants to help you by revealing and unraveling your unique situation. It is God's intention that we are healed of our wounds so we can pass legacy on to the next generation.

TURNING WOUNDS INTO WARRIOR BADGES

An open wound in the natural leads to infections, which left untreated leads to death. It's the same in our spiritual life, too. The death that inevitably happens affects our life, and it affects the legacy we can pass on in the future.

In the natural, if we take care of our body, it will heal itself of the day-to-day wounds and even more major conditions which may leave a scar. If we bathe, eat properly, sleep, and exercise, then the body will respond with healing. It's the same with our spirit—if we get in the Word, worship, and fellowship with the Lord, then our spirit will maintain its defense against spiritual wounds. Our day-to-day issues will be somewhat recollected but no longer major setbacks. And our longer-term healings will develop into scars, the testimonies of healing for others to see. They are your warrior badges. The key for this to happen is forgiveness.

Once we've acknowledged our wounds and the abuses that have caused them, then we recognize our way forward starts with forgiveness. This forgiveness can be directed outward to those who have hurt us, and it can also be directed inward, in the form of our own internal repentance of partnering with sin, bitterness, resentment, and unbelief, and then forgiving ourselves for hurting ourselves.

Forgiveness is not forgetting, and it's certainly not going back to abusive wound-causing situations. Forgiveness is letting ourselves go free because forgiveness is a curse breaker! What we're saying with it is that we acknowledge the wrong and we forgo our right to seek satisfaction for the offense. We're giving God the right to give us back healing and peace because we're no longer in His place as judge.

Forgiveness breaks generational curses and the cycles of abuse. It stops the legal doorway for that abuse to manifest through us because we're removing the access entirely. What we don't forgive we become. Unforgiveness, resentment, and judgements are all legal doorways to demonic influence. As much as we can justify it, a recognized wound alone will *not* set us free. A demonic legacy will begin to operate in our life. We're carrying something around that is chaining us to the past, which will start to dictate our future.

We must take ownership of where we are at right now. We must decide to walk through this and become free. Recognize the symptoms, acknowledge the wounds, give them to God, and pray for Him to help. We might need to ask God to help us even *want* to forgive because we need help just thinking about the idea of letting wounds go. That's okay! God is here for us, no matter our situation. It is His desire that we become free and whole.

We have no more tantrums, lack of trust, and harboring offenses and judgments; instead, we begin cutting the ties and foregoing our right to judgment. Recognize that forgiveness is a decision, not a feeling. Don't let yourself get discouraged. It is likely that you will have to keep choosing forgiveness as the feelings of hurt subside. But continue to press on, because your future is dependent on doing the hard work today to reap the rewards of tomorrow.

LOVE IS NOT STUPID

I say that love is not stupid in response to the naïve sentiment of the modern church that everything can get covered in grace and forgiveness without any standard or consequence. And while grace and forgiveness are essential pillars of kingdom culture, they are not complete on their own.

To qualify this somewhat controversial thought, I believe that grace and love is only qualified through the lens of truth. True grace and love can never be applied until truth has been embraced. Grace is not ignoring truth but a response to an acknowledgment of the truth, especially in the situation of sin or wrongdoing. Love is not giving someone grace who refuses to take responsibility for his or her own actions.

Love may be walking in forgiveness while understanding that the individual is not interested in being honest and embracing truth that leads to humility and repentance. Rather, in a lot of cases, the offender would rather demand his or her "grace rights" and cover everything over and move on without consequence. But that's not love, at least not kingdom love. Jesus gave mercy and grace to the thief on the cross, but the thief still died for his crimes in society.

I am not inciting a judgment mentality but a real culture of grace, mercy, truth, and love.

Why am I discussing this? Well, relational boundaries have been significantly blurred due to compromised teaching and sloppy grace culture in much of the church today. When sin grows in the church, the teaching around grace warps to enable and accept more than it should.

This makes way for people who have been taught incorrectly to end up in situations relationally in which people in their lives are violating trust and integrity and even walking in levels of abuse. These people are then compelled to keep accepting this poor treatment and look the other way in the name of love and grace.

But this is a twisted love culture and not one Jesus recommended. Love isn't stupid. Walking in love also means having love and respect for yourself. And you must learn how to love, value, and honor yourself before you can ever give these attributes and treatment to another. If an individual lives unhealed and never learns to value themselves through the eyes of Jesus, which is kingdom identity and purpose, they will live in a posture of insecurity and be open for cycles of being mistreated by peers and unhealed leaders and father figures.

A healed person does not keep leaning back into cycles of abuse answered with cheap grace. When we know what healing looks like, we won't invite that abuse back into our lives. Rather, we will move forward.

We see this clearly in our day-to-day interactions with leaders. The most extreme example of this is when leaders fall, and they do not authentically humble themselves and repent to people who followed and trusted them. I have seen these leaders fight tooth and nail, rewriting the story, character assassinating everyone who knows the truth, and, like King Saul, doing everything to look good in front of people instead of walking right before God.

This false concept of grace has empowered pride to carry on without addressing the event or decision that hurt people and betrayed integrity. Everyone sins, but when a leader has significant failure, love doesn't just look the other way. Grace, mercy, and restoration must be the heart, hope, and lens through which a fall is seen. But when an individual repeats these traits or refuses to deal with the issue, we must acknowledge that even God has requirements through which grace and mercy are administered. We must also hold a standard.

In cases where a father or leader walks in failure and refuses to be humble, I counsel you to discuss with the Holy Spirit the need to walk away from this counterculture of the kingdom of God. When someone refuses to walk in humility when sin has happened, especially in leadership, when they say statements like "It's in the past," or, "It's under the blood," but there hasn't been repentance to a congregation or individuals, it's likely just a big show to push everyone away and remain unaccountable. This ultimately abuses people's trust and inflicts wounds in trusting followers.

Love isn't stupid. When there is significant unhealthy behavior or failure that has been covered up without authentic repentance, then that is the time to walk in love and care for yourself and build boundaries and maybe even cut ties. Refusing or ignoring this basic personal boundary will place you in harm's way to live under abusive patterns and sabotage your path, and, worse still, teach you to adopt these traits and mindsets into your own life.

WOUNDS AND LEGACY

The reason I feel strongly that the Holy Spirit wanted me to address this topic is because He wants access again to bless generations.

*Curses are passed down by legal right,
but legacy is passed down by agreement.*

We cannot wholeheartedly come into agreement with legacy if we are already committed to curses. We know that the devil is a lawyer, and he will exercise his rights to wounds in you to make you miserable today and to cripple and destroy your influence tomorrow. And God has had enough.

Some of these areas may have touched some sensitive places in your heart and memory. Maybe you felt pain and a connection while reading this, identifying with some of the hurtful wounds described in this chapter. Pain is an acknowledgment of an existing wound, not a healed scar. When we are healed, we can remember the experience, but it doesn't hurt anymore. Just because something happened in the past that inflicted pain and wounded your heart does not mean that healing has come because time has passed. Time does not heal all wounds.

So how do we get healed from the wounds of those who hurt us? Particularly those in leadership and fathering or mothering roles that impacted us negatively? This unfortunately negatively influences how most people see and interact with authority, leaders, and father figures.

Without healing, people are bound to the wounds they carry like a prison of emotional pain that gets triggered anytime a person, situation, or comment reminds them of the wound. For some, it isn't explosive trigger reactions but rather cyclical destructive patterns in life. Obviously, the answer is that we need Jesus to heal us and set us free. But the crucial detail to grasp is that this prison of pain is locked and the key to being open is a partnering between Jesus and you. Forgiveness isn't God's job—it's ours.

Jesus taught us to pray to forgive us our trespassers as we forgive those who trespass against us (see Matthew 6:9–13). To put it differently, "God, please forgive my sins; I understand that I must forgive those who hurt and sin against me—it's connected." If we refuse forgiveness toward others, then God is restrained from being able to forgive us of our sins. Jesus can't just heal the wounds in our life if that wound is directly connected to active unforgiveness.

We must turn the key of forgiveness in the prison door of our emotional pain. We must choose to forgive. It sets us free from the pain. Forgiveness does not validate the offender or validate their wrongdoing. It sets us free from that person living in the mental real estate of our mind. Do not be a prisoner to the past. Decide to release yourself and walk in innocent purity.

Forgiveness can feel like a weak surrender to a hostile aggressor or grievance. However, forgiveness is the great weapon of freedom. Forgiveness means to forgo or relinquish the right of vengeance. What forgiveness is ultimately doing is removing hatred from your heart and handing the court case to God, where He can bring justice like you never could. But by the time it happens, you have moved on and should be praying for mercy and even blessing on those who caused the wound.

Forgiveness can be a real process; it is not always resolved in speaking the words one time, but rather in the commitment to forgive that person and give your pain to Jesus and calling on His mercy, grace, and healing over and over again. You must war for the peace and purity of your heart.

If a father or a mother betrayed you or hurt you, that cannot be your excuse for the end of your legacy. You will need to heal and trust another father or mother, and God will bring you a better spiritual parent. Do not punish the good people of today because of the wounds put on you by the broken people of yesterday.

Walk with Jesus. Pursue healing and forgiveness. Wear healed scars like medals of God's faithfulness, not festering wounds that will repeat more brokenness. Forgiveness is the doorway to healing.

Healed sons become great fathers.
Healed daughters become great mothers.

Only healed leaders can produce true disciples who further God's kingdom vision of legacy in the earth today.

HOW WE RETURN TO LEGACY

SECTION IV

WE HAVE WALKED THROUGH A DIFFICULT CONVERSATION TOGETHER, but in this section we are transitioning from dysfunction to heaven's solutions. In many cases people can point the finger at problems in the church or poorly stewarded culture, but it takes the heart of God to be able to not only identify the root issues and dysfunction, but also to present a hopeful solution and path forward back to health.

> This final segment of the book outlines the way we can return to the fullness of our purpose as sons and daughters of the King, as the bride of Christ. It will give us a detailed outline of how we can return to a culture and model that God has designed for us to live in. It is a how-to section with practical solutions and actions we can take to see legacy restored in our relationships.

Here I offer a roadmap to return to the old pathways God built and entrusted to us to steward His story in our lives and dream for the world.

> Christ in you is truly the hope of glory, and the way we can hold fast to God's culture and not reinvent the wheel that is already perfect will determine just how far we can see the great commissions' intention reach Jesus' desired outcome.

Returning to legacy is going to take humble hearts that are willing to relearn and reform our habits and culture that have slowly wandered to a lower level of existence, back to all God dreamed we would be.

CHAPTER 18

THE HOPE OF THE WORLD

Now that we've covered God's intention with humanity, Jesus's Great Commission to make disciples of all the nations, the current state of the church, and our spiritual relationships, I want to bring us back to the initial question at hand: What is legacy? And why does it matter?

Everything God does is generational; He is the God of generational culture. The writer of Proverbs tells us, "A godly man leaves an inheritance to his children's children" (Proverbs 13:22). Legacy is the generational wealth that is transferred as a heritage and stewarded as an inheritance. The legacy giver is giving his wisdom, experience, and wealth to the receiver, while the legacy receiver is receiving what he did not cultivate. But, in turn, the receiver should develop what's been handed to him to do the same again and pass the legacy on to the next generation.

We recognize that wherever we go, we bring God's kingdom, which is a kingdom of God's DNA that we want multiplied generationally. God blessed Abraham with the anointing of a king and a father, a patriarch, and in turn Abraham blessed Isaac, and Isaac blessed Jacob. Jacob then raised Joseph who saved a nation and the crucial lineage of promise. God established David, and the wealth he gathered empowered his son Solomon to build God's temple.

Like an investment, the older generation has high hopes that this new generation would not only carry legacy well, but that they would increase the inherited wealth of knowledge and wisdom they have stewarded and gathered themselves. This older generation has an expectation that this will not create a selfish and lazy mentality that now they can relax and live in an entitlement posture, but rather that this younger generation would honor and steward this extreme privilege with all diligence to increase what was handed to them, not to live off it.

> *Legacy is about creating strong men and women, not giving weak men and women opportunities that they don't deserve.*

Hard times create strong men. Strong men create good times. Good times create weak men, and then weak men create hard times. So, what's the hazard to legacy?

Strong men and women forge ahead in kingdom progress, but often we don't know how to regulate how much privilege we give to those who follow. We must learn to empower them but not from a place of empathy, love, and compassion, trying to save them from the challenges and struggles we faced, thinking that we can help people avoid the pain that we walked through. It was the pain that we walked through that offered us the opportunity to grow and mature. If we bestow someone with elevation without qualification, then that will create an entitled tyrant who becomes engorged in good times and ultimately breaks the progress that we have laid the foundation for.

The problem with generations handed huge wealth and peace is that ease and the abundance of peace, if not understood and valued, will create a lazy and thankless generation. Like the prodigal son, they will squander their inheritance to the point of poverty, slavery, and dependency.

LEGACY MATTERS

The scriptures refer to "Christ in you, the hope of glory" (Colossians 1:27). I often picture all the generations of believers who are now in heaven, their generation is done and their race completed, but now they stand in heaven's glory watching what we will do with Jesus, with the building blocks they laid down in advance for us to now build on. The hope of glory is now the living generation of believers receiving and honoring the legacy of the gospel in such a way that the kingdom grows and increases, rather than becoming stagnant or neglected.

Legacy matters—it always has. It is not a selfish entitlement; it's a kingdom honor and privilege. The enemy understands the unstoppable power of an older generation who can mentor and train an upcoming one with all faith and excitement, for the sons to run as well and even further than the fathers themselves.

This equation of legacy will only ever be a viable transfer if this generation of sons and daughters are able to posture like Peter and let an older, wiser, and more seasoned generation wash their feet. Peter needed Jesus to let Him wash his feet, letting Jesus touch the uncomfortable, the most undignified and vulnerable part of him. We need Jesus to touch the humiliating places in us and lower ourselves in a vulnerable posture to do so, so that we understand the submission we need and the humility we will grow into.

His picture of foot washing was a symbolic act of fathering and discipleship in which the father knelt and put his hands onto the most unclean part of a person. Jesus used His hands to wash Peter's feet, which had all the refuse from the dusty streets. When Peter realized what was happening, he began to refuse Jesus because this was so humiliating that a master would wash his student's feet. It probably made Peter feel exposed, vulnerable, and humiliated. And that's when Jesus said if Peter didn't let Jesus wash his feet, then he would have no part in Jesus (see John 13:8).

From a discipleship and legacy perspective, a father is going to have to risk his dignity and reputation to reach into broken and flawed places in his disciple's lives so that healing can come, reformation can occur, and life be restored. But this can be threatening to someone who doesn't understand that this is the only way discipleship can happen.

Jesus is telling us that this is how we build legacy. We only get a double portion if we steward well what we were handed. Serving a father is not just about being in the room, then walking it out, having your feet washed and then on to the next experience. We will have to pass tests. No one can escape the tests that are coming that will prove our future, escaping the storms, the pain that ultimately proves the soul in legacy. Likewise, you must pass your own tests. You will have to run well by decision. Tests never show up when you want them to or at a time of convenience.

Walking beside a father gave me the ability to learn. I did not just learn from his speaking and counseling, but he enabled me to pass tests of pain, pressure, and persecution because that's what was going to prove me. I was shown that by handling the pressure, I would also walk in greater works.

This is the only way that God's kingdom works. It is not a culture of self-promotion, selfish gain, or becoming the greatest name in a lineage. Rather, it is one of humility, service to the one King, and a laid-down life to build a harvest worthy of His sacrifice on Calvary.

THE KINGDOM LAMP OF GENERATIONAL LEGACY

If we can learn to steward with all diligence and run with endurance the race set before us, to carry the heavenly baton in our generation, then the kingdom lamp of generational legacy and guidance will never grow dim. In doing this, the light of God's kingdom will shine for all to see the strengthening and expanding of territories. This is an authentic picture of the kingdom.

When Jesus anointed His apostles, He was not initiating a decrepit monastic order that would hide from the world. Rather, He was initiating a group of men who would move into regions and cities to convert, disciple, and influence—to the point that the culture and ambiance of the city would shift into a kingdom culture (see Matthew 10:1–2). This is why the world spoke of Christians, saying, "these are they that turn the world upside down" (Acts 17:6). And the word *Christian* was not a self-generated brilliant branding campaign but rather one that the unsaved gave to believers—it simply meant one that "was like Christ." Originally, the early church named themselves as The Way.

Legacy has been sabotaged by the desire for numbers over truth, the desire for popularity over purity, and the need for approval and relevancy with the world over hearing, "Well done, good and faithful servants," from the Father.

The devil has not had to attack the church from the outside; he has systematically weakened it from inside, removing its legacy that was laid down and paid for in the blood of martyrs and saints who gave all, Jesus being the chief of these, over the decades and centuries past.

We have lost our reverence for the old paths of God, the unchanging cultures in pursuit of the new and more shiny approaches that seem successful. In fact, most of the viewed modern successes have been the church's greatest failures. When an inheritance is passed along, it is the result of someone's existence. At the end of their life, it is the fruit of their labor. The sacrifice to build a better future will live on in the story of the children's lives long after that father has passed on.

When a father passes an inheritance to the next generation that he has worked so hard to compile, he is not giving away spending money for a few weeks of fun. His entire life is attached to those funds; his eager focus is fixed in the hope that his children will take that legacy and not just exist but build on it. It is his hope that it would then catapult them further than he went, that it would allow them to get breakthrough and success beyond what he experienced.

There is a sacredness to this inheritance because it's a different type of money. This wasn't money earned in the past week's wages or a loan that was repaid. This is a life's work being entrusted with the expectation that it will carry on the family legacy and dream for a better future. And this money must be treated with that level of respect and honor.

In the kingdom, there are seasoned fathers and mothers who have deep wealth stored up from lifetimes of serving Jesus and walking with the Holy Spirit. These people are wise farmers who are looking with great expectation for those they can train and raise up, those who will walk with honor and reverence in stewarding the relationship and the legacy. It cannot be those who are self-seeking or ambitious, but rather the humble and sold out. Those who will not squander the privilege of being disciples and fashioned for service and greatness in the kingdom.

Many well-seasoned ministers, mothers, and fathers are not content to just minister and serve—there comes a point where the spiritual focus changes to "this must multiply."

As the global body in the last fifty years, we've seen a huge season of "the singular man of God" where there were many congregants and few kingdom participators. However, we are in a new season, and many must rise to do the work of God's kingdom. For that to happen, many must walk through being trained, discipled, and submitting to healthy leadership.

> *Success without a successor is a lonely failure that looks good for a short season.*

Having groupies or enthusiastic followers is not enough; we must become fishers of men, like Jesus told the disciples. And then we must school them in the way of the kingdom through a lifestyle of community and family relationship.

In biblical times, oxen were used to plow the ground to make it ready for crops to be sown. When a young ox was introduced to the team, it was not paired with another young ox. It was yoked together with an older ox that knew how to pull the plow and work with the farmer. The older ox was not moved by the erratic energy of the younger ox, but rather pulled the plow steadily and kept the younger in line until the younger ox was broken in and trained. This is why Jesus invites us to take up His yoke and learn from Him.

> *Zeal never trumps wisdom. This is the way of the kingdom.*

Legacy looks like the wisdom of Solomon being walked in today because the person who raised us taught us all they knew, corrected us when we were out of line, loved us, believed in us, shared their mistakes and failures with us, and guided us through our journey with Jesus to a point of maturity. Paul said it like this, "My dear children, for whom I am again in the pains of childbirth until Christ is formed in you" (Galatians 4:19 NIV).

But what if that wasn't just a couple of elites in your church who got close to the pastor? What if that was the normal culture saturated through your entire church, your kingdom community? If we can shift things to see this, then we can see the world transformed through the revealing of sons and daughters of God to all of creation.

Legacy passes the values of everything learned and gained from one life to another. In the Old Covenant, one successor or student passed on his legacy to the next successor. This was a time of addition. But we now live in the New Covenant, which is a time of multiplication. For example, Jesus raised twelve. Peter saw three thousand added to the church on the day of Pentecost. And from there onward, we see great increases in numbers because the Holy Spirit was released to anoint many instead of a few.

Legacy looks like everyone with a tongue of fire. It looks like every person in the body of Christ leading at least one person because someone led them, and it's a natural progression to help others grow. Legacy looks like every person stewarding God's vision as a team, not competitors and not as independent orphans. We need each other. The seasoned need the young, and the young need the seasoned. The hearts of the fathers must turn to the hearts of the sons, and the hearts of the sons must turn to the hearts of the fathers.

THE HOPE OF THE WORLD

We have recognized the disconnect between mothers and fathers, and then allowed the Holy Spirit to turn our hearts toward the next generation. The hope of the world and the hope of heaven is that kingdom generations would live connected in a unified passing of the baton of legacy. This results in growing the kingdom, not weakening it.

We know that Jesus said a kingdom divided against itself would not stand (see Matthew 12:25). In other words, division is the prequel to conquest. When generations of fathers either do not know or refuse to live connected and in service to the coming generation, there is a measure of agreement with the brokenness that results in being divided. This gives the enemy the upper hand.

The hearts of sons and daughters must equally recognize this disconnect and embrace the grace of this opportunity for restoration. This must be done, even if that means cultural and regional tradition and the fallout of disconnection is broken for the first time in many generations. While a father or a mother can pursue a son or daughter to steward them and help raise them, the heart of the son or daughter must choose to also embrace and respond by turning their hearts toward fathers and mothers. If both fathers and sons don't turn toward each other, then this will remain a disconnect.

We need to stop and recognize that the keys to the success of the younger generation often lie in the ranks of the older generation within our church or community, and equally, the keys to the significance and purpose of the older generation lie within the ranks of the next generation. To build legacy in your church is an intentional endeavor, utilizing everyone in the room.

Kingdom legacy has never happened by accident; it only results from intentional and purposeful design, taking specific steps in hopes of specific outcomes. Choosing to build a legacy is choosing to build lives and utilize those lives into their functional purposes by training them through this immersive discipleship culture. True legacy building honors everyone's purpose.

What does your family, church, or community look like five to ten years from now as a result of building legacy in both the younger and the older generation? How will it change the world you live in? Malachi 4 tells us that God will send His servant Elijah the prophet to bring the hearts of the fathers to the sons, and the hearts of the mothers to the daughters. Malachi is referring to the spirit of prophecy, which is needed to call out the fathers and sons.

The prophetic voice is required to speak to turn the hearts of the parents to the children and the hearts of the children to the parents. If this doesn't happen, then God will strike the earth with a curse. The curse is a world with a church not in unity, not passing on generational anointings of wisdom, and each generation starting to build again from ground level rather than building on the foundations of the previous generation. It looks like a world without hope.

The prophetic voice is required

Jesus said, "You are the light of the world, a city on a hill" (see Matthew 5:14–16). If we as kingdom people lose our potency by dishonoring Jesus's model, what hope is there for the world? Jesus is clearly declaring an urgent need for fathers and sons to come together, and maybe this book is like the voice of Elijah calling out your need to partner with this in your life.

Successful leaders leave a legacy

Successful leaders leave a legacy by empowering and mentoring those around them and by raising them up under mature guidance into each person's calling. The opposite of this is a person who wants to stop people from growing by creating dependence on the leader. These so-called leaders are usually cowardly tyrants.

One of the most tragic things I have seen is people who have seen great fruit in their lives and ministries, but as they approach the final chapters of their ministry, there are no successors around them. There is no one who has been trained in the ways and in wisdom to ensure the continuation of the heavenly mandate and mission.

I always say that success without at least one successor is failure. Fathers cry out, "You need me," while sons cry back, "You need me." But legacy looks like this—sons cry to fathers, "I need you," and fathers cry to sons, "I need you." We need to understand that both parties need each other to feel valued.

UNIQUE INDIVIDUALS

There is a fallacy of the loss of identity in discipleship.

Many people forfeit the benefit of an authentic discipling relationship because the submission covering causes them to trust their fears. Fears that suggest that coming into a close, accountable, submitted relationship will pigeonhole them into the identity and function of the father or mother role. These people fear they will lose themselves and somehow never get an opportunity to grow and develop.

Unfortunately, there are legitimate examples of leaders who simply see people as servants and subjects rather than sons and successors. I'm sure we have all been to or been a part of a church where everyone looked and acted the same. This looks more like cloning than the kingdom. Spiritual inheritance doesn't look like the same haircut, mannerisms, or mimicry. We think by the way many imitate their leaders that there was credibility to it, but I absolutely disagree.

While honor and value are paramount, and while the influence of those who lead you will most likely cause you to do a few similar things, God created you to be unique on purpose. I do not try to get people to purchase the same car, wear similar style of clothes, or talk like I do. My sons don't need to preach the same way I do or have the same type of business acumen as me.

What I value is that each of my natural sons, and my spiritual sons and daughters, have their own unique identity in Christ. I am not their maker; I am their caretaker. While I am a spiritual father, I am not their God. So, my job is to cultivate character, integrity, and walk them through life's challenges, and thus champion their victories. My job is not to force them into looking and sounding like me. My role is to steward them toward their calling and purpose, not to control them into being a slave. It is not my purpose to only show affirmation if they are fulfilling my needs.

While it's true that God will never give you your own ministry until you have been faithful with another's, it's also true that this should never be taken advantage of (see Luke 16:12). The goal is that sons and daughters receive my anointing and mantle without pressuring it to be expressed in a specific way. It needs to be a natural product of their walk with God.

Do you remember the instance when young David came to the battlefield of Elah? Where Goliath the giant was taunting the armies of Israel? He volunteered to fight the Philistine, and when he did so, King Saul took him into his tent and offered to put his armor on him, which was an endearing act. However, the armor didn't fit David. And so, David went out against Goliath with the weaponry he knew.

This is an important point to examine. While it is not good for leaders to influence in such a way that only mimicry is rewarded and acknowledged, it is also important to know that trying to copy your leader's mannerisms, preferences, and style will not make you anointed or more holy. And it certainly will not bypass your need to spend time seeking God on your own to establish your own identity, calling, and anointing.

With all the podcasts and teaching available today, it's easy to learn the language and recycle what we hear. It may fool many people, but it won't fool God. Eventually, like the sons of Sceva (see Acts 19:11–20), we will find ourselves in a situation where the enemy calls our bluff and our unauthentic quotes and associations will not be sufficient.

Many people believe that getting close to a pastor, minister, or ministry gives them spiritual credibility. This is simply not true. It wasn't true for Judas or for

Demas, the disciple of Paul who backslid to the world (see 2 Timothy 4:10). None of this takes away the incredible value and honor of spiritual parents and mentors, however. I will submit to and honor my mentors, mothers, and fathers who have poured wisdom, counsel, guidance, and spiritual DNA into my life well after they graduate to heaven. This is the way of the kingdom.

A son or daughter should never lose his or her personality in pursuit of being mentored, but an authentic spiritual father or mother will challenge many aspects that at first appear to be personality that are really character or culture issues that will sabotage destinies. So, while some areas will drop out of your life and you will become another person because Jesus is changing your character, you will also remain who God created you to be without wearing Saul's armor.

CONCLUSION

The Father delights to establish the son's honor and moments of recognition. "Come, sit by My side," He invites us. There is something powerful when fathers stop what they are doing to solely focus on championing their son's or daughter's moments. And the same is true for mothers. A father will support his son from the front row of a service while his son preaches or ministers or performs or competes in a sports event. It's not just honoring the child; it's viewing the future potential extension of his or her legacy.

Sons become an extension of a father's legacy, but too often that treasure is tainted in a moment where it should be cherished. Fathers cannot allow jealousy of how well their sons are doing to steal their God-given role to coach, encourage, and guide their sons into success.

A father will be faced with the decision to genuinely celebrate his child's success or to resent it in a moment of jealous contemplation.

The greatest joy I can have for my sons is to see them go further, to do better, to exceed the successes and limits that I achieved in my life. My goal is to build a platform as high and integrally solid as I can with my life, and from that platform my sons can construct a structure that builds upon the inheritance of my life.

The hope of the world lies in the generational inheritance that is passed from fathers to sons, from mothers to daughters. God's plan of discipleship is dependent on it. As we begin to see legacy passed on from one generation to the next, we have greater hope that God's dream of discipleship is being fulfilled.

CHAPTER 19

HEALING THE GENERATIONS

IT IS TRUE THAT WHAT IS ON THE HEAD COMES ON THE BODY. What and who we submit to has a significant ability to influence our atmospheres and spiritual inheritances. This is one of the reasons why the topic of legacy is so crucial at this time in history. It is about what is being passed on and what is being received between generations.

Jeremiah tells us, "The fathers have eaten sour grapes, and the children's teeth have been set on edge" (31:29). Allowing generational sins to invite curses into spiritual lineage cannot be tolerated or allowed if we are to fulfill the dream of God's heart. We hold a sacred responsibility to steward the Great Commission. So, our only real response to this state of generational curses is to break them and destroy the poison and sting of these imposters in legacy.

HEALING GENERATIONAL CURSES

Often curses can exist from previous generations that have an impact on the subsequent generations if they are left in place. Curses can arise from various causes, but these can be categorized into three main types: sin, spoken curses, and witchcraft.

Sin
The Bible is clear that certain sins, like murder, perversion, terrible crimes, adultery, and the like open a curse into multiple generations. God even says He will visit the

sins of the fathers on the children to the fourth and fifth generations (see Exodus 20:5–6). Demons get attached to bloodlines to corrupt legacy in family trees.

As someone who has pastored for many years, I can tell you that while working with people I often see the same sin strongholds appear in sons and grandsons as a result of their dad's and grandfather's sins. For instance, rage and violence in a dad often appear in the family for generations to come. Alcoholism and substance abuse are another example that is often seen. And sadly, it can often be because instead of being a protector to the legacy of his bloodline, a dad's weakness or compromise opened the door for the enemy to transit to the following generations.

The same can be found in churches, denominations, and movements as well.

Spoken Curses

As believers, we can sometimes forget the consistent advice and warnings we received through the Scriptures, specifically around the power of the tongue and words. Words can bring life or death; words can raise up or limit and contain. Words can be released in seconds and can create years of chaos.

Negative words, which are words that speak death, are types of curses. And these are a serious thing in the eyes of God. There are generations that can be difficult or not embrace the older generation well, and this agitates the older generation to the point in which power statements are made that begin to release negative pronouncements over the younger generation. These are statements like, "They are good for nothing," or, "They will never do anything great."

These types of statements said with sincere intent are released over and over, and they begin to form an alliance with demonic intent to stifle the potential and purpose of an upcoming generation. They also create a powerful rift between generations in which a message of doubt and mistrust is sent to divide the connection needed for legacy.

Witchcraft

If parents have either dabbled in or been heavily involved in any way around the occult, satanism, freemasonry, the illuminati, new age, or any form of divination, then it will attract demonic activity and oppression. This can even invite various levels of demonic possession, which can bring with it a range of hallmarks that can include torment, nightmares, destructive habits and traits, calamity, as well as generational health issues.

Witchcraft of any kind is defined as an activity in the spiritual realm that is illegal with God. It is a perverted agreement with the demonic underworld. This type of activity invites generational demonic curses into bloodlines.

*****

While I have taken some time to describe curses, I am not here to give honor or glory to the enemy. But equally, we must take seriously the destructive power that these curses can wield in people's lives and lineage.

The first step in breaking any generational curse is recognizing and identifying them. Often, over time and through familiarity, these are not recognized but embraced as personality traits, family tradition, or culture, which allows for these strongholds to remain and replicate unchecked. But thank God that He has given us the anointing, which is His power entrusted to us, that breaks the yoke of bondage. This means God's power in us, when utilized correctly, destroys the power and stronghold of every demonic chain and curse.

While some curses evident in people's lives can be extreme and obvious, many go unchecked as just white noise or "bad luck" in people's day-to-day world. To catch a thief, we must recognize that an individual is a thief and not just a regular person. This is how the enemy gets away with so much chaos in so many believers' lives—he blends into their peripheral vision and goes unnoticed.

We need the Spirit of God's revelation to make us aware that certain traits and characteristics are not natural or just bad circumstances. Once God has shown us these and we have recognized these traits as the evidence of a curse, our only natural response is to go to war in partnership with God to root out this evil intruder.

I want to discuss a few key steps that are important to put into practice.

HEALING NEGLECTED SONS

I want to examine the tragic element of neglected sons who grow up and become fathers themselves and repeat the cycle. These sons can often grow emotional spines and muscles that are lopsided and deformed in compensation for the absence of a healthy father figure in their world.

When a child is in formative phases of growth and there is a void of affirmation, guidance, and wisdom, specifically from a constant father-figure role, it creates an insecurity that often can influence negative development in one of two ways: either forming an introverted insecurity or developing an extroverted egotistical confidence. Both traits are dangerous and toxic, and both often have resentful sentiments toward the dad they never knew or who was never there. This is a tragic result of the neglect and abandonment of a father's crucial role.

In the case of many, the son can grow up despite circumstances and push through with perspectives like, "I made my own way," or, "I will show him and grow despite of him." And while this may appear as an underdog success story, the tragedy strikes in these people's inability to relate to authority figures in their journey. But the devastating fallout hits when these sons grow and become fathers themselves and struggle to know how to relate to their own sons.

People always idealize that they will never emulate the father who hurt them, but without healing they repeat the cycle. Many people get stuck in moments with beautiful children of their own, not knowing how to connect and relate to them. They live present but detached, or, worse yet, they run like their own father did and leave another generation fatherless. They will wake up to the fact that it was resentment and hatred of their father, and the base instincts of survival, that got them through those difficult years. But, in truth, they never escaped the pain of abandonment, insignificance, or feeling lonely or unloved.

This is one of the devil's primary weapons against a generation. That's why Malachi says that if the hearts of fathers and sons would not turn to each other, then God would strike the earth with a curse. Unfortunately, this level of disconnect between a father and a son even later in life causes pain that challenges identity and worth deep in the core of an individual. This, of course, can be avoided, but it must be done so intentionally—it is not something that we simply grow out of.

The awakening to this absence is the first step toward healing. Processing the grief and letting go of the demonic torment that speaks, "I wasn't lovable or worthy of my dad's presence," is important to healing. In this process, grief is healthy as long as it's not our destination.

In the midst of this grief, forgiveness must take place. No matter what was done, no matter how traumatic the absence or the neglect, if we do not choose to forgive, then we remain captive to the wounds that keep us enslaved to the past. Forgiveness is the power tool that sets us free from what wounded our soul.

Giving God our emotions and pain is the next key to healing. If we do not allow God's love to come and occupy the place in our heart that was wounded, then we are trying to self-heal. And that's not a viable option in the kingdom. Once we choose to forgive, however, we need God's strength to maintain that choice, and equally we have to invite love and healing into every area of our heart and soul that was wounded and ask God to make us whole and be our Father.

I remember in my early twenties breaking down crying in my apartment with God as I came to a moment of clarity about the pain and betrayal in my life with my biological dad. I realized how deep the pain was in my heart. I stopped and wept and sobbed as I called out to God, "God, I'm calling on You to come and heal me. I can speak to the Holy Spirit, I can speak to Jesus, but I cannot even say the name *Father*, because that's a hurtful word to me."

I was so hurt by my own dad that I didn't even feel confident that I wanted to be a dad myself. I never wanted another child to experience what I had experienced. That moment for me was a breaking point, a point of grace and love that came crashing in on a lot of my emotions and painful wounds and memories. After that, it was a daily decision I had to return to. God came and began to heal me and make me whole, bit by bit.

Having a bad history with neglect or absence from a father in your life is not a life sentence to be cursed and doomed. There is powerful and effective freedom and healing that breaks the curse of this type of emotional and identity trauma damaged in our formative years. We just need to bring it all to God's loving arms and let Him set us free.

If not set free and healed, these wounds can create a tyrannical or abusive characteristic or trait in a fathering sense, but also relationally, in the workplace or even in society. It's disturbing where unhealed wounds can take a person. Time doesn't heal these wounds, only Jesus can do that!

It reminds me of that 1970s song "Cat's in the Cradle." The song starts describing the life of a little boy born to a busy dad who is always at work, a dad who could never make time for his son. Whether it was throwing a ball or playing in the yard to important moments in life, as the song progresses it tells the horrible tale of that dad now grown older, finally has time to be with his now grown son. But the son has grown himself and is now too busy for his dad with all his own work. The generational cycle repeating itself. It is truly tragic.

This highlights the destruction waiting if fathers refuse to love and steward the growing generation and foster development. And equally, it is the inevitable outcome if sons and daughters refuse to embrace fathers and mothers for whom God has made them to be in their lives.

It's important that discipleship in this legacy is not a factory-style production line that lacks personal love and care. In Jesus, we see compassion expressed in love and standards. He loved His disciples and showed them so much grace even though they were not walking on a spiritual level of maturity anywhere near His. We see the humanity and vulnerable love with which Jesus loved His team.

And yet His message was not watered down. He rebuked Peter for blurting out a demonic sentiment in the garden, He had compassion on the crowds and the sick, and He showed Peter mercy on the beach after Peter's biggest failure. Jesus showed parental love to His disciples. He held high standards of righteousness and didn't apologize for them. And yet, Jesus didn't make it too hard for everyday people, His disciples, to access this kingdom around Him.

Jesus stewarded well His disciples, who frankly had a long way to go even at His crucifixion. But He stewarded them as a parent nurtures and cultivates his children. When children know that they are loved, it will instill in them a confidence and nurture that nothing else can impart. A child who feels loved will excel and develop in such a way that it accelerates development compared to a child without love. And a child with love will be able to embrace correction and instruction when it happens so much better than in the absence of that type of love. Love makes way for a healthy development of a biological or spiritual son or daughter.

HEALING A GENERATION

God has a plan to fill the earth with sons and daughters. Where there has been generation disconnection, there are rifts in this legacy lineage. These rifts must be repaired, at least from today forward.

You may be reading this, and you're in ministry, maybe even have a few younger people around you who are looking for guidance and a path to their own growth. And this book is striking you with the missing pieces of where you have not had a father or healthy mentor in your journey. Maybe you did have one and you were deeply wounded and devastated by the lack of care. Someone else's failure is not your dismissal of the need for fathering; rather, it's the proof of that need even more!

My counsel to you is to seek out a healthy father or mother to speak into your life and ministry. Those following you depend on it and don't even know it. If the curse of generational disconnects is going to break somewhere, let it heal with you. Your sons in the Lord will never know how to honor and receive from you if they cannot see you honoring an older father leading you. You are fooling yourself if you believe you can lead sons where you have not been led.

Take the thread of your commitment and sew generations back together in your life. The curse of generational disconnects must be broken in the healing found in your pursuit and honor of fathers. Once this is set right in your life, you can go about healing a generation by setting a right example of how a father walks, affirming sons, validating and recognizing who they are. You will also bless and impart anointing to those around you who are mature enough to steward it. In fact, your ceilings will become their floors.

Once a son recognizes that your success is connected to his success, the partnering of generations can be fully embraced. Understanding each person's role will lead to better stewardship of legacy, thus building unity between father and son, healing the generations. Let's heal generations together. It's going to take all of us.

A TRUE FATHER IN THE FAITH

Fathers who genuinely desire sons to exceed them are the fathers this rising generation needs. Sadly, the past season of the church has been one where empires of men's greatness have been built in the name of churches and ministries. There have been emperors and not ministers and stewards who have been leading. There are individuals more interested in retaining notoriety than legacy. That all needs to stop. None of this will have any credit in heaven. There is no crown or reward for that behavior. We must transition to a kingdom mindset in the body of Christ and not an individual one of great speakers and ministers that are the "church celebrities" of the moment.

Paul referred to Timothy as a true son in the faith, but what's a true father in the faith? A true father in the faith looks like Jesus, a person who is not threatened for his followers to go further than him and do greater works than he has done. But equally, a father in the faith must train his sons for the long haul and not just train them to take care of him in the moment.

A father must train his sons that if they do go further than him, they will likely pay a higher price. So, he must instill in them resolve, purity, endurance, and a hunger for truth. If a son lacks these basic qualities, he will recant his commitment at the first sign of hardship or trial.

A true father in the faith is preparing a runner, not a sprinter, to start and finish the marathon of his own calling. We need sons who finish their race. And those sons need to see fathers finish well, running true, in humility and reality, with strength and courage, ever growing in their walk in Jesus, serving the King and those given to them. Sons who finish well had fathers who showed them the way.

This is how we heal generations—we raise fathers who believe in their sons and champion them to run further than ever before. We have many teachers, but few fathers. Only a father will tell you what a teacher is afraid to say. Teachers want to impart information; fathers want to establish wisdom. There is a huge difference between the two.

AFFIRMING THE NEXT GENERATION

The reality is that in eternity past, Jesus is and was fathered by His Father. He said He and His Father were one. Among other things, this essentially means that Jesus's nature is a fathering nature. Jesus fathered His disciples and cared for them in a parental sense. He raised them and trained them by example, teaching them how to live and carry on the legacy of the kingdom.

Fathers and mothers bring identity and a powerful affirmation to sons and daughters. They add a strong sense of security and stability to their children.

Fathers present a role model for sons to follow and daughters to look for in their husbands. Fathers bring wise counsel and guidance in seasons when their children are at the ages of choosing for themselves in various areas. Fathers do not have followers; they produce and raise up and empower sons who follow the model.

Mothers bring a deep, authentic nurturing and nourishing to sons and daughters. One of the most powerful things a mother can do is to never speak badly of the children's father, even in a conflict, or in a separated or divorced situation. Speaking badly of the children's father does something to a child's psychology that disconnects them from potential legacy that they will likely not get from anyone else. United together, there is a model carved into the makeup of sons and daughters as they grow and mature.

Inheritance is not just merely a monetary principle that the family wealth is passed from parents to children. It is also a passing on of gained ground, spiritually speaking, with the older generation teaching and transferring keys, lessons, and freedoms gained through their journey to the next generation that will empower their sons and daughters to go further and gain more ground than they ever saw.

Although Moses never entered the Promised Land, the entire journey of his life made way for Canaan. Moses embarked on a journey with God long before the children of Israel ever were freed from their chains. The foundations in his life, being raised in Pharaoh's royal court, dealing with the rage of his heart that drove him to kill an Egyptian in his younger years, being banished from Egypt, meeting God at the burning bush, being sent to Egypt by God to see Israel freed, and on to seeing the power of God demonstrated against the grip of Pharaoh's hold of God's people, developed his relationship with God.

Seeing all the great deeds done built a platform for him, and, from this platform, Moses was able to instruct Aaron and anoint Joshua to then lead as Moses passed not only the baton of leadership but also the many years of mentored leadership to his team. This then catapulted them to succeed onward and further than Moses was able to see in his lifetime.

Joshua was able to learn and glean from the wisdom and lessons that he saw and heard from Moses, his spiritual father. Moses did not sabotage Joshua's succession; he didn't compete with Joshua. How much does it cheapen a father's meaning if he begins to emulate Saul by cutting down, disqualifying, or competing with his natural or spiritual legacy?

AUTHENTIC MOTHERING AND FATHERING

There is an unannounced apprenticeship in the unrealized classroom. Oftentimes, we do not realize the potency of our actions. When my boys were very little, it was easy to just live and have conversations with a mentality that they did not understand what was being spoken or taking place. But the reality is that everyone is watching you, even if it is not necessarily conscious. Especially children—they are always watching us, and even more so the children we are responsible for.

I knew that my children would mimic my words and actions, but I never really realized just how much until I saw and listened to my children repeating my statements and actions. We were made in such a way to replicate the thing we submit to or are influenced heavily by. And much of the time, we don't know how much we are being influenced.

As my children grow, they will have certain traits, gestures, thought processes, perspectives, and statements that will have my impression for life. Equally, spiritual parenting isn't a classroom or a sixteen-week discipleship course—it's a lifestyle of costly love, care, and patience poured out on sons and daughters.

In our church, we have walked many people through their unique personal struggles, strongholds, and challenges by loving them where they are at. We realize that we cannot take someone who has no background with God and a broken past and simply love, mentor, and parent them through their journey, with no mess. In the first few years, it will be messy and tough. Love is many times misrepresented in the church, saying that it's a beautiful thing. But it can also be tough on the spiritual parents and confronting to the son or daughter. The reality is that through someone's brokenness, if we can continue staying where we are without giving up or abandoning the person, then they will begin to open up and trust us a little more.

Initially, there will be more intrigue than trust. But over time—and I mean years—if put into practice, the individual will become healthier and more stable. The wisdom we carry will have stabilized them and trained them. I find this part to be phenomenal. Over the course of time and training, the mentee has come to a level of being mature. And the imprint of the parent's stewarded spiritual DNA has transferred.

My wife and I have spiritual children that we have walked through deep healing and the mess of life. We didn't take them on with the premise of them becoming our apprentices; we took them on by posturing ourselves as parents. It's easy to fight hate, but it's impossible to fight love. Over long periods of time, love wins with these individuals, and what used to get them all twisted up in their hearts no longer has power to touch them. As time continues, they become stable and established enough to help others.

Some of them have come from so much brokenness that, like my story, mentoring or helping someone else was an impossible thought. But something has happened. In the years of receiving care, love, and wisdom they were unwittingly being trained on how to care for others. On how to endure and have longsuffering. On how to never give up on someone, to believe and hope for the best. They were being trained in how to pray someone through a dark season when the enemy was doing everything to attack. This is the huge difference between classroom discipleship and authentic fathering or mothering.

Do you remember when you were little watching your mother or father making your favorite meal in the kitchen? You were a receiver; you were probably not taking notes about the recipe when you were five years old. You were in an environment where you were absorbing and observing them preparing those ingredients. When you moved out on your own, the time came when you craved that food, and based on what you had encountered, you re-created that meal and surprised yourself.

Influence isn't about what classroom you are in; it's about who is caring and speaking into your life.

If you submit to the right person, you will find yourself doing the same things for people in your future. This principle works in both positive and negative aspects. We don't want to give out fish; we want to teach others how to fish. This is taught by sons living life with dads and daughters walking with mothers.

I grew up in what I thought was a good home that became broken in my late teens. When I thought about becoming a father, I was scared and intimidated because I didn't know how to relate to kids, and I sure didn't want to hurt a child by not being a good father, like I had been hurt. I had to pursue my heavenly Father to discover what a good father looked like. In the process I was changed. But I was not just changed, I was marked with aspects of His nature. I am now confident in being a good father because I receive from a good Father.

ENCOURAGE YOUR SONS AND DAUGHTERS

Every son needs to hear his father speak life and belief into his calling and worth. A statement like, "The world needs to hear what God has placed in your heart," is a statement that encourages and empowers sons to rise to the challenge of their calling and destiny. Never underestimate the life-giving breath of a father's encouragement and support.

Fathers, the sons around you need to hear you breathe life into them, many of whom never had a dad who loved them. They are trusting you with their destiny by submitting to you as their leader and father.

Sometimes we can be caught up with the process of shaping them that it's easy to forget to stop and have moments of encouragement. The truth is that it is a lot of work raising sons and daughters. But never let it become a chore—keep it a family atmosphere. Don't get so caught up in the correction and adjustment aspects of shaping a son that you lose the soft heart needed in a father. If you do find your heart getting hard, maybe it's time to revisit your intimacy levels with the Father and your own personal boundaries to ensure you are refreshed so that you can offer your son the grace, love, compassion, and mercy that he deserves in the process.

There will be times when your children will keep making the same mistakes, pushing against you, and reverting to old cultures. That can be frustrating and cause you to question your progress and resolve to continue pouring into a son. And while some do need to be assessed if they are still walking within the parameters of the discipleship understanding, a lot of the time we must stop and remember the grace we needed when we were where they are today, monitoring our personal well-being—physically, mentally, and spiritually. Make sure you are always in a space that even when correction is needed, you can also authentically offer encouragement, grace, and love. This is how we'll heal the generations through kingdom legacy.

CHAPTER 20
MY PERSONAL JOURNEY

DISCIPLESHIP IS NOT MERELY ABOUT DEVELOPING SOMEONE'S GIFTS—that's coaching. While discipleship does develop gifts, it also hones character, it shapes values and culture, it tempers endurance, and, most importantly, it strives to see Jesus formed more and more in someone's life, character, and decisions. In this chapter, I want to share with you my story of discipleship so that we can see how discipleship plays out as the vehicle of kingdom legacy. Then in the last chapter, we'll develop the thought even further.

My personal journey has afforded me the insight in the values I've written about in this book from both terrible experiences and good experiences surrounding discipleship. I've been under fathers through various seasons of my life, who were both good and bad, but mainly not so good. I want to remind you that if you are committed to a consistent walk with God, even if you are under an unhealthy or dysfunctional father, you can grow and learn from his good examples, bad examples, and mistakes. God causes all things to work together for our good (see Romans 8:28). And so we don't become self-righteous but remember that we all make mistakes and need grace. This is not an excuse to become critical.

Until I was twenty-one, I grew up in a church never really hearing leaders talk about their personal journey, and especially not about their mistakes and struggles. They were stoic and distant from the people in a way that was intimidating. I guess it was a strong face they wanted to present to the people.

This upbringing in church massively impacted my view of Father God. I deeply knew that God was real, but the image these leaders portrayed was so intimidating and was subconsciously training me that the way that they interacted with me was how God interacted with me as well.

The problem was that it created a model of important people who were apparently close to God, who never seemed to have ever struggled with conquering sin in their lives. So, it established an infallible culture in the leadership. In general, the people in the church were afraid to approach these leaders with questions or concerns. Even worse, they were afraid to confess any sin because the way it would be handled was harsh and judgmental, lacking any grace and mercy.

The problem with this culture was that anyone hopeful of being raised up had to start acting like these pastors, leaders, and elders just to be accepted, which was unnatural. They had to talk, act, and behave in a way that they lost their individual identities, and they looked like what I would describe as clones. They learned behavior so that acceptance and approval would be given to them.

The tragic fallout of a culture that shamed and punished sin that was confessed or discovered was that people become sophisticatedly secretive and sin became well hidden. And in the darkness of secrecy, sin degenerates and hideous evil starts to become present, but very few people know anything is wrong. Years later, hideous scandals of every kind emerged with damaged lives still traumatized and they were still trying to put their life back together.

During my last few years in this church, I saw some significant hypocrisy in the leadership. There were some serious conflicts with kingdom culture, and asking about it resulted in me being put in my place as a young man. Through a series of hurtful events from this leadership team, I became deeply wounded, I left the church, and walked away. I said that if this is what God is, then I don't want it. The abuse from these fathers caused me to walk away from God.

I was ostracized and excommunicated as a result, which put a strain on my family relationships. I backslid and went extremely deep into the world and everything the world told me it had to offer. In truth, I was deeply hurt, both from church and from a series of heartbreaks at home. Around the same time, my father had made some tragic decisions both morally and financially—decisions which impacted the family dynamic forever. Our family home and all the funds I had ever saved and invested into the family business—all of it was gone in a matter of days.

LOYALTY TO A FATHER

In a short period of time, all the father role models were tarnished for me. In the midst of this season of brokenness, I had an encounter with Jesus that changed my life. This encounter rescued me and put me back on the path toward my Father God, a moment that allowed me to become soft again to hearing His voice.

About a year later, I met a man I heard God clearly speak to me about: "This is the man you will be with for the next season of your life." I started following this man, doing life with him, and serving him. Despite the pain and hurt from father figures in my life up to that point, I made a conscious decision to be faithful and trust this man because I had heard God's voice and chose to be faithful to it.

I served this father faithfully with my whole heart, both in our local church and around the world at various places when he would travel and preach. I would do this at my own expense—I saw it as a privilege to serve him in this way. This relationship taught me about the importance of fathers being fathered. But this spiritual father had no father covering himself. He had not authentically been discipled.

I witnessed a regular habit of positioning to be closely associated with big ministry names that gave him public validation, but he never got close enough to where they could see how he truly behaved in his life. He didn't trust them and found reasons to keep all relationships at a surface level. All leaders need deeper connections, a support system to keep them honest and to guide them. I would pray every day that God would bring someone who would be able to help him and speak into his life as a father. I now know that to be a huge orphan trait—coveting the association, validation, and approval of others but despising the accountability and the need to submit to another's authority.

My loyalty to this father was birthed out of obedience to God, so when this leader was abrasive or harsh, I was able to stand in the midst of it because my heart toward him was loyal and honoring. At times, I had to walk through being mistreated. I was faithful to the voice that told me I was to be with him for that next season of life. And here is a massive point for this generation to rediscover: Most people go where it feels good to be shaped and trained, but I pursued where God told me to be. And when things were difficult, unpleasant, and frankly abusive, I didn't just leave for greener pastures; I stayed faithful to where God had put me and prayed for the man I was placed under.

Understanding that easy environments mostly don't create strong, resilient sons is crucial to grasping the fact that looking for a soft and comfortable place to sit and serve and walk into an easy destiny doesn't exist. This is all confirmed looking at biblical history. Not a single great man or woman was birthed in the kingdom in that way.

I believe the lack of fathering led this leader to an ultimately devastating moral decision, which severed our relationship and disqualified his ability to remain in ministry. I served him faithfully like I was serving Jesus Himself. God used that season to fashion me into someone with endurance. I learned what not to become in that season.

For me, this was one of the more tragic moments in my life. I never wanted to see my leader fail. My hope and prayer were for him to be healed and know true fathering. It was obvious that this was a compounding and painful repeated wound. Watching him fall was disappointing for me personally because it was another instance where I had seen fathers fail, which you might be able to identify with.

For a son who has been deeply hurt by his father, the unfortunate natural default is to not trust fathers or people in authority again. But I knew that was not a wise option. While I could no longer follow the model that my previous pastor had been living, I knew that I needed to come under the covering of a seasoned father. This was my opportunity to walk away from submission to authority, but instead I called a man of God whom I highly respected. A man I knew God could use to speak the truth, guide, and counsel me.

The fallout from this situation was that I had to step into a role where I became responsible for the members of our church. At the time God really encouraged me by visitation, which equipped me to step into the next season of pastoring. I took this seriously because when my previous pastor was disqualified, I was then installed as the lead role. I knew that my new responsibility was exponentially increased in the way that I stewarded myself and the people around me. I refused to be an independent leader. A father who is not submitted to another voice risks becoming a disaster. I witnessed this with my own spiritual father and so I refused to repeat his error, learning from his mistakes.

We must be careful we are not loyal to compromise or sin. I loved this man, even though he had been unkind over the years—my heart toward him had always been love. So, this broke my heart.

When leaders don't have actual fathers, they become free agents. They remain unaccountable and, unfortunately, their messes just take on larger scales. In this situation my former pastor connected himself to a ministry that required no authentic repentance and therefore no genuine restoration from him. He went on to a new ministry and made similar messes.

As fathers, our goal must be to address issues and walk through true repentance so that restoration before God and others can take place. Countless lives have been destroyed because of the story I have briefly shared. But the true tragedy is that this is the model of much of our country club churches. It enables broken ministers to keep reproducing brokenness and destruction.

Ministry country clubs don't validate ministers or protect congregations; they cover up grotesque sins and call it grace and restoration, only for the individuals to repeat sins and make bigger messes with more damaged people. The real tragedy is the example it leaves to those impressionable followers who, if not filled with the fear of the Lord, have high chances of catching the impartation of compromise and follow a similar path. Or they go on to reject God altogether.

FROM A SON TO A FATHER

As time continued, the Lord brought three voices into my life as we planted a new church (one apostolic, one prophetic, and one pastoral—which is a powerful governance council). My pastor falling was not my graduation or absolution from needing a father, but rather a greater need to pursue it even more!

In the midst of a painful transitionary and turbulent time, I had a clear grasp that as sons become leaders, and leaders progress to significant roles like lead pastor, the need for wise counsel grows exponentially. This is not just for the lead role to walk well for their own person, but equally and even more significantly because every single person trusting the integrity, purity, and wisdom on this lead role depends massively on the dependability of the lead role's walk.

We should never excuse our need for a fathering or mothering voice in our life. If we have got this far in life without it, then we should start now. Independence is not a kingdom attribute. No matter how significant I ever become, I will always pursue the voice of a father in my life to speak wisdom, counsel, and guidance.

During this season, my discipleship dynamic changed. I shifted from being a son to becoming a father. But here's where I really want you to grasp how the kingdom works. While Jesus came in the full power and authority of the Godhead, He was meek and mild and identified as a reflection and messenger of the Father. While He was the full expression of heaven sent to earth, He primarily presented Himself as a Son. If we are to learn from Jesus, even in the fullness of our call, the correct posture is son, not an emperor or a dictator.

I have learned lessons in my discipleship journey over the years. Much of my journey has been learning lessons about what not to do, and how not to lead, father, and behave. Now I am in a season where I'm leading and discipling others and being myself submitted to and being discipled and advised by others. We never graduate from discipleship. There should always be a voice of a father in our life. We only enter new levels of accountability and wisdom from advisors as our call and responsibility grows. May we always be teachable, willing to learn, submit to, and be advised by others, transparent and accountable. This creates a kingdom that is safer for those who lead and those who are led. Never follow a leader who isn't following a leader.

One of the best examples that I give to people when explaining the process and purpose of discipleship is the sculpting of an image out of a block of granite. Most people see a rectangular block of quarry stone, no different from any other stone. To the block of stone, there is a feeling of intentional significant purpose and potential. But to the sculptor, she sees the finished image within the lifeless block of stone. The sculptor sees the block in its current state, sees the fullness of potential in the sculpture that could be carved out of the stone, and finally understands what must be removed from the block to reveal the potential.

If it's not already obvious, a true father is a sculptor who can see a disciple's potential but also realize his current condition and progress in life. A father is a sculptor who looks in hope at who someone can become, someone who looks in love and truth at everything in his life that needs to change, develop, or be removed for that potential to be realized. He understands that every time he holds the hammer and chisel of instruction, example, or correction, the opportunity for another chunk of granite can be removed from the block.

The disciple must understand that this is love and care, even though it may feel abrasive and confronting at times. Once the granite block understands that the sculptor is more interested in establishing its potential purpose and shape, then the block will not resent and despise the impact of the chiseling. Once a son realizes this important detail, he will stop fighting and resisting the father's input, correction, and guidance.

A TRUE HONOR

Discipleship should not be a hard, scary place full of fear and difficult conversations. There must be joy and life in the journey. Discipleship around Jesus was full of adventure and excitement, as well as wonder and awe, along with moments of sincere fear of the Lord. Apprentices who are invited to serve along the seasoned can see and witness how things are handled and discover how certain scenarios are stewarded. This is always an invitation to learn by proximity rather than by a textbook. This should be an exciting experience, full of expectation and honor.

It's such an honor to be invited into the proximity of a father; it should never become familiar to a disciple. It's an honor to the disciple's potential and future to be invested in like that, and also, it's an honor to the father to be able to invite a younger disciple into his environment. I would encourage every young disciple, no matter what phase of discipleship you are in, to be hungry for your call. Don't be ambitious to get there. Don't allow yourself to be so focused on getting to ministry that you forget to enjoy the season and moment of discipleship that you are in.

Don't end up having so much ambition that you are pushing to get past mere discipleship to the next season of your calling, or you will at some point begin to think your father is holding you back. At this point, you will be in danger of seeing them as an obstacle to overcome rather than a doorway inviting you through a process.

Ambition must not be found in you. The Lord will be at war with ambition in you and will use circumstances to starve that out. If not, it could be your ruin. Do everything you can to make sure your heart is postured right through this period of your discipleship. Embrace the process, but not with a heavy stoic religious approach. Do it joyfully and have fun along the journey. Fulfilling God's dream of discipling the nations depends on it.

CHAPTER 21

DISCIPLESHIP: THE VEHICLE OF LEGACY

IF LEGACY IS THE TREASURE WE ARE TO INHERIT, then discipleship is the delivery vehicle by which that treasure is delivered. There are two discipleship influences in your life: the first is God's discipleship of you and the second is the spiritual father or mother God will give you. The God-given father or mother will disciple you in partnership with the Holy Spirit as a practical role model and mentor figure. They will disciple you in the Word of God and how to live in your day-to-day life.

This discipleship is not for the elite or exclusively those called to ministry; it is for everyone who enters the kingdom of God. I wrote this book to define what discipleship is, the discipleship that Jesus modeled and instructed us all to walk in. This message is on the heart of God because, over time, the meaning and implementation of what discipleship is has been extremely blurred, particularly in the last century.

Is it any wonder that there are so many opinions as to what discipleship is? To some it is a church course for getting new members. To others it's a six-to-twelve-week, part-time, one-night-a-week course at the local church to convey theology and informational teachings around Christian principles and beliefs. Or for others it is a school where a student sits and absorbs knowledge on topics such as biblical history, eschatology, and specific books of the Bible. But the truth is that although each of these have their place, none of them are authentic discipleship on their own.

In Matthew 28, Jesus refers twice to making disciples. It's important we recognize He did not say that we are to build schools or emphasize classroom settings. And although He did say we are to teach, He was not referring to knowledge-based institutions. Jesus did have large-crowd teaching moments; however, He did not major on a model that focused on a classroom scenario. Jesus demonstrated a model of an immersion of His close followers in which they were invited into His everyday life, not just His microphone moments.

Jesus's model of discipleship involved Matthew, John, Peter, James, and all the others, including Judas Iscariot, into His personal world. The guys saw Jesus at His greatest and at His most painful moments. They did well at times, and they also failed horribly at times. But despite their flaws, Jesus stayed faithful to each of them.

When Jesus told the team that they were to make disciples of all nations, He had spent three and a half years discipling them. He wasn't now changing the model to an institutional mass-production model; He was saying to each of them, "As I have allowed you to walk up close with Me, so you need to now replicate and make sons and daughters that follow My life mirrored in you."

When the modern church offers a twelve-week discipleship program or a three-year discipleship school, then we are confusing the narrative of discipleship. And we are thus contributing to a dilution of the potency of what kingdom participation looks like.

AN INTERACTIVE RELATIONSHIP

A few years ago, I sat on a panel at one of the largest Bible schools in the United States. On it with me was a well-known individual in the Christian community. The individual stated in the panel interview that she was "fathered and mentored" by a famous individual. The person went on to say that she never met this individual, but she was fathered through his teachings via books and sermons. I was so taken back at what I was hearing that I could barely believe that it was being said to so many impressionable students who were eager to learn.

Everything was wrong about that statement. Here's why. The nemesis of discipleship, fathering, and sonship is the independent, orphan culture of isolation. Orphans want all the recognition and status of a son who has served and been trained by a father but with no commitment. They want the knowledge and the promotion without the accountability. Being fathered or mothered is not an isolated, remote learning experience. It is an interactive relationship.

The church has degenerated toward a corporate structure of mass production that turns a brand-new Christian into an apparent mature warrior leader within a few short months or years, and all that without the proximity, insight, or accountability of a seasoned mentor, father, or mother. We have become a culture that only tolerates certain levels of complements and despises any correction that so easily offends. Healthy correction is a pathway to maturity and wisdom. This rejection of wisdom ensures a tragic future for fools.

This individual was speaking to so many impressionable students who willingly trusted what this person was saying so they could figure out how to forge their own path. Now, because of this person's prestige, thousands of young people eager to serve the Lord have been given permission to get credibility by associating with certain names. Think about this: they are teaching the next generation to listen to podcasts and watch YouTube videos of teaching from well-known people in the Christian community. They watch their teachings, but they never meet these people in real life.

The Bible is clear when it instructs us to "recognize those who labor among you and are over you in the Lord and admonish you, and to esteem them very highly in love for their work's sake" (1 Thessalonians 5:12–13). This means we don't blindly follow celebrities, especially when we have no idea about who they are in their private lives. The next generation is following stage and microphone personalities who could have all forms of addictions, sin issues, and compromise in their private lives.

Subscribing to a social-media voice or podcast is not discipleship. The faster we learn and understand this, the faster we can reclaim true kingdom culture. This instance in which this individual was so boldly and confidently giving everyone who was listening permission to be isolated orphans, one could understand why I was so shocked. This is why this generation is disconnected from authentic relationship with a more seasoned generation. This is why we have novices being raised up into positions of notoriety and falling into the same condemnation as the devil (see 1 Timothy 3:6).

Discipleship is a side-by-side walk in faith and life. The younger with the seasoned. I love how the Apostle Paul refers to Timothy as a "true son in the faith," who worked side by side with Paul as a son with his father. To think that every single leader, father, or mother has the same approach to discipleship and mentoring, let alone the focus and goals for the outcome of their sons or daughters, doesn't make sense.

Paul clearly stated his desire concerning discipleship focus when he labored over the Galatians until Christ was formed in them (see Galatians 4:19). The goal that Paul would pour into his sons and daughters so that they would look like the nature and character of Jesus should be every spiritual parent's desire for the ones they lead. This goal should be a constant without compromise.

Let's delve deeper into an important detail.

ONE SIZE DOES NOT FIT ALL

Of course, there is the core kingdom focus in our culture that reflects the nature of the King; however, it does not stop there. The Scriptures tell us: "And God said, Let the earth put forth grass, herbs yielding seed, and fruit-trees bearing fruit after their kind, wherein is the seed thereof, upon the earth: and it was so. And the earth brought forth grass, herbs yielding seed after their kind, and trees bearing fruit, wherein is the seed thereof, after their kind: and God saw that it was good" (Genesis 1:11–12 KJV).

So how does this passage apply to discipleship? God is a God who is not plain, boring, or short-sighted. He created the earth and everything in it using a great range of variations, from terrain to plants and crops to fish, animals, and birds. Not forgetting people, not just racial or cultural variations, but everyone's gifting, calling, and personality. Humanity descended from Adam and Eve with huge flavor and variations in our individuality and uniqueness.

With all this uniqueness and diversity, we need to understand that not everyone will relate to your specific calling and gifting. They can be understood somewhat, but we have an inherent desire to be understood by those we are led by. For example, someone who is called to be a multimillionaire cannot necessarily expect to reach his or her full potential being mentored by someone who has never even had a hundred thousand dollars in their bank account. An athlete cannot expect to be trained well and make it to the Olympics with a coach who has never competed himself.

In the same way, when it comes to the kingdom of God, we must understand that one size does not fit all. Although a seasoned evangelist can somewhat relate to and understand a young prophet, that young prophet will not receive an optimized mentoring from the seasoned evangelist because the focus and goals of an evangelist are different than the goals of a prophet. And not just the goals but also understanding the inherent strengths and weaknesses and the developmental journey specific to the unique offices. Both fathers and sons and mothers and daughters need to understand that it's helpful to recognize that this matters immensely.

Here are a few notes that outline some of the apostolic profiles that each one of us fit into, which are like personality traits in the body of Christ. These are not just a description of leaders in senior roles; these traits are across the room in a local church—some dormant, some juvenile, some semi-developed, and others in the maturing process as well as the seasoned.

The apostle is known as a sent one. He has a discipleship focus of strategic development, multiplication, and leadership development. The prophet, known as a guide, has a discipleship focus of reformation and restoration. The evangelist is known as a gatherer and primarily has a discipleship focus of conversion, then retention and maturation of disciples for more outreach. The pastor is known as the guard, and he will have a discipleship focus of transformational and spiritual nourishment. Then lastly, the teacher is the equipper and has a discipleship focus on Bible literacy and worldview.

Once we grasp the concept of the diverse focal values of each apostolic office, it becomes clear that destiny must be walked into by the masterful care of someone who is already seasoned in the call or office that sons and daughters feel called to.

A knife cannot be forged in a garden
and a crop cannot be grown in a kiln.

Environment and influence are everything concerning your destiny.

This principle applies to any field, such as professional careers, not just ministry or kingdom culture. For instance, I love fishing and hunting, and if I wish to catch a certain fish or hunt an animal outside of my personal region or experience, then I will look for a friend or connection that not only has experience and knowledge but also personal success in hunting or fishing that species. I could try myself, but it could take me years to get the success that it could take just hours or days to get if I had an expert show me the way. If I really pay attention to my time with that expert rather than just being served, I will learn the skills it took them years to acquire. I can then glean from their time with me and further my own abilities in that sport.

If you want to see the direction of someone's life, examine those they call closest friends. But equally important is to look at who is leading them.

> *Remember a leader always calls people higher toward who they are, not just forward.*

True fathers and mothers have the amazing ability to leave indelible markings in the DNA and lives of those they lead, in mindsets, value systems, principles, characteristics, integrity, financial management, and sexual purity.

We need to pay attention to who is in our lives because there are people who are key doorways to our future. We may need an apostolic father or mother who also walks in multimillion-dollar marketplace success. It may not be as simple as subscribing to a course; we need a personal voice of a seasoned and successful mentor.

DISCIPLESHIP FOCUS MATTERS

Sons and daughters, in your pursuit to get mentored, I recommend waiting on and partnering with your heavenly Father to send you to the right person. I would also urge you to narrow the influential voices in your life so you do not end up with confusing options. While developing your character, you need to have a single, clear, mature voice to guide you.

The Bible says, "You have many teachers but not many fathers" (see 1 Corinthians 4:15). Wisdom becomes confusing to be loyal to if several conflicting voices are speaking at once. Don't try to adopt several voices, as this is a sign to fathers and mothers that they are just an optional advisory voice in your multichoice selection column.

There was a young man in my church who would always come to me with the appearance of great sincerity asking for advice. He wanted to be affirmed that he came to me for counsel and would often tell others that he sought my counsel. But there was always a check in my spirit when I talked with him. I had a profound sense that he was not as sincere as he would like me to believe. Even with that said, I would give him basic counsel and scriptural advice as any good pastor should.

However, as time went on, I began to hear that this young man was making the rounds to several different pastors, ministers, or peers. His strategy was to keep asking people that he somewhat esteemed until either he had a majority consensus or until he received the answer that suited his cause or agreed with what he had already decided.

Let me be clear—this is not discipleship. This is an orphan pretending to be submitted, making the rounds, abusively working the system. It is an orphan navigating around authentic relationships and sonship. As I saw more and more of this behavior from him, I began to withdraw my voice. My time was a poor investment into his life, given the fact he didn't really want my counsel. As a father, I value my own time and dignity not to cater to that type of poor stewardship.

We need to allow the Holy Spirit to heal our wounds and lead us into leadership and mentoring we can trust Him in. Don't avoid maturing and sonship by romancing and engaging many voices but never actually sitting down under one voice. It's good to have teachers and influencers that educate you and even advise you, but don't think that having three fathers will go well. It doesn't in the natural and it doesn't in the spiritual either. Have many teachers and advisors but try to limit your father to one. Elisha was the disciple of Elijah, not Elijah *and* Jehu. Ask the Holy Spirit to lead you into the relationship that will propel you into who you are called to be.

Fathers and mothers, don't waste your time with those who are using you as a casual option or one of many voices. You are looking for those in whom your seeds of wisdom will bear fruit that remains, not people who will trash your pearls.

Most people in life hate submission to authority. But healthy submission to God-given authority is a key component in heavenly kingdom culture. Because most people do not like submission, and yes, that includes people in the church, it causes most people to never walk in true discipleship.

In business, my goal is to mature my employees much like a fathering role. I've been in business since I was twenty-one years old, so I have plenty of experience. I've made lots of mistakes as with anyone in business, and over time I've been able to fine tune the operations of my various businesses. In that world, pulling additional staff in around you is key to growing your operation or enterprise.

Now when new staff come on board at a company, they have to learn the basics of operations and company protocols. But my goal isn't to create robots that know how to repeat prices, protocols, and policies to staff and clientele. My goal is that they would work around me in such a way that after a year or two, they would know how I would respond, value, or problem solve in almost all situations within the company.

My goal is not merely that these values and concepts would be grasped; my goal is that they have taken so much ownership of their role and presence in the company that they are responding out of values adopted and imparted. They now have personal focused values that look exactly like the company culture. They don't need to ask about most questions because they have been so well trained that they know what needs to be done.

DISCIPLED BY GOD

We have already said that there are two discipleship relationships that are important in our lives: our relational discipleship with God, and our discipleship with a spiritual father or mother.

It's important to recognize that your discipleship focus with God should be your foundation in your life.

Our primary discipleship is with God. That means intimate relationship with Jesus, the Holy Spirit, and Father God. And no, you cannot pick your favorite of the three—you must be relational with each of them to the point that each of their voices becomes distinct and they each can encourage, exhort, and correct you. Discipleship is not just about the warm fuzzies of proximity. It has important facets like correction, thus challenging and confronting our dysfunction and unhealthy attributes.

> THEN [JESUS] SAID TO THEM ALL, "If anyone desires to come after Me, let him deny himself, and take up his cross daily, and follow Me. For whoever desires to save his life will lose it, but whoever loses his life for My sake will save it. For what profit is it to a man if he gains the whole world, and is himself destroyed or lost? For whoever is ashamed of Me and My words, of him the Son of Man will be ashamed when He comes in His own glory, and in His Father's, and of the holy angels. But I tell you truly, there are some standing here who shall not taste death till they see the kingdom of God." (Luke 9:23–27)

We will never get authentic impartation from a spiritual father that we refuse to get from Jesus privately. Human nature is broken, and somehow many people act out a lifestyle and approach to this that assumes to get anointing and promotion from people in influence. And somehow, they completely disregard the pursuit of Jesus in their private love relationship.

Being discipled by a father or a mother is not and never will be a replacement to an intimate relationship with God that disciples us into His image.

Jesus said He was the way, the truth, and the life, and that no one comes to the Father but through Him. Another way of looking at this is to understand we won't get into heaven through our leader's relationship with God. The Word of God clearly instructs us that we must each work out our own salvation with fear and trembling. We must walk out our own faith relationship in the healthy fear of the Lord.

God has no grandchildren; we don't get into the family by association. Being discipled by a spiritual father or mother is never a substitute or replacement to an authentic relationship and discipleship with God the Father, Jesus, and the Holy Spirit. We must learn to listen to the Holy Spirit and develop a relationship with Him. He is sent to be our teacher.

Jesus, prior to ascending into heaven after His resurrection, said that He must go so the Holy Spirit can come to us. He described the Holy Spirit as a guide, a teacher, a comforter, and a counselor. He said that the Holy Spirit would lead and guide us into all truth. It's important that we do not substitute men or women for our fundamental dependance of guidance, counsel, and instruction through relationship with the Spirit and heart of God. Jesus is the perfect reflection of the Father. And the Holy Spirit perfectly represents Jesus. Although each of the three in the Godhead have a slightly differing interaction with us, if we see Jesus then have seen them all.

Ultimately, believers should learn to hear God's voice for themselves. A lot of young believers often struggle with this, and so they have the need for leaders who can guide them so they don't shipwreck their lives.

God has built a principle that I have observed around His guidance and voice. God will speak to us as individuals, and if we are not listening, then He will speak to leaders and father figures who are tasked with warning us. If we refuse to listen to these voices, we will ultimately learn by the confrontation of difficult circumstances and consequences. This highlights the urgency to be teachable and softhearted, ready to hear God's voice personally, and the voice of wisdom inside discipleship.

We ultimately must cultivate our personal discipleship relationship with the person of God so we don't miss His voice when He is speaking. Jesus reminds us, "My sheep hear My voice" (see John 10:27–28)

THE DISCIPLESHIP HEART OF GOD

I encourage you to pause and read the passage out of Ezekiel 34:1–15, which reveals what a shepherd, pastor, and a father is called to do. Notice how the passage starts by God speaking out against the shepherds—the leaders, pastors, fathers, and mothers. He speaks to the fact that they were using their position for their own gain with complete disregard for their "sheep" or their congregation, for their sons and daughters.

The first half of this passage clearly labels the bad shepherd in God's view. Those leaders who have used, abused, fed themselves, and left the sheep for half dead. God responds with a stern and serious response coming against these self-serving fathers. An eye-opening response from the Good Shepherd Himself, don't you think?

The second half of the passage highlights what true fathering looks like. God is coming to heal wounds and bind up the bruises of His people. Now if you know anything about animals, when an animal is wounded, cut, or bruised, it doesn't need candy coated conversation; rather, it needs its wounds to be handled and touched in the process of healing. The problem is that touching the wound is painful and threatening to the animal. The animal often has trouble separating the feeling of its pain in an open wound with the pain of that same wound being handled by the shepherd in the process of being medically treated, ultimately to save the sheep's life.

The sheep will often fight violently for its life, not realizing that the pain being experienced is the life-threatening wound being treated and healed. This is the most difficult part of discipleship in a legacy context.

Coming back to the understanding that most people don't embrace submission, which makes this process of addressing wounds a volatile risk for fathers and mothers. For this reason, many fathers and mothers don't address a lot of wounds because they don't want to be hurt themselves. Instead, they keep their "discipleship relationships" to a positive-only approach. This completely misses the whole concept of discipleship and falls grossly short of heaven's intent for legacy.

It's not our strengths that will take us further that we must be concerned about. It's our wounds and dysfunction that will sabotage us from ever getting to our destiny. And almost one hundred percent of the time, these wounds and dysfunction cannot be seen by the son or daughter. They are only apparent in perspective to the more mature and seasoned father or mother. Anyone can see faults, but only someone seasoned in the love of God can see them and have the heart and understanding about how to see these wounds redeemed and healed.

God demonstrated this heart perfectly in this passage of Ezekiel.

BEING DISCIPLED BY A MATURE MOTHER OR FATHER

The second form of discipleship is the one with seasoned men and women whom we must submit to in relationship. Paul wrote: "But I trust in the Lord Jesus to send Timothy to you shortly, that I also may be encouraged when I know your state. For I have no one like-minded, who will sincerely care for your state. For all seek their own, not the things which are of Christ Jesus. *But you know his proven character, that as a son with his father he served with me in the gospel*" (Philippians 2:19–22).

Elisha was already established and set up with the family business. He had to humble himself and detach from a *title* he thought he had, the *knowledge* he thought he had, the *value* he thought he had, and the *security* he thought he had, *to get a mantle* that he did not have. First Kings 19:19–21 tells us:

> So he departed from there, and found Elisha the son of Shaphat, who was plowing with twelve yoke of oxen before him, and he was with the twelfth. Then Elijah passed by him and threw his mantle on him. And he left the oxen and ran after Elijah, and said, "Please let me kiss my father and my mother, and then I will follow you." And he said to him, "Go back again, for what have I done to you?" So Elisha turned back from him, and took a yoke of oxen and slaughtered them and boiled their flesh, using the oxen's equipment, and gave it to the people, and they ate. Then he arose and followed Elijah, and became his servant.

It's important to note that Elisha didn't get the mantle of Elijah when Elijah threw his cloak on him as he passed by. He got it years later after walking next to the man of God, being taught, corrected, trained, and anointed. Elijah schooled Elisha for almost a decade. This goes against a lot of today's current popular church culture. In today's culture we see short-term courses labeled as discipleship. People go on a discipleship training program and think that this will cause an impartation.

The problem is that we live in a generation that wants to get approved and get promoted fast.

But the reality is that heaven's process takes significant time and is not just a fast pass.

To succeed, you must be discipled, mentored, and schooled by a seasoned father or mother. This mentorship isn't just an association with a person of influence; it's an immersion of key people into your life.

You cannot substitute with being taught by a peer. There is a sharpening that happens with brothers, as iron sharpens iron.

But there's a raising that happens with fathers in a way a brother never can (see Hebrews 12:3–11).

It's being fathered or mothered by someone who is mature beyond you. But it's not just being mentored from the aspect of the skills and gifting development around the office of your calling. Mentorship benefits growth in all the areas of your life. For instance, the men I disciple are schooled on character, excellence, integrity, finances, relational stewardship, even down to small details like keeping their home or bedroom clean and tidy, dressing with excellence, and having good hygiene.

This may seem extreme to some; however, you can have the greatest word from God but if you have not been trained on how to present and carry yourself with excellence, then who is going to take you seriously? Human nature is always looking for a reason to dismiss someone who is representing God's truth.

The way that we are trained to prepare our character is just as important as the gift we must learn to operate.

Not preparing and being trained in these areas would be like painting a valuable painting over a piece of rotting canvas. Eventually all the skill and effort that was invested into the artistic painting will be of no value because the canvas that the art was expressed on was flawed, corrupted, or compromised and would eventually come to nothing. Everything would be wasted.

Being authentically discipled is one of the main key ingredients that will bring success in your journey and office. Baptism was a moment we committed to Christ. Commitment to discipleship is the moment we are assured in the trajectory of our future. We must acknowledge that all are called but, like the Scripture tells us, only a few are chosen by God. The separating factor is how people intentionally posture themselves to honor, steward, and immerse themselves in relational discipleship with God and a spiritual father and mother.

CONCLUSION

Discipleship is the vehicle God uses to transport His story, legacy, and hope for the world. And so, this vehicle matters in your life. You are not going to get to your destiny on your own. In fact, God's built it this way. Independence will block you from being able to embrace a father and listen to his wisdom.

If either of these two discipleships is missing in your life—discipleship with God or discipleship with a mother or father—I would encourage you to pursue God for a father or mother to disciple you. And really, and more importantly, pursue God for more intimacy with God's heart so that He will shape you as your heavenly Father.

"Many are called and few are chosen" (Matthew 22:14). Choosing happens because a person is qualified. The primary distinction to the qualified is individuals embracing discipleship with God *and* fathers and mothers. May God establish you in His legacy that has been passed on from fathers and mothers in the faith.

LONG LIVE LEGACY

In this book I have covered God's elaborate dream that He partnered with us in covenant and gave us His legacy to pass on to the next generation. We've seen how Jesus went to extensive lengths to demonstrate the heart and nature of the Father. We also discussed how Jesus then perfectly replicated His relationship with the Father by mentoring the disciples and teaching the masses. And finally, He commissioned the church and empowered us as believers to live as He lived.

Jesus has sent us into the world to see as many people as possible come to the same encounter of His goodness. He has made it abundantly clear that relational discipleship was His vehicle to save the world, empowered by all He did and said.

We have studied the early church and we've studied the modern church. We've seen both the strength in God's intentions, and we've seen some of the shortcomings of the modern church that are sabotaging this effectiveness in our past and current generations. I hope that as you have read this book, it has become incredibly apparent to you that God's desire for optimum effectiveness over us individually and as the church is that we would be disciples trained and raised into mature sons and daughters of God.

Returning to this model of authentic discipleship legacy empowers us individually to reach our full, God-dreamed potential. And in doing so, this causes entire churches to be strengthened, resourced, and grown. Just like with the ancient Phoenician apostle that the Scriptures were referring to, our job is to bring heaven to earth and populate heaven's culture in our cities and nations.

All this is an amazing mission statement, but it is going to require the cost of discipleship. It is going to require us leaving our comfort zones of blending into the church pews and becoming vulnerable in these fathering and mothering relationships that raise us higher, show us the way, and coach us toward our purpose. If we as individuals and even as entire churches can grasp this and implement it in our lives, then we will soar back into God's dream, both personally and corporately as the church.

It is my intention in the sequel to 'Legacy' to take you through a journey of practical application of both fathering and mothering, as well as becoming a son and a daughter, as we reestablish this culture in the modern church. Meet me in the next book as we restore kingdom culture and your personal response and contribution to Jesus receiving the rewards of His suffering.

Legacy is God's dream and your inheritance. My prayer is that you run a race worthy of this high calling on your life and steward the privilege of partnering with God's great plan to save the world.

Blessings,

Andrew Billings

About The Author

Andrew Billings

Andrew Billings, has a profound calling to serve the body of Christ, preparing believers for the present times and the days ahead. After being raised in a church-going family Andrew had a powerful encounter with Jesus that changed his life and ignited a passion for serving the kingdom.

Since then, he has dedicated his life to this cause with unwavering commitment. Central to his message is the belief that healthy fathers raise healthy sons and healthy mothers raise healthy daughters, in both a spiritual and biological sense.

As a Father, Andrew, along with his wife and their three sons, have taken seriously God's call to create environments that reflect God's heart for immersive discipleship culture. The goal always being to reflect the timeless model seen in Jesus' ministry, integrating family and team into the mission. Their commitment to Fathering and Mothering the next generation an advocation for the church to return to these foundational principles to fulfill Jesus' vision.

As a Son, Andrew has devoted himself to being led by his Heavenly father. A commitment that has taken him from his homeland of New Zealand to becoming a missionary to the United States early in His marriage where Andrew and his wife Rebekah planted and led a local church for over a decade. Andrew's ministry has taken him around the globe as an itinerant minister where he has been able to serve the international body of Christ. As an accomplished author of several books and the founder of multiple academies that train and equip believers in various pursuits and giftings, Andrew has been able to serve both the local and the international church.

In service to the church as a minister and the marketplace as a businessman, Andrew has engaged in demonstrating that the kingdom of God is present both within the church and equally the business world. Insights into innovation and business strategy highlight his belief that there is no separation between these two in service to God's Kingdom.

Andrew's ministry spans a diverse range of expressions and authentic discipleship remains the heartbeat of Andrew's calling to the body of Christ. This devotion to Jesus enables Andrew to give all in his pursuit of restoration of Jesus' Church. It is his sincere hope that you find your feet on the road of your destiny in Christ, and that the resources available through Andrew Billings Ministries continue to encourage and strengthen you in these days and the days ahead.

Andrew Billings

Andrew Billings Ministries

Join an online academy, attend an in person event, read other books by Andrew, and follow him on socials for impactful livestreams, messages, and more.

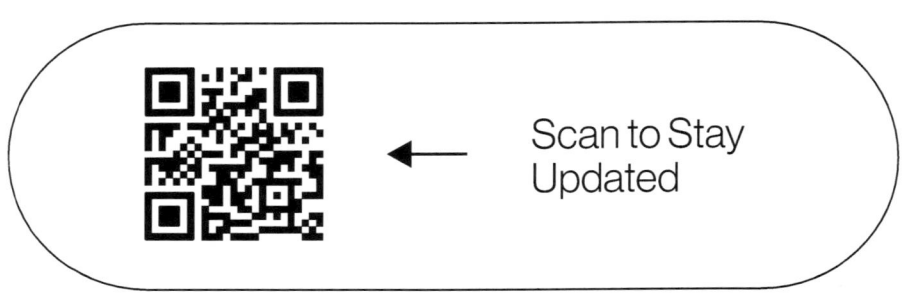

Scan to Stay Updated

AndrewBillings.org

Books
Buy Andrew's books and be the first to access new releases.

Academies
Curriculum created to equip the body.

Speaking
Discover when Andrew is speaking near you.

Events
Join Andrew at one of his in-person events.

      @AndrewBillingsMinistries